STAR
CHILDREN
AWAKENING

ANNA GŁOWACZ

STAR CHILDREN

AWAKENING

Vol. II

It is only when you become one with your
soul that you can fully become yourself.
You are it, you feel with it...
You become love and light having the
power of illuminating even the darkest
obscurity.

Star Children Consciousness, Volume 2

By Anna Glowacz

All material contained herein is Copyright

Copyright © Anna Glowacz, 2021

Written by Anna Glowacz

Published by YRIAH
Cover art by Tyrone Roshantha; Damian Buczniewicz
Illustrated by Damian Buczniewicz, inst: @damianartdb
Translated by Hanna Taboła; Noemi Rojek

YRIAH.COM

Any resemblance to persons living or dead is purely coincidental.
Based on transmissions from Semi Semjase Evolet...

Prologue

After a several days journey to the past, during which I remembered many important details about the true history of civilization, Semjase let us breathe a little. She hasn't taken us anywhere for weeks.

Kal and I knew that it was only the beginning of our journey. A prologue to the events that are yet to come. We felt our calling to this earthly task given to us, and this feeling was increasing every day. We were becoming the task. I felt that way, even though it could sound a little irrational. I was proud of myself and I was dreaming for us to succeed. The fate of humanity depended on that. Nothing was the same as it used to be for us. The time has come to open the eyes of others, to show them the truth in its entirety, no matter if beautiful, or hurtful at times. Nothing was only black and white, I understood that completely now. Humanity had to make its own choice – and dependent on that, each and every one will write their own path, in order to follow it.

Kal and I spent these few weeks on us and our love. We spent every free moment together. Of course, we couldn't help but talk about our mission. But we tried as much as we could to enjoy the here and now, even if for a little while. With every coming day we felt our connection getting deeper. It made us happy, and the energy of love growing in us was shining around just like a lighthouse. We have seen changes in people more than once, people who we saw unintentionally entering into our light zone. The harmony and feeling of instant love were overflowing them and it was showing on their faces. It showed a smile, and peace.

When Kal was not around, I'd sit and write everything Semjase taught us so far, to a textual file who was about to become a book telling the history of humanity. I was still wondering if this way of sharing the truth will be right. But every time I'd come to a point that I was confident; writing about it was the best way, because it would allow all the information to reach as much people as possible in the whole world, in a short time. I felt inside of me that the universe supported me. The leading energy was always close to me. I felt it with my heart and body. When I would sit and write, my fingers would run over the keyboard so smoothly, that I was amazed myself. In the midst of the creating process, I felt shivers over my body more than once. Pleasant and warm feelings would let me know that I was going the right way. I loved this kind of feeling.

Lately, I would feel more and more squeaking in my ears while I would write. But it didn't bother me, it was more like music played just for my ears. Mommy would watch this creative process with a smile on her face and pride. She didn't even ask if I needed help. She knew perfectly that if I needed it, I would have asked immediately. She and Daddy took my task of showing the truth with great recognition. They would read everything I wrote. Whenever I would ask how it's going, they would answer in agreement, that the time is being fulfilled. I knew then, that I am on the right path.

Time would pass by, and I slowly started to miss my encounters with Semjase. Her person, as well as places she would take Kal and myself to, were so magical that we wanted to spend more and more time with her and Mother Earth inside of these beautiful spaces. My dreams were slowly becoming mine. Memories would pass by my head like movies from the past. It would let me complete my knowledge already given to me by Semjase. I went to many places that we visited together with her.

The dweeb gave up, and he surprised me with it. He didn't show up anymore and didn't take me on interrogations. It clearly hit him, that even I don't own any information about the matrix of Shiru. I didn't miss him, I just felt a little sad that I'm not able to help him. I was just thinking about that, when in my head I heard the voice of Semjase:

But you're helping, Smaisi. What you do is helping all nations, not only those who are human.

I was glad to hear her.

I know that sometimes I just forget, I replied. Is it time yet?, I asked, hoping deep in my heart that her answer will be positive.

Soon, my dear. Now I am far away. I have to do something, much is happening at the time. As soon as I will be back, we will return to our lessons.

I will be waiting, I replied and I came back to writing.

I felt the eyes of Semjase on me. She was standing behind me, reading what I managed to type on the file these last minutes.

A true writing gift is slumbering inside of you. Congratulations for the idea. Many will benefit from it. Many will read this book and it will lead them on the right path. You will save millions. Write, dear child! Let your fingers burn to pour memories out. Let your soul feel and write from the heart, let the Creator of everything that exists, inspire you and lead you throughout the pages of this book. When she said it, I was filled with a wave of warmth. Soon after, Semjase disappeared and I didn't feel her presence anymore.

When Kal came into the room, I was sunk in my new writing world. I didn't pay attention to him – I was reminiscing, and my fingers danced on the keyboard in a unique dance of the truth.

Chapter 1

*"The Light
You can fully manifest your light when you have walked through the
darkest corners of Yourself, because the shadow is used to express the light
fully and in fact is a part of it..."*

Damian Buczniewicz

Energetic attack — Astral attachment

It was the evening. I was sitting with Kal in my room and we were listening to music, talking casually about subjects that were completely not connected with either the past or the future. We just were present. Immersed in the here and now that was forgotten by so many. I loved spending time with him. He always understood me so perfectly. The words were not actually necessary for that. We were uttering them out of earthly habit. And even though we had been together for a few months, I felt, and I was even sure, that it was him. I was in great spirits and I was just audibly laughing at Kal's joke, when this happened.

I could feel a wave of darkness overwhelming me. As if the whole space around me was filled with darkness. It was engulfing me. Before I managed to react in any way, it was already too late. The shadow intruded on me and my body froze and arched within a few seconds. I felt immense fear. The pain pierced through me, from the head to the tips of my toes. I was not able to choke anything out, I could not even move. Any attempts to react in any way were ending up with further waves of pain. I did not have any idea what was going on. I was slowly panicking. Kal was looking at me terrified. He did not wait long. When I gave him a begging look, he immediately ran downstairs for my parents. I was wriggling on the bed trying to fight it. This thing, this energy though, it was stronger than I was. It was keeping me in snares, not giving me any chance for release. It was tightening and thickening around.

"You won't change humans," it hissed into my ear and I felt cold in its area. " You can't save them. They belong to us," it added.

Then I felt not only fear but also slowly intensifying anger in me. This was evil as well though. The being was feeding on my energy that my body was just generating for it. I tried to calm down and fill myself up with love and light. In vain. I was too weak. Too horrified.

When my parents ran into the room, the being suddenly released me from its incapacitating grip. My body relaxed a bit, however, I still remained in the energy of that being. I felt bad there. So bad that I sobbed.

Mommy ran up to me and held me tight. Daddy sat by our side and embraced both of us with his arm. I could feel how he was cleansing with light me and the whole space around. Kal was standing at the doorstep and was looking absentmindedly. His face was pale as a wall. I already knew that he felt that too. Not as intensely as I did, but he was in it with me.

"What was that?" I asked when I managed to calm myself down slightly.

Kal was sitting on the chair and was not saying anything. I could feel he was trying to understand what had just occurred and who the creature that managed to enter our astral field was.

"Reptilians," Mommy started, "It wasn't alone. There have been many of them. A single entity wouldn't have enough energy to pass through your protective field. Since you started talking with Semjase and getting to know the truth and, consequently, decided to pass it on, you are a threat to them, Smaisi. And a huge one; to all the reptilian nations as well as to those who feed on human energy. You know very well that an awake and conscious human, who is connected to the power and light of his or her soul, ceases to be food for them.

9

"I guess it's time," Mommy interjected and said that more to Daddy rather than to me. I felt though that this was about me.

"It's time for what?" I asked.

"For you to learn how to protect yourself so that such situations won't happen to you again. So that in the event of the attack you know how to react. I shall take you to my beloved friend Maria. She is a wonderful woman with a pure heart. You will see. I'm sure that you will like her and She will teach you how to create a protective field. She will also teach you many other things and they will be very important and useful skills...

"Can I join in?" Kal asked shyly.

"Of course. We'll take you too. It couldn't be otherwise," Mommy answered him and I could see she was looking at him like at a son.

I noticed that Kal was slightly moved. He sensed Mommy's affection.

"I'll call her today and I'll book a first session for you," she continued, "Maria has been asking for some time if you are ready. You already are and, what's more, as today's events have proved, it's high time for that too".

"Thank you, Mommy" I declared hoping that I would learn everything fast enough in order not to experience such attacks again.

I could still feel shivers running down my body. The energy of this entity was fading under the influence of light that Daddy wrapped me up with, but this was happening very slowly. As if it was leaving the stench behind that evaporates only with time to let you enjoy the neutral smell of the air again.

My parents, having ensured that everything is ok, left me and Kal alone. They started re-securing the house so that I could feel safe until I built up a desired protective shield that was sufficient for me.

Kal was speaking little. I was not sure if it was out of shock, or perhaps fear was eating him up. I could sense conflicting emotions in him. Similar emotions were filling me up as well.

"I think it will be better if we let it go," I suggested. "It happened and it's done, there's no point returning to that, it's the past that doesn't count".

"You're right," he replied, "Let's rather focus on raising our vibrations so that it won't happen again. Even though they've attacked you directly I could feel everything inside me. I don't even want to know how intense your feelings were," he summed up and hugged me tightly.

Despite the attempts to redirect my attention to positive things, the negative vibrations that this entity had seeded in me, were making me unable to shake it off. Kal could sense that. He stood up, grabbed my hand and pulled me towards the door.

"I reckon it will be better if we stay home where it's safe," I suggested.

"I can feel that Mother Earth can help us," Kal announced, responding to the expression of fear on my face. "You can't get stuck in this low vibration because this only lays the route to you for them. This feeds them. Remember that."

Kal was right. I could not disagree with him. I obediently followed him into the garden. We sat on the ground and laid our hands on it. I closed my eyes and connected to Mother Earth asking her for cleansing of all the negative feelings that were still inside me. It was only after a moment that I started to feel a tingling sensation in my palms; at first, it was very subtle, with time, I could feel it stronger. I went into this connection deeper visualizing how I travel inside the Earth to the place where its matter merges with its symbiote. When I did that, I started to feel that Mother Earth smoothly and fast sucks out all the energy of fear and anger that was flowing out of my hands. It was getting better and better and after a few minutes I managed to relax completely. Filled with harmony and light, with the feeling that the cleansing was finished, I disconnected. Delighted, I thanked Earth and turned to face the house. My parents were standing at the threshold, glancing at me with pride.

"This is exactly how you do it, Smaisi. Exactly like that!" Daddy approached me and patted me on my back, "This was a great idea," he added with pride in his voice.

11

"It was Kal who suggested that," I confessed, not wanting to claim his merit.

"Kal is experienced with Mother Earth. He connected with her many times. Even earlier, when he wasn't quite aware of that," Daddy noted and I could see this was a gentle shock for Kal that actually brought satisfaction to him.

"When is Semjase going to return?" I asked. " I miss her and our conversations."

"She'll be back soon. Don't worry yourself. You are safe now. We've let our defenses down with Daddy but we won't let this situation happen again," Mommy said in response.

"Have you already called Mrs. Maria?" I wanted to know. I realized that the ability to protect yourself and the knowledge how to do that would be useful for everyone, not only myself. Difficult times were coming. I knew that the beings of dark, especially those who parasitize on human energy would be desperately looking for the opportunity to attach to someone's energy.

"Yes, Smaisi. I've spoken to her. We're going to visit her tonight."

"So quick?" I was surprised.

"She's been waiting for this for a long time. And the Universe is still taking care of you because today is her day off."

"That's wonderful!" I was happy. None ever would be allowed to enter my space without my consent.

Kal was still sitting on the ground, as if joined with it. He was not paying attention to our conversations that were taking place right behind his back.

"Let's leave him here", Daddy recommended. "He's talking well".

"Talking?" I inquired further, I was not sure if I heard it correctly.

"Yes, Smaisi. Talking. Go home and give him some space," he pushed me lightly before I could resist and closed the door behind me.

Kal looked relaxed and peaceful so I trusted that If anything was going on it was positive and he would surely tell me all about it soon.

I was not mistaken. As soon as he entered the house he almost attacked me with his excitement about the experiences he'd had a moment before. It turned out that he talked with Mother Earth and she thanked him for the trust he had for her. She told him that he could always count on her. She knew as well that she could rely on him and the changes that would take place on Earth thanks to the merit and hard work of star children. I felt a light prick of jealousy when he was describing this. I regretted I had not been taking part in that conversation.

"Of course, you were," Kal read my thoughts. "You can enter this at any given moment. You are me. Always remember that".

Suddenly, Mommy rushed into the room announcing that it was time. Excited about the close encounter with Mrs. Maria, I completely forgot about the experience Kal had without me. I focused on creating my own experiences in the not distant future of mine.

The journey there took us over an hour. During that time, Mommy told us a bit about Mrs. Maria. About who she was and about her terrestrial and extraterrestrial experiences. I was thrilled by the multitude of her trips and the vastness of her knowledge that she had gained. She had been working on awakening human consciousness for decades because she was the star child of the earlier generations. She had the gift of energy healing. She was simply unique.

When we arrived, at the entrance of a small house stood an old woman. Her hair was cut short and was black and gray. It was not the hair that drew the attention though, it was her beaming smile and beautiful warmth radiating from her even from afar. I immediately recognized a beautiful soul in her filled with light and love only to the whole existence...

"Welcome, my loves," She greeted my parents warmly and glanced at me and Kal. "The same... this is just unbelievable. You two are always the same. It's impossible to confuse you with anyone", she cuddled us in turns and invited us home.

The energy of love that the woman was radiating with was so intimidating that I was unable to utter a word. I nodded only and followed my parents that were already disappearing at the doorstep. I had the impression that the whole house was filled with that energy and incredibly bright light. Nothing that was dark could not pass through the walls of this house. It was shielded so well.

"The house always has the energy of its dwellers," Mrs. Maria suddenly said. "Only in a place where the energy of many vibrations meet, there is the need of filling the space with light.

"Mrs. Maria, I'm so glad that I can meet you..." I started.

"Call me Majka," she requested, interrupting me. "I'm happy too, Smaisi that I can meet you again in this time that is so interesting for Earth and the whole galaxy. I've been waiting for this day for ages, since Semjase visited me and told me about you. You're very important for her. First..."

When I wanted to ask her what she meant saying "first", Daddy quickly joined the conversation asking if Majka still had this delicious white elderberry tincture which works so well on his digestion. It appeared quite weird to me, as I had never heard before that Daddy had ever had any stomach problems.

"Screwball," Kal whispered into my ear, and I only nodded in agreement.

I was already coding in my head the wording "first".

Majka pointed us to the living room and asked us to sit comfortably. Soon she entered carrying a tray with cups and a kettle of steamy water. Next to the cups, there was a tiny glass filled with almost transparent liquid. Daddy reached for it immediately. Majka poured a cup of tea for each of us. I could not recognize any particular smell in it, despite my knowledge of various teas.

"This is the mixture of herbs and flowers from my garden, Smaisi. You won't find here one but the whole range of aromas. Believe me though, you will enjoy the composition of them. I don't know anyone who would not enjoy it. Although..." Majka glanced at Daddy. "Your dad still prefers the tincture for a starter".

"Daddy is peculiar," I laughed.

"That's true, and that makes him so special. Each of us is

special. With the whole spectrum of advantages and disadvantages. Let me, before we move to the practice, pass on to you the basic knowledge that will help you move in the astral planes with the complete understanding of these spaces and the multidimensional energy relationships. This is quite important".

"Of course, we're used to elaborate lectures," Kal interjected and smirked under his breath.

"I'm not surprised. Semjase tells stories and teaches very beautifully. Everyone would love to have such a teacher. Let's see then what you can learn from me", Maja beamed and having checked if everyone was ready to listen, she started: "I would like to mention a few matters. Namely the activation of DNA on a multidimensional level and how to safely travel using your astral body. So, if you're ready, let's begin".

Everyone nodded because we could not wait listening to Majka's story. I was suspecting that her knowledge was much broader than Kal and I had thought. My parents though had already been aware of that for a long time.

"Good then... DNA is the availability and ability from zero point in time, it's a sort of a starting point leading to the restoration of the natural human abilities, telepathic communication, travels to other dimensions, and the exploration of your past and future generations. People need to always remember that they are multidimensional beings, existing in many realities and planes simultaneously. It is in DNA that humans have the memory of their all experiences encoded from all the timelines that they have existed — planets, star systems, galaxies, universes, spaces and dimensions in which they exist at the same time in a so-called connection with the source of all that is. Humans, having incarnated on Gaia, start their life without the remembrance of who they actually are and who they were in previous incarnations. They are surrounded by low vibrations of the third density of Earth that constantly influence them and they are prone to the control of technology that they don't always understand. In order to access the memory of your soul, therefore, one needs to break through all those artificially created blockages that have been put

15

up for humanity for a long time. When this is achieved, there is a connection of sensing and perception on the symbiote level activated, which is the soul, which allows to restore the memories from the parallel incarnations and the connection to the astral body. Only few people know that the hard work and commitment, that the meditating monks are characterised with, are not necessary. The astral body during meditation requires the accumulation of an enormous amount of energy so as to colloquially get out of the body. I know how hard it is to let yourself live the way the monks do, whose whole life is based on practice and they live as individuals who are almost completely secluded. I want to, therefore, show you easier techniques and practices that enable the connection to your astral body on a daily basis. It's a sort of a conscious half sleep in which the human brain works on alpha waves. I want to pass on to you too the way to activate your dormant DNA strands and enable fuller access to the consciousness of your being."

"How cool!" Kal shouted out enthusiastically.

Mrs. Maja smiled under her breath.

"Drink," she advised him pointing to his cup of tea that was still full.

Kal took a solid sip and Majka nodded with approval. This tea had to have some sort of deeper importance.

"Astral body is located in the human shell," she continued. "So it is important to restore the bacterial flora to its natural form. One should get rid of all the remains of food and bacteria that influence the human body. It is necessary to cleanse the intestines, even do an enema, rinse the stomach, obtain pH of the organism on the level of 6.5 so that you can experience the true connection with your astral body. This process allows for closure of the energy portals which other entities can have access to, the entities that want to draw energy from humans and influence their consciousness. The biological shell plays a crucial role here — it's a temple for every being, therefore, one needs to care for it and nurture it well. Without the body, your soul would have no home and wouldn't experience life on a physical plane."

16

"Does this tea have anything to do with this?" I asked.

"Not entirely. It clears your mind. The work with your body you need to start yourself, so that it is brought back to its natural harmony and a point in which the connection with the symbiote is clear and uninterrupted.

"How to achieve that?" I thought I was eating healthy and naturally. My parents always took care of that. Perhaps there was something more I could do that I had not been aware of before.

"Drink a lot of clean water. It's best to program it before drinking, by generating the feeling of love from the energy of the heart. The same applies to food. The higher the vibration of food, the easier and better the connection that leads to individual experiences. You can cook for yourself with the intention of internal transformation, cleansing, connection and growth — this is one of the most wonderful things that you can do for yourself. That's why, it is said that the best cook is the one who loves what he or she cooks. In those dishes there is a powerful high-vibrational energy of love instilled.

"How does this take place?" Kal wanted to find out.

"Thanks to the intention and your own thought assigned to the dish. In this way you code your own energy and it penetrates to the structure of the food. One can say that by eating it you supply yourself with your own light.

"Is it then not possible to awaken your consciousness of your soul and connect with it without such cleansing?" Kal asked again. He was focused a little less on the body cleansing than I, that was possibly the reason why this was bothering him. He started to like Mommy's juices not long ago. The green color and weird taste stopped disturbing him and he started to pour more helpings.

"Without energetic cleansing and proper body care, the connection to other dimensions is impossible or highly hindered. Therefore, the fruits and vegetables are the best for us, they are what your diet should be based on. By cleaning your biological shell you will activate your DNA strands that will allow you to experience other realms and offer access to your inner wisdom that is always at your fingertips, from the zero point in time. However,

I would like to first explain in greater detail the relationship with the sun and its energy, which is the so-called "primordial energy". This is a creation, which is omnipresent and it floods all the realms and spaces including you.

"Mommy taught me the sun meditation," I boasted, "These are very high vibrational energies triggering access to the consciousness of the soul. I was able to connect with it the first time."

"Wonderful. You have a gift for that, dear child. Like for many other things that you don't know yet about. Everything at the right time. And of course you're right, Smaisi. In the dimension we currently exist in, the physical manifestation of this energy is the Central Sun from where the light codes and energies are sent out. This happens so that the energy can communicate with you, so that it can help you connect with the part of existence that is inside of you all the time and forever. These energies are like an unimaginably enormous cobweb of the universe through which all sort of information is transmitted. The threads of this cobweb — let's call them multidimensional lines — are located in our solar system and on one of them there is the sun. It is, therefore, one of the energy joints on the lines of the multidimensional.

"This means that there are more joints," Kal spoke this time.

"Of course, yes. Each of these energies has their own source and codes assigned to it. The sun is the manifestation of the group of beings from the same family of symbiote beings, which means those that do not possess matter, who are the higher energies from higher dimensions of consciousness. These beings connected with each other and decided to gather all their codes of light, that is the experiences from all the currents of time, in order to merge and share their experiences with the rest of the beings. The sun is a portal which the beings walk through to incarnate in this solar system. Including the Earth as well."

"This is quite complicated. What kind of family of beings do you mean?" I asked. I did not want to show too much self-confidence. I already knew that this knowledge would be passed on by me and I needed to do it with the utmost integrity.

"This family is made up of our ancestors and those before them, as well as multidimensional incarnations among which are even your own incarnations on other timelines. These beings have access to you via the sun and they'd love to connect with you and transmit onto you information, experiences, and teach you beautiful abilities. Information is written in the space. Humans need to learn how to reach it. Everyone has access to that. In the sun, there are many civilizations and amazing cities which you can gain access to after a proper internal integration and activation of additional DNA strands. The sun is a group of beings that makes up a collective from the thirteenth dimension. They are one of a kind in this space. With their help you are able to travel wherever you desire because they have a complete set of light codes to other realities and dimensions, that is a sort of a set of symbiote energies that allow for multidimensional exploration."

"This is something I wouldn't have probably figured myself out," I remarked. Since I came to Majka's house, I was tormented by weird emotions. On the one hand, I really wanted to be there, but on the other hand — which I was surprised with — I felt anxious. Some sort of tiny internal part of me wanted to just run away from there.

Mrs. Maja continued her small lecture and I switched to listening and trying to ignore my feelings.

"You need to know that the energy of the sun is the best for cleansing the mental programs that are coded deeply into your central nervous system. It allows you to clean the peripheral nervous system from the patterns that block your infinite potential. Humans also have an unlimited point of observation but it is blinded by the workings of the human belief system that they need to cleanse themselves from so as to unlock that ability. That's why, working with the sun and the sun meditation is the fundamental exercise. This opens up the possibility to restore your full potential.

"How to do it exactly?" Kal inquired.

I thought that I already knew that since I first — and last time — connected to the higher realms via the meditation with the sunset. I remembered my Mom's intervention, nevertheless. I even began to consider if I had been able to return to reality without her help.

"It's a very good question, dear boy. You need to know exactly how to do it so that it's absolutely safe for the physical body. Always, absolutely always, when you enter the multidimensional space or the astral realm, it is incredibly important to stick to the safety rules. Otherwise, such a journey can end up not very well. Just like on Earth, there are a sort of health and safety rules that need to be strictly adhered to."

"Can you teach us Majka?" I requested. I was already sure that during that meditation on that day I did not follow any rules.

"Of course, my loves. I'll present to you for now two techniques for meditation with the sun — with closed and opened eyes — they will be sufficient for a start. Ready?"

"I have an impression that always," Kal laughed out and me and my parents joined him.

"Kal is always ready for the next dosage of knowledge," I summed up.

"And are you not?" Majka chuckled. "This only proves that he doesn't notice any barriers that could be standing in the way of the full awakening of his consciousness. If you were blocking the information or doubting it guided by the ego, you would put a sort of a block on the channelled messages from the worlds of higher energies. However, if you open yourself to the knowledge and feel its vibration with your heart, it will always tell you if the knowledge is true or not. This is resonance. The heart resonates only with the truth to which your soul has access to.

"I understand." I smiled at Mrs Majka giving her a signal, at the same time, that I also am ready to absorb new knowledge without any blockages.

"Great. So... when you're outside, close your eyes and face the sun. Visualize a portal that is located thirty centimeters away, that is letting through a beam of light photons into your head. Next, imagine that you extend that light stream and direct it towards the back of your head where the pineal gland is located.

This way of meditating leads to the stimulation of not only the left, but also the right hemisphere of the brain. This is the way of creating new synaptic pathways and connections that lead to the synchronization of brainwaves and clearing of the core of the brain that is responsible for the subconscious programming. This is the process of tuning the brain frequency to different brainwaves. You start to feel with the parts of the brain that you haven't used before. If you feel any tickling or itching sensation, or electrical impulses in your body during this process that cause distractions at the moments in which you practically catch a better connection, this is a sign that your nervous system and the programs of the subscious as well as all the other personalities that let you know about themselves, they try to distract you from exploration. It happens so because when you learn who you really are, you won't need them anymore, you'll gain a new, fresh perspective on the surrounding reality. We will move to the health and safety rules. Meditation with the eyes closed can be done at the beginning for no longer than a few minutes. The maximum of ten minutes for a start but, in the course of the time, you should extend that process, and remember to always focus on your body and feeling. The sun rays stimulate the pineal gland, if you feel any vibrations, it means that you start to properly work with those energies and the connection is being opened.

"I think I know now what I'm going to do tomorrow," Kal summed up.

"Remember about the rules and caution," Majeczka reminded him.

Even I read it as a plan for the whole day.

"Yes, of course. Only ten minutes for a start," Kal announced to calm us down.

"Very well. Let's move to a more difficult meditation then, namely the one that is conducted with the eyes open. You can do it only during the sunrise or sunset, when the UV radiation is equal to zero so as not to harm yourself. You start such a meditation from ten seconds and every next day you add another ten seconds to the previous time. If you miss a day, next time you add ten

21

second to the time you spent before. And so on the tenth day you stop at the hundred seconds of looking at the sun. Next, you take a three days break. After this break, which is the eleventh day of the practice, the time span of sun gazing will amount to hundred and ten seconds. In this way, your eyes will adjust to the sunlight without any health complications. You gaze directly into the sun every time. After nine months you can even reach forty-five minutes. Connected to the sun energy with the threads in this way you will start to see the energy in the air. It will be visible for you and perceptive in the form of a sort of a diamond powder that is shining and vibrating beautifully. By absorbing more light, you stimulate your third eye which will enable you to perceive many interesting things that are not only in this space, but also in the multidimension."

"So we have a plan for spending our every evening for the next nine months." Kal summed up, proud of himself and you could sense he was completely serious.

"That would be for sure a practice that you would certainly appreciate in time. Your symbiote, that is your soul reached the Earth through the sun, remember that. Therefore, you have such a beautiful connection with it. It is like a portal for you. The sun contains the DNA codes that allow for the further activation process in the human body, these are human codes, including Shiru codes. And one more thing. I sincerely ask you, while meditating with the sun do not try to push anything because you won't achieve anything by that. The mind has to be calmed down. The healing and DNA activation is a process, in many cases very long one, not a one time event, believe me."

"Is spending time in the sun throughout the day also activating a process of transformation or is it only the sun meditation and direct connection?" I enquired, because Daddy was always saying that a day without an hour spent outside in fresh air is a wasted day. I already knew that, whatever Daddy said, it was not accidental.

"Of course, it is. Really, I recommend you spend the minimum of an hour a day in the sunlight because not only your eyes, which are the portal to your brain, absorb the light, but also your whole being. Your skin, your hair. Everything. You absorb light codes with your whole body. On the other hand, the connection and the sun meditation allow for a quick stimulation of the pineal gland, the clearing of unnecessary programs, and the activation of additional DNA strands."

"The myth about the harmfulness of the sun has just been debunked," Kal announced that with such an elevated tone of voice as if he was just making a speech for millions of viewers in public television.

"Well said. Don't let anyone persuade you that the sun is harmful. This is one of the myths of the old world and a program that was meant to cause fear in order to move you away from the process of ascension and remembrance of who you are. The energy of the sun can bring miracles in the process of the awakening of consciousness. After some time of raising your vibrations and accumulating energy, it's quite possible that you will hear the bell or other sounds which may initially sound weird. Please, do not be afraid of that. These are transformations of the DNA strands and the effects of an update, which will be taking place.

"Do these sounds mean anything in particular?" Kal asked suddenly and I sensed that this question had a solid foundation in his personal experiences…

"If you hear ringing in your right ear, in the central part of it, this means a telepathic contact and the sending of data from the light resonance, but if the sounds is located more at the back of your head, behind the right ear, this means that the system of domination and control is using their etheric frequencies to block the signal."

"So…" Kal pondered.

I guess Majeczka immediately sensed what he might have meant by that.

"The bell above the right ear is responsible for the transmission of information and creating some sort of a bridge. While this bell is ringing, your code is transforming the structure of the brain — it merges the aspect of perceiving and processing so that your biological brain can process more information, and also so that you can effectively awaken your gifts for multidimensional perception. The bell above your left ear induces the interaction with high-dimensional beings whom the soul connections are made with. These can be not only positive, but also negative beings, this will mainly be dependent on your internal intentions which, being the energy, bombard your aura with the cloak of energy so as to repel or attract other beings. Therefore, it is of utmost importance to clear the intentions of anger and negativity from your consciousness and all the timelines in order to become a sovereign being and experience only those contacts that you want to allow yourself. The bells in your ears are, therefore, a sign of feeling and hearing higher vibrations and a sort of a bridge to the telepathic communication between worlds that you can't perceive with your eyes yet. This connection is a wonderful tool on the journey of retrieval of your consciousness. So as to support this process, you can also meditate on those sounds and synchronize your brain hemispheres with their help. By shifting your consciousness to the side where the sound is less audible, you will strengthen it with your focus. After the sound is balanced, you can search for other tones. After the appearance of three of them, it starts to be really loud. The sound or the tone is nothing else but a sound vibration which flows down and covers with a beautiful protective cloak like a cocoon. From this point, it is not a long way to reach the ability of creating mimicry around you. The connection to higher energies is indeed something incredible. It's a stream of inexhaustible information in which one would like to swim and dive into eternally. At first you will encounter blocks in your capabilities. Your biological body will be letting you know if it is able to absorb more energy or not".

"How will we know what kind of beings and information we have drawn to us?" I asked. I already knew then that the sole unawareness that you can draw both good and bad energies can create many problems.

"It's mainly a matter of your vibration. It's very crucial for

24

you to remember that you need to take care of your safety at all times. Because of the technologies and false geometrical pattern that is spread across the Earth plane, you can get lost very easily. This pattern leads to the dimensions created by the system of dominance and control which, believe my word, you wouldn't prefer to sightsee. That's why it is so important to stay in your heart space and be guided by the love for the whole creation. This love, this light inside of you is your protection. Every night, completely unaware, you experience a few astral travels, but the majority of people don't remember them though because they are so cut off their frequency of light."

"Can you somehow get protection against these dark energies?" I enquired, because deep inside me I could still feel that this knowledge would be useful for me. I still had this weird anxiety in me. As if the dark entity that had attacked me, did not leave me in fact. I had the impression that I was in the space that I did not belong to. As if I was very far away from home.

"Of course, there are many ways of protecting not only yourself, but also the space where you are. You can do it by, for example, placing crystals in every corner of your bed or place where you sleep. If you have never worked with the crystals, start doing it. It doesn't matter what crystals, you can use any of them."

"How does this protection work?" I kept asking further.

"It works so because the beings from the crystals create a protective shield during your astral travels. This barrier doesn't let negative energies in and direct you to the right stream of light frequency so that you can dream with the energy of Gaia. It is with her that you have a connection unconditionally and she won't let anything bad happen to you. You need to know as well that dreaming with Gaia leads eventually to the exploration of a so-called earthly Akasha and to gaining insight into other incarnations, both the past and the future ones. These are the records of the evolution of your soul and experiences that it chose on the path of its learning across dimensions and timelines.

"The subconscious is important as well," Daddy interrupted. "It's extremely important to reprogram your subconscious in a positive way so that it helps you. Therefore, use your conscious intentions in order to create new neural pathways which, in time, will become really strong and will create automatic patterns of thoughts that lead to behaviours that will stay with you for the rest of your lives. For example — let the smile of a stranger automatically trigger a smile on your face and the sadness of your neighbor — the eagerness to help him or her. These are the pathways that if blazed on systematically in the same way they will become a trail for you that is worth following. Create only beautiful paths, for the ones that you have created will arrange your life here.

"Nju-en is right," Majeczka spoke again. All that time she was watching me carefully. I did not know why. Or maybe I knew. I was suspecting that she knew something that my own consciousness was afraid of at that moment. "The subconscious mind guides us in ninety, or even ninety-five percent of time, and the conscious mind in five up to ten percent. That's why you need persistence and effort to create a new scheme. I would like to emphasize that this requires a strong character and self-discipline. It's not that easy and not many succeed for the first time. You can't give in after the first obstacle encountered."

"How fast can you create such a new pathway as a pattern for the subconscious behaviour?" Kal asked who had a technical and detailed approach to everything.

"Great question. Of course I'll answer. Every decision of yours and every action will create new neural pathways and after twenty one days of a repeated model of action or reaction, the neural pathway will be strong and crystallized enough in order for the habit to appear more automatically. It will get rooted in your subconscious mind and merge with who you are, who you want to be for yourselves and others.

"I hardly ever remember my dreams. They are some sort of flashes. I never really manage to remember it from the beginning till the end. Why does it happen?" Kal seemed to be focused. He was inquisitive and inquiring. I knew that night he would use the whole knowledge that Mrs. Majka was teaching us. I was proud of him. I could not focus to the extent I wanted. I could feel that all the time. That was weird ...

"It's very important for you to get to the point in which you without any effort will be able to remember every scene and every microsecond from every experience from your astral travels done while sleeping. This leads to the retrieval of your access to the memories of your soul. And what follows is that this gives you access to every type of psychic abilities — from telepathic abilities and contacts with other beings to biolocation and travels to different places and dimensions. These abilities depend on, to a great extent, what your DNA is holding".

"I was writing down my dreams," I said shyly.

"Very well, Smaisi. You cannot even imagine how extraordinarily important is having a dream record! Fill it up every time you wake up. Straightaway I forewarn you that every of the mechanical patterns set off from your central neurological system after you wake up. As a result of this, there appear all sorts of thoughts about work, preparing a morning coffee, the worries about the next day, pressure in the bladder, so on and so forth. Don't give away your power to those subconscious patterns and focus on remembering what you have experienced during your sleep. You are the rulers of your reality, take full control and don't fall into the embrace of the dominance system immediately after you wake up. Ideally, lie down peacefully and try to remember the whole astral trip that you have experienced. Step by step. Ideally, you can do it backwards. Start always from remembering the last memory and go backwards to remember the whole. If you will have difficulties in synchronizing with this beam of light that enables the exploration of the memories — send the energy from every chakra to the root chakra starting from the crown chakra. This will stabilize the connection with the frequency of light of Mother Gaia. And remember that those moments after you wake up are yours and only yours. Please don't let yourself get caught up in the automatic patterns. Use the alpha waves for your growth. These memories and the remembrance of the memory of your soul will lead you to the retrieval of your heritage, and it's high time for that. After some time of resonance and experience you will notice a certain pattern. It will allow you to dive into these processes more deeply. Remember that your ego keeps taking control and creates the illusion that you don't need to do it because you will remember what you have dreamt of. Nothing is more misleading than that. Look out for this trap! There's no real growth without the notes. And the intention you set before sleep is substantial as well. Repeat this exercise every day like a mantra and you will soon see the results. Always, I repeat, always create your own intention."

"These are very useful pieces of information! Thank you!" Kal summed up and only then did I notice that he was meticulously scribbling down some notes.

Majka was still watching me carefully. At one moment, she suddenly grabbed her phone. Mommy started to wriggle nervously on the chair which made me a little anxious. I had not seen her acting this way for a long time and since we arrived at Mrs. Majka's house had been mysteriously calm and taciturn.

"Come, son. I will need you." Mrs. Majka's words were seemingly normal, but I sensed a hidden message in them.

Although I did not know what the message was, I was sure that Mommy knew exactly. Not wanting to be kept unaware, I looked empathically at Mommy first, and next at Mrs. Majeczka. She understood instantly what I meant by that.

"You will need my son's help, Smaisi. The entity that has visited you today, is still with you. It's an energy hookup. I sense that your soul let this happen so that you know what it feels like when you're not alone, when someone pulls energy out of you and sucks you into the space of low vibration, fear and anger. This happened so that in future you will be able to react quickly. The more you can, the more entities will want to stop you in your actions, even though your light will be brighter and brighter. There will always be beings powerful and persistent enough to wait for the right moment to infiltrate your energy. These are the traps of the low vibrations. However, living on Earth, you won't be able to avoid them completely. This is just impossible. I will teach you today how to light yourself up in the garden of your soul so that

28

your light becomes almost electrifying so that you become almost invisible. This will help you minimize the risk of energy hookups. But before I do it, I want my son to set your light soul free from the hookup that has been made. I want you to be yourself fully and synchronized in your light energy when you will be creating the oasis of peace and safety which you can enter at any time."

I already knew very well what was going on. My impressions were right. However my consciousness and ego directed by the thoughts of this entity were trying to reject this truth, I felt something was not right all the time. I was hoping that Majka's son would come in no time and release me from this distraught that I was going through being not in my vibration.

Chapter 2

"I Am

You conceive what there is, You are everything and nothing at the same time. The illusion, the fun that is called life's a temporary forgetfulness of who you really are. The way you perceive Yourself, that is everything that is around you depends on Your level of consciousness that can be compared to the ocean that consists of countless amounts of water drops. Apart from the ocean, you are the water drop too, connecting with the ocean you become it too and the ocean will always be a part of you and you will be a part of the ocean. Is it possible then to get off your path?

You can temporarily get disoriented , however, you will always get back on the trail. This is also part of this journey. You create always and continually, in every moment beyond time in Here and Now. This game, you can only win because you are the game."

Damian Buczniewicz

The garden of the soul — your inner light is you

We were sitting mostly in silence anticipating the arrival of Majka's son, whom she had told us about only that his name was Mariusz and he had been helping the souls in the astral plane for decades. He had the ability to penetrate into the astral plane and multi-dimensional and to see everything that was there. No entity was able to hide from him regardless of the space it was located in. He scanned the human energetic body like an earthly X-ray device. He was repairing what was damaged, bringing back the correct energetics and detaching any hooked up entities. He could merge the soul if it had been divided into pieces and located in different spaces. I had no idea how he was doing this and what the way of chasing away the low-vibrational energies and energetic parasites was, but I really wanted his magical powers, as that was how I perceived them at that time, to work on me as well so that they could liberate me and retrieve my old myself. I hoped that my soul had permitted this one time episode only for the purpose of my learning and growth and that I would not have to go through that again. While I was dwelling on considerations and hopes, the front doors flanged open letting in already freezing fall air.

Into the living room, where we had been sitting, entered a man that had a nice appearance and a big smile on his face. First, he approached his mother and hugged her tightly. In the air were floating vibrations of respect and their mutual love. Only after that did he look at us and greeted one by one with everyone. When his eyes stopped on me, I was sure that he already knew that I was the reason for his immediate visit at Majka's house. He sat comfortably at one of the armchairs and stared at me. I felt the tormenting emotions inside me. They were not mine. The being that hooked up on me was afraid. It already knew what was coming.

"There are many of them, mom. I will need your support," said Majka's son and I shivered.

Kal was sitting motionless and he completely did not know how to act. I sensed that he could not get over the fact that the whole negative energy was focused on me. I knew that he would have bravely taken this blow on himself, without a blink of an eye, If only he could have.

"Smaisi, relax." Mariusz interrupted my thoughts. "Do not cross your arms or your legs. You can close your eyes if you want to."

I did what he had told me. Soon after a while I felt a light hit at my body,

"I entered your space," he continued, "You have a strong aura and protection. It must have been difficult for them to get through you...", he suddenly stopped." These are Carians," he announced after a while. "There are many of them. They'd been waiting patiently for the moment of your weakness. They had been accumulating energy and forces to pierce through. I can see cords attached to your chest, heart, and spine. One of them comes out of your head. These cords look like dark thick threads. They are the connection between your energy body and these entities. I will need to cut off these connections. Do you agree to that?"

I froze. I wanted to shout out loud that of course I did, but my voice got stuck in my throat. Mariusz noticed that.

"Smaisi, fight with them. Do you want me to cut off these cords?" his tone of voice was not pleading, it was commanding.

I surrendered to that. I focused with all my might on the light inside me and I spit out:

"Yes, I allow that!"

Perhaps it was only my imagination, but I felt like the connections one by one disconnect between me and those Carian beings and the cords are falling slowly down on the ground like hairs coming out of the ponytail. Gradually, I started to feel greater and greater relief.

"I give each and every one of them two possibilities. I open two portals. They will decide if they want to go to the light or the darkness, which is exactly where they came from," Majka's son was telling me.

Honestly, I was not even considering what they would choose. I was so happy with my freedom again, that everything else for this one short moment was completely irrelevant. It was only after all the emotions subsided and I did not feel Mariusz in my space, I asked timidly:

"What did they choose?" I do not know what I wanted to hear and what I was counting on. The curiosity arose in me about what had happened to those beings that enslaved me.

"They chose the darkness, Smaisi. They are Carians. It was not a surprise for me at all."

"Why did you allow them to choose if you knew what they would choose?"

"It's not difficult to judge. I offer light to every being. These

are my rules," he admitted honestly. I liked his attitude. It was noble and righteous.

"Do at least some of them choose it?" I inquired. I was curious if the tunnel leading to light had ever been chosen thanks to Mariusz's amazing will who was giving everyone an opportunity to connect with the Source again.

"You would be surprised, how many of them have chosen light," he responded.

I did not expect that. I had not even known until then that they had a choice.

"Their mind, which to a great extent is collective, does not allow that and blocks the possibility to choose light because that's what you've been thinking of, right?" Mariusz asked, but before I could answer anything, he continued: "It happens though, that the individuals are so strong and they have such a strong connection to their own self that they choose light, despite the blocks imposed on the collective. Not everyone likes to cause pain. More and more beings want to follow the light, because they know that the time is coming that there will be no pace for them on Earth and, in turn, the energy that is food for them. Everything that is dark will be fought off by the light. Or at least that's one of the timelines if humans choose right."

"If..." I repeated quitely.

"Only the belief in that choice will propel and motivate us to be doing what we've been doing," he summed up. "I don't think I'm needed here anymore."

"How about you telling us some interesting stories connected with the release of the souls?" Kal requested with an almost pleading tone of voice, "I'm sure it's much better than any science-fiction movie."

"That's true. It is really interesting sometimes. Let it be, then. I'll tell you one of such stories. But only one because I know that this being would permit that."

"Is that a secret?" I was surprised.

"You can say that. What happens to every soul belongs to them. The soul decides, just like you've had to decide today. I couldn't have done that without your conscious consent and your free will."

"I understand now," I responded. "They tried to influence my free will."

"I know, that's why I was so stubbornly and with emphasis influencing it on the other side. The light always wins over the darkness, Smaisi. Regardless of how dark it is. Even a small spark can light it up."

Both Kal and I sat comfortably and were ready for an interesting story. My parents were curious too. I was suspecting that they did not often have the opportunity to listen to Mariusz's stories. And they must have been really special.

"The release I'm about to tell you concerns my friend Yriah" he began.

Immediately I realized that we had met her before. I became even more interested in this story. For I knew that it was connected with the incarnation of a cherub on Earth.

"It was a time when the forces of darkness were particularly imprinting everyone, and the beings that descended on Earth to incarnate and help in waking the rest up were hit the hardest," Mariusz went on, "None of the protective barriers were able to keep these forces away for long. They always found a way to sneak in. That was when Yriah called me for help. We had been friends before. One day she sensed that something was not right. Her vibrations fell down and the physical body was affected in a painful way. Almost immediately I went into the astral world to see what was going on there. It turned out her assumptions were right. Despite the powerful protection she had due to her mission on Earth, the dark beings captured her soul and locked in a huge cage in their low-vibrational space. Even though she was still in her light cocoon , they managed to pull her into the place that was meant to gradually lower her vibration and to eventually enable their direct hookup. I released her from the gate she was held at and something struck me. I took her up high to the place that was a blue and white cloud. We met there with a character which filled Yriah up with the energy of power to fight. It seemed that she was floating in an indigo color through which one could see the most distant galaxies. I could feel inside me that this wasn't enough and something was telling me that I should take her to Kalikena. This is a planet inhabited called by the beings of Earth the dragons. We were welcomed warmly and Yriah received from them a light armor that was to protect her. The dragons knew that Yriah was very important for them. At the beginning we didn't know why. Only after some time did we learn that her being had a dragon aspect and the roots of her origin go far, up to Saturia. It became clear to us that somehow she was one of them and the dragons offered her help to protect her."

When Mariusz finished his story tears were welling up in my eyes. This was such an amazing story that I wanted to dive in it for a little longer.

"I remember perfectly the moment when I told Yriah about her origin," he added. "She was so excited that the information was lifting her up high, raising her vibrations. What I love the most in what I do is the fact that I can see beings merging their soul, growing, becoming more beautiful, and following their destiny. There's nothing more beautiful and graceful than that. I think that this is enough of an impression for today. You're about to travel to the astral world with my mother and this will also exhaust you slightly."

Mariusz said goodbye to everyone and left us with Majeczka. My emotions were gradually returning to the original state — the state of my vibration. I felt completely myself again.

"I think you're finally ready for your first guided astral travel," said Majeczka. "Perhaps not entirely the first one because you've been in many spaces not even once, but the one we will create, will be forever only yours. I would like you to sit on a couch comfortably," as she was saying that she stood up and approached a huge oak wardrobe. She took out two huge thick blankets and gave them to us.

"What is it for?" Kal was surprised.

"While entering the astral world and being in the alpha state frequency you send out part of your energy into that space. The body stays here, completely still. This causes the loss of warmth and a sense of coldness. This is more to make you comfortable. At the frequency of alpha waves you will be aware of what's happening in both spaces. This is not complete hypnosis. Nothing like that. This is consciously appearing in a higher realm without full out of body experience."

Hearing that, I wrapped myself up tightly with the blanket that my parents laughed out loud. They immediately calmed out after seeing Majeczka's meaningful look. You could hear soft music in the background.

"Close your eyes, clear your mind," Majka began calmly. "Relax. Take three deep breaths and breathe out slowly. With every consecutive breath let your body become more and more relaxed, the muscles become lazy, calmed down, " Majka went on and I breathed in deeply and let the air out.

I could feel that with this breath any tension in my body was released. I felt blissful.

"Now, the breath returns to your normal pace," Majeczka continued. "You sit comfortably, you feel safe. Your eyes are closed all the time. Now look with your inner energetic eye. High above you there appears to be a beautiful sky. It's a sunny summer-time day — it's warm and nice. You notice two white clouds, just like the ones during the nice weather. What do they remind you of? Just notice that only... In your sky there's also sun and it has just sent a gift to you. Receive it. Maybe it's a thing or maybe only a thought that comes to your mind... Notice it and remember. It's yours..." she said quietly.

I looked at the sun. Out of its disk there flew out a bird. I looked at it closely and I saw a white dove flying in my direction. It sat on my arm and cooed quietly. I was about to say something but I held back and focused on what Mrs. Majka was saying.

"And now look around. This is the garden of your soul. The garden is you. Only you know what it looks like. Your garden is your sanctuary. In this garden, none can harm you and you cannot harm anyone. This is the zone of your unconditional safety. Even if a mosquito sits on your nose, remember that you can't kill it. If in your garden, there would appear a huge lion, you don't need to be afraid of it. It won't threaten you because it knows, just like you do, that this place is safe for everyone. You can walk towards it and hug it. Do it now..." she requested with a serene tone of voice.

I saw that right next to me there lied an enormous lion. Its majestic mane was asking to dip the fingers in it and comb its hair. Pushed by the desire and convinced that I was safe — I did that. The lion leaned towards me as if giving me permission for what I was about to do. Its mane was soft and warm. After a while I cuddled the lion and he was purring quietly in content. I felt only the energy of love around."

"In your garden there is a beautiful meadow, look for it, "Majeczka went on.

With a tinge of sadness I left the lion lying on the grass, I looked around and continued listening.

"It's filled with alluring colorful flowers. Or perhaps these are crops? Only you know how this looks. It's yours. Can you see it now? It's pretty, isn't it? There is a small hill in the middle of the meadow. Can you see it? Go in this direction. This is your own hill. Sit on it like in a chair."

I did what Majka instructed and I sat comfortably on the tiny hill. My meadow was almost entirely filled with red poppies. They were stretching around for hundreds of meters creating a beautiful carpet. This view was breath-taking."

"Are you sitting comfortably?" she asked. "Now have a look, on the ground right under your feet there are opening two little holes. This is Mother Earth opening to you. Anything that is low vibrational, whole anger and whole sadness will be absorbed by her, and this energy will be transmuted into a positive one."

I immediately noticed two tiny holes in the ground. I was even wondering if I can see Gaia through them.

"Look up now," Majka continued. "On your head there has begun to fall delightful light. Bright, clear, golden." She was speaking in a way that I saw it and almost immediately felt soft tingling and warmth on my head — as if the light was filling me up with energy. "The light is filling you up slowly. At first, it lights up your brain. Your left and right hemisphere. Both of them are shining equally bright. It's very important for them to shine equally. The light is flowing down and and lights up respectively your eyes, ears, your sinus and cheeks. Your whole head is now beautifully and evenly lightened up and the light is still descending onto you, lighting up your chest. And her by the principle of a line. What is above the line is beautifully lightened up, and what's below it, is still gray and soiled. The light pushes all the gray down and from your feet... " she suspended her voice to take a deep breath. "Can you see anything? Perhaps there's a gray smoke coming out of them, or perhaps soiled water flows on the ground or tar? Simply notice that anything that is bad is getting cleansed and taken by Mother Earth. And the light is still bright inside of you. It reached your arms and hands, now it's filling up the lungs and is shining too. And it doesn't matter how particular organs look like — each of them is equally lightened up. And now focus on the places when something was hurting, bothering. Bring there as much light as it's possible."

I could exactly see and feel everything that she was saying. At first I had the impression that I was only imagining that, but when I started to feel warmth gradually embracing my whole body and filling it up it hit me that the energy of the Source is really inside me.

"The lovely light has reached your loins and is splitting into your two legs," Majka went on. "It's highlighting your thighs, calves up to your feet. Your whole body is now highlighted. You're shining. The holes in the ground are closing now and everything that was dark and gray doesn't belong to you anymore. And now stand on the hill and notice that the light is still flowing onto your head. It thickens inside of you, filling you up more and more until it starts to overflow your body. It embraces you creating around you a sphere of light. Take care of the fact that the light is equally intense in every place, so that its rim is even. And now look at yourself. How beautifully shining you are. This light — it's you! It's inside of you. Remember that always. It will protect you always."

I could see myself closed in a lovely sphere of light. I was warm and cozy inside of it. I did not want to come out of it. I tuned with the light completely and kept it inside of me, I hugged it with love.

"And now forget about your light." Majka said suddenly. "It's inside of you all the time so you don't need to visualize it anymore. It's you and you are it. Take a walk in your garden. What can you see? Everything that is there, reflects your emotions, your feelings. If there's something not right, the garden will show you that. You are not alone here though. You have your energetic guardian that will always help you. Look, on the right there is a huge flowery bush. It's taller than you and so wide that it's impossible to see what's behind it. What are its flowers? Are there many of them? Simply notice that, " she requested and I saw it immediately. "Now, walk around your bush. Before you find your dearest friend, your spiritual and energetic guardian. He's there. Go and greet him. He's been waiting for you for long.

My bush was full of wonderful pink flowers with five petals. There were so many of them that it was hard to notice the green of its leaves. I hesitantly walked around it. I did to know what to expect. However, as soon as I was behind it a tall man appeared in front of me. He was in a shimmering armor, the silver and gold were mixing with one another. His hair was blonde and wonderful blue-azure eyes. On his back there were enormous beautiful white wings. He was covered by a rainbow aura that I could not take my eyes of.

"Hello, Smaisi." he spoke to me and I could not believe how realistic he was. "I've been waiting for this meeting. My name is Nael."

"Hello, Nael. You're a winged light being," I noted. I was moved that such a being was my guardian.

"Yes, Smaisi. To be precise, a seraphin." he explained.

"The angel of love," I said as if to myself but he could hear me exactly. He beamed.

"Come closer, Smaisi." he requested so I approached him closer. "I connect with you with my light and my immense love for you" he announced and from his chest there shot out a beam of

bright light and love filling me up to the rim. "I love you and I bless you. I will always protect you during your earthly journey. You can always turn to me and I shall help you."

I felt that I should do the same. So I sent a beam of beautiful bright light from my heart to his.

"We're connected." I said calmly because I could feel this connection very well inside me. As if I was never to be lonely again.

"Yes, Smaisi, It was always like that, you've never been alone and I was always by your side, ensuring that you reach exactly where you are — the place of our meeting. Only now will you be aware that I am beside you and awareness is a huge power of creation. You can always come to the garden to talk to me or call me when you need help or support. I will always answer your call."

"Does Kal have you as his guardian too?" I was curious if the fact that we were halves of the same soul mattered.

"No, Smaisi. Kal has his own guardian. In fact, every person has a few guardians. Not only one. Many of them incarnate on Earth to keep an eye on you in matter.

"What do you mean by that?" I inquired.

"Kal is your guardian, and you're his. Isn't it obvious for you? The next one you'll meet soon." he said quite mysteriously.

I was about to ask for details but I sensed that he would not tell me anything more on this subject.

"Next time" he promised.

At the same time I heard Majka's voice again:

"The music's over and you're leaving your garden."

Suddenly I stopped hearing the music in the background. I sensed intuitively that the time spent in the garden finished.

"Move your body slightly, your arms and legs. Open your eyes. And you're here." she finished.

I opened my eyes and I looked directly at Mrs. Majeczka who was sitting in front of me smiling brightly.

"How was it?" she asked.

"Amazing!" Kal answered before me.

I was curious how his guardian looked, I was sure he would tell me all about it.

"Wonderful" I responded only, equalizing my enthusiasm with the one that Kal bursted out with. It was only then that I felt lightness inside me. That was incredible. As if all my problems were suddenly gone.

"Because they're gone." Majka responded as if reading my mind. "You lightened them all up. You're light, there's no room for grays in it. Remember that the light will always illuminate the darkness regardless of how scary it might be. And you, my dear lady, together with the other star children are the light for the people. Look at the darkness they are plagued with. It's time to become the lighthouse that illuminates their way to life that they've always longed for. Now that you know how to illuminate yourself, go and illuminate the whole world. You have the power inside you to do that. And you Kal, too," she added so that Kal did not feel omitted in any way. "If you ever need help, you know where you can find me. The doors of this house will always be open wide for you."

We chatted with Mrs. Maja for some time. It was getting late though and it was time for our return home. I was glad I got there. I felt… — I could not even describe it correctly — liberated. All the evil and fear that captured me after the morning energetic attack — were completely gone. What is more, I had that certainty that they would never return. Nothing and none could ever wade through my light.

Chapter 3

"Creation

"Thoughts create reality. Under the condition that you identify with them, you give them power. The majority of people are oblivious of the fact that they identify with their thoughts. The stream of thoughts can be so strong, that the person can be unaware of the fact that it flows through him or her. The vast majority of thoughts do not belong to us. It is the creation of the stream that absorbs the person into the depths of often absurd creations."

Damian Buczniewicz

The perspective of the fifth dimension of consciousness

Since meeting Majka I have entered my garden of soul almost every day. I went back to distant incarnations with my memories and Nael assisted me. I was definitely better at traveling into the past at that moment. I was slowly missing Semjase. Three weeks have passed since our last meeting. I was focused on writing everything down but I felt that I was ready for another dose of knowledge and I knew that only she could offer me that.

I attended the school because I had to. I did not want to begin to stand out suddenly. I was happy I had Kal and that I was not alone in all that. Since the meditation in the garden of soul, Kal was often thoughtful. As if he was still processing everything that happened there, including the day before when the meeting with Majka was kind of pressurized by the circumstances. He entered the garden just like me, but he did that less often. He focused on broadening his knowledge about the extraterrestrial beings and the identification of them. He wrote down their agendas, origin and tried to draw out the lines of genetic codes, creating huge families of beings by doing so. In this regard he reminded me of Daddy a little.

That evening I was sitting alone, jotting down on the computer the memories from my last visit in the garden.

"Are you ready?" I heard a familiar voice and I almost jumped up happily.

"Are you back?" I asked, craving for a confirmation.

"Yes, Smaisi. I'll see you tonight." Semjase confirmed and disappeared.

I suppose I had never been getting ready and eating dinner so quickly in my life before. My parents were looking at me oddly, probably they were suspecting what the origin of my behaviour was. It was only when I was walking, or rather running upstairs, I heard a bit ironic tone of Mommy's voice:

"Enjoy your trip, dear daughter." She always knew when and what to say.

I crawled under the duvet and sleep almost immediately took over me. Semjase's teachings about calming the mind were not in vain and despite enormous excitement I managed to control the thoughts so that I could fall asleep without any obstacles. The trips to the garden of the soul also taught me that. After these few weeks, I could calmly say with my hand on my heart that I was quite good and efficient at that.

As soon as I felt the sand under my feet I knew where I was. The sound of the sea waves was again echoing in my ears so beautifully with a tune I missed that I started to dance spontaneously on the beach, spinning around with a childlike joy. Then, someone caught me and began to guide me in the dance. I did not need to open my eyes to know it was Kal who found me. His lips softly touching mine were only the confirmation.

"I adore you like this," he whispered into my ear.

"Like what?" I inquired, wanting him to say it out loud.

"Well... that free..." he replied.

This word was a perfect description of how I felt then. In that space, there were no barriers, rules, or programs. I was completely myself and I could feel with my entire self the freedom of my being.

"Welcome."

Semjase's loud voice brought us back into order. We knew that the romantic moment was over and it was time for a lesson.

"I've been missing you so much," I whispered uncontrollably.

"I could feel your emotions, Smaisi. I missed you too. Sometimes there is that moment though when I need to complete a task in many other spaces which makes me too busy."

"Of course, we understand. Simply we just like our nightly meetings," Kal tuned in.

"We had adventures." I confessed immediately.

"I know, Smaisi. Nothing happens without a reason and it was the same in this case. Every experience — regardless of the fact if it's on a physical, spiritual, or astral plane — it has its purpose. It's another step without which further climbing wouldn't be possible. Your protective shield was lowered for a bit so that you could experience certain things and learn more. Now you know how you can protect yourself on your own. You don't need anyone else to do that for you. Your wisdom is a sufficient protection on its own."

"Where are you taking us today?" I asked.

"To the very source of every existence" she answered mysteriously and I got shivers all over my body.

"That's what I was waiting for," Kal added and sat comfortably on the sandy beach.

Semjase and I did the same. Then, something incredible happened. From the distant corners of the beach small creatures started to approach us. Water turtles, crabs — there were hundreds of them. They stopped near us as if waiting for Semjase's story.

"It's become very crowded," I laughed.

"Don't be surprised, they want to hear too" Semjase replied, amused and then one of the crabs pinched me lightly on my hand.

"Au" I winced and glanced at the crab with a slightly angry look and it crawled up on my lap and lied comfortably.

"I guess he was flirting with you," Kal suggested and all three of us burst out with the laughter that sound of which echoed far over the ocean or at least this was the impression that it gave.

"Today, my beloved, I would like to tell you what the symbiote is. I've already used this name in my previous stories a few times. Today though we will dive into this subject — into the origin of each of us. You already know that this term is equal to the word 'soul'. So, what is the soul? Where does it come from and how does it incarnate in the matter in order to create intelligent physical organisms?"

"Oh, I would love to learn about that!" Kal was ready for everything as always.

I felt that his brain was focused on listening and remembering. Nothing and none could interrupt him at that moment.

"I'm glad that you so willingly approach every subject." You could notice that Semjase liked to teach, to remind us of what we already knew so well but was forgotten. With every day I knew more and more and the more I knew the greater the craving was although I was aware that I would never learn everything. The earthly time was simply too short for that, or at least the one that humans had in one incarnation.

"The soul is a subtle and etheric form of your being. The souls are born and exist for hundreds of years, and there are also such souls that can boast about millions of years of evolution in different incarnations and physical densities. The soul is assigned to the reality in a given space and undeniably exists completely independently from the physical body which, as you already know, is changeable. It is only a container in which the symbiote has a chance to experience while being in the process of growth. Every soul in the universe is assigned and their existence is not dependent on their level of vibration or the stage of evolution that the given being is at. What is more, you need to know that the symbiote can exist in forty levels of vibrations and frequencies that intertwine

47

simultaneously in a given dimension and space. And there are billions of such dimensions. The soul is multidimensional and can have experiences in many spaces at the same time."

"Hmmm..." I pondered.

"What's on your mind, Smaisi?" Kal asked me.

"How to illustrate the existence of the soul in multidimensional space?"

"It's quite easy. That's what I've been actually thinking about lately," Kal responded to me, and both Semjase and I looked at him questioningly, unable to wait what his mind had come up with. "What are you looking at?" he puffed up, "Imagine that the soul exists in the universe in which there is no time and everything is happening at the same time — here and now. The soul hangs a very long rope on prana, plans from the beginning till the end what it exactly wants to experience. On that rope, it hangs its clothes, that is, the bodies for the specific incarnations and assigns them to time — a linear one this time — that exists on the planet that it wants to incarnate. And so, it will become the 'trousers' that will be on Earth in the twenties, but at the same time it will be a 't-shirt' that incarnates in the body of a cat in the ancient times, and somewhere else it will plan an incarnation on Mars in times — let's say — a thousand years from now in the future and it will hand a 'sock' on a rope. This rope is really very very long and everything hanging there dries out, that is, experiences those incarnations at the same time. When all of the clothes dry out, the soul ends its process of evolution. And although in the linear time the whole process lasts eons, for the soul it all happened simultaneously. It hung the washing, it dried out and was placed back in the closet as its experiences."

I was looking at Kal with my mouth wide open and Semjase did not look different from me at all.

"I wouldn't have figured that out better than you, Kal" she praised him.

"Where, apart from Earth, do the souls incarnate most often?" Kal asked, changing the subject completely. He wanted to know as much as he could in the shortest period of time, even though he had described to us quite vividly that something like time does not exist.

"Only in this universe there exist four billions of star systems, but only half of them are the worlds where there is life. The rest of two billions of planets is not in the spectrum of human perception. It happens because, in the vast majority, the human consciousness simply does not resonate with them. All of these worlds are connected with each other and create a common multidimensionality of vibrations and frequencies."

"And what about those who do resonate?" I wanted to find out more, having noticed that Semjase used the word 'majority'.

"You're very alert today, Smaisi. I'm very glad. So, it depends on the degree of the spiritual consciousness of a given being. The greater the degree, the greater the activity of connections between the physical body, mind, and the soul. You need to be aware of the fact that the soul has a constant connection with the heart chakra, but it doesn't dwell directly in the physical body. It dwells in one of the subtle bodies of a human."

"And where exactly that is?" I continued asking.

"Every soul is beautiful and vibrates only in their unique frequency. It weighs only twenty-one grams and is located directly above your heads. The symbiote is nothing else but the source that directly activates and powers the pineal gland in your brain. It's the connection to your Higher self.

"When does the connection take place between the symbiote and the physical body?" I asked because I was curious if it happens on the day of birth or perhaps earlier.

"That's a good question, Smaisi. The symbiote descends from the space and the soul is created during the act of love, that is, already during the act of conceiving a new life. During this act, in the magnetic field of the woman's womb there is released a very powerful energy. One day I will describe it to you in greater detail. Thanks to this energy, the symbiote is absorbed and it creates the soul and tunes and adjusts the energy to the physical-entity form. In this way, the conception takes place. And that's how the next incarnation of a given soul and the possibility to experience begin in a new body. Humans call this life, unaware that life doesn't exist only in the purely physical form, which is the way they are able to perceive it. I would like to mention here that reincarnation is an illusion and lasts only up to the fourth density, from the fifth density there is no physical body, and so there is no death either. Everything is connected with the two-track evolution taking place from the first to the fourth density where the body and the symbiote evolve independently. The fifth density is the state of existence in which you lose the physical shell entirely. This is the state that is absolutely etheric, in this state you are the existence itself. A human connects to some degree with the fifth density during sleep. This state can approximately show you how the existence in ether looks like and how you feel it, that is, what is ahead of you after the so-called transition — the illusion of death which, in fact, does not exist."

"This is one of the topics which will be the most difficult for the people, not even to understand, but to acknowledge. The lack of existence of death according to their own understanding," Kal summed up everything.

"You're right, that's why, it's so paramount to pass on to them exactly everything from the beginning till the end. So that they can arrange everything in their own minds and so that, thanks to this, it could make sense for them."

"I understand you will help us?" I asked.

"Of course, Smaisi. That's why I'm here. Today we will very broadly address many topics that unite as a whole. And for the birth of the symbiote and the moment when it settles in the physical body, I shall have a separate transmission. Many of the pieces of information that I want to bring up today are partially familiar to you, the others though are completely alien to you at the moment. They will constitute a very important complement of your current knowledge, because they will help you in the overall understanding. It will change your perception."

I could feel that Kal focused on listening. I did the same and looked around quickly. There was no sand around us anymore. The small land-sea animals were whirling around, trying to find a place for themselves as close as it was possible next to Semjase. I got amused by this. As if they were choosing the best seats in the cinema theater. On my lap there was not one but a dozen small crabs. They were politely waiting for the next part of the story. Kal could not complain about their lack of attention either. Even Semjase looked as if she was wearing a crab dress flowing for tens of meters on the sandy beach. It looked magical. In addition, this dress was teeming with life and the richness of colors — from yellow-brown, through orange and red shades. You could feel the high vibrations of these beings and the huge love filling them up from inside. I had the impression that they were there for a reason.

"They've come here for a lesson too. Just the way they have planned. I can speak every language and the transmissions are comprehensible for all the creatures to the same degree. Are you ready then?" she asked, "They already are!"

"Always and everywhere, Semjase" I replied.

Kal only nodded. He was always ready anyway. Even if you suddenly woke him up in the middle of the night, he would be ready. He was like a sponge absorbing the knowledge and he had never enough of that.

"Let's begin, my beloved. I want you to be aware of the fact that entering higher dimensions of consciousness requires from humans and their beings a fundamental change in perception of time and space, as well as a completely different perception of multidimensionality, frequencies and vibrations that surround us all the time. Regardless of the space we're currently in. There are many paths that allow humans the insight into other dimensions, however, sometimes you need to face many challenges to achieve that and be able to not only perceive them, but also become their integral part so as to exist in them. For this moment, the human biological physical shell is somewhat assigned to the frequency which you are in. Humans are, therefore, anchored in the third and fourth dimension of consciousness. They are quite well familiar with the three-dimensionality of your world. Since they resonate with it the most — they are somewhat absorbed, programmed this way to move around and do not cross some forbidden by other

51

nations borders. The fourth dimension is a bit more difficult for them to grasp and perceive. There are, however, those — and there are more and more of them — who succeed in that."

"Why is it so difficult?" Kal asked.

"The human neurological system is very well tuned into the frequency of this reality, in which you currently are, that is, to the third dimension. The whole system of your perception, that is the brain, the mind and body too, is synchronized with the physical reality of your world. Every biological challenge is dependent on your ability to navigate in the reality that surrounds you. What's more, your body, mind and consciousness are anchored in the linear perception of time. The body and mind are somewhat enclosed within, and it's difficult to break through to higher spaces. It doesn't concern the consciousness, though, that connects to the soul and for which all the spaces of multidimensionality are equally accessible. The high dimensional states of consciousness, to which you need to only find access to again, are not bound by these restrictions. They are absolutely free from spatial and time-orientated restrictions. It happens mainly because the high dimensional etheric body, which the soul is, has no mass or physicality and, as a result of this, it isn't subject in any way to the action of gravitational fields. Hence, this can result in some disorientation when you enter higher dimensions and suddenly you notice a huge fluidity in penetrating different levels of reality. This is a difficult part. As to everything, you need to simply get used to it, especially when your ego will tell you repeatedly that it's not possible."

"Why do I feel that the gravitational fields are more important here than I think?,,," Kal interrupted.

Semjase was not even surprised by how accurately he analyzed everything, although, in my opinion, it was a highly developed intuition and increasing connection to the wisdom that he already knew so well. The memory of his soul was coming back at an alarmingly fast pace because he could open to it without creating any blocks. I knew that since the meeting with Majka he had practiced whenever he could.

"You're right, Kal. As a matter of fact, as always recently," Semjase laughed out. "The gravitational fields influence to a great degree the time and the perception of it. There is no doubt. What's more, your perception of time is conditioned top down. It's imposed on you in some way and assigned to your existence on Earth. The mixture of gravitational fields and social conditions created by the reptilian nations as the only truth, created in majority of humans a sense of being caged by the limitations of time and space. This is a program that you've been simply closed by. However, this program, like every other, can be successfully switched off. For, you need to notice that your experience of reality and the ability to perceive the space around you is actually dependent on the level of consciousness you are at and, primarily, which of these levels have you decided to identify with. When you identify with higher states of consciousness, crossing the imposed norms, the barrier crumbles and, in this way, you free yourself from the limitations of time and space. Then, you can navigate in this more fluid reality and exist in it. In a place, where time and space are not stiff matter or a rule. I would like you to remember the relations and specification of dimensions. Nju-en described seven dimensions to you. I would like to refer to the twelve-dimensional model, of which the part above the seventh dimension is not known to you yet. However, let's refresh them all shortly again, for the record. Perhaps I will be able to add something that has been omitted before, and even if not, it will ground your knowledge and understanding."

"Let's not mention that to Daddy, because it may upset him" I said to Kal.

He only laughed out and nodded as a sign of a just made agreement.

"Alright," Semjase continued, "At the beginning I would like to refer to you directly, which doesn't change the fact that it concerns the whole collective of human beings; therefore, anyone can identify with the knowledge I'm about to pass on. So, the part of a human which is in a physical body exists in the third dimension. For, this dimension is based on matter which you know perfectly well already. You are able to move in it, although, sometimes for some people it comes out oddly and they don't fully use the possibilities that the matter provides. When you enter the garden of the soul, you sink with your consciousness into the fourth dimension. The fourth dimension is by many called the astral plane. These two levels — material and physical — comprise what can be called a lower world of creation."

"What a beautiful name" I interjected because it seemed to me particularly charming.

"This is only called beautifully, but it is not so positive for humanity. I'm about to explain to you why. The lower world of creation consists of the levels on which the separation takes place. These are the only levels on which the illusion of good and evil can be sustained and where you can feel separated from the spirit and other beings dwelling the same spaces. Humans are really good at this. They got engrossed in duality so much that it became the only thing that exists. It needs to be admitted that the separation initiated by reptilian races was very successful. However, the era of separation is ending and humanity will enter a new age."

"Is it ending already? Have you not said that there still remains a dozen years to awaken for humanity?" I inquired further, slightly frightened by the fact that perhaps for those a few weeks, when Semjase was gone, there had occurred drastic changes in the collective timeline.

"The fact that there remained this amount of time for humanity to raise their vibrations doesn't mean that Earth is not introducing its changes. They will be slow, but will be more and more noticeable for humans.After a few years of increasing cataclysms and natural anomalies it will occur to people that this is not another instance but a part of the process of transition which they have no influence on.This planet has been evolving and vibrating on the lower astral level, currently though the matrix of the third dimension has been completely closed and it has already entered the fourth dimension. Any transformations that are taking place, will be more and more felt for humans. They will perceive it at times as dreaming. They will find more and more of a problem in identifying if they are awake or perhaps stuck in their own dream. It is noticed by the human perception in a way as if the objects were changing. The time will come, and it's not that distant, when these breakdowns on the continuum will cease to be surprising and disrupting — in the exact same way as it happens in a dream state. What's more, the borders will start to blur so much that while dreaming your state will change too. These two layers will overlap and finally after a night's sleep you will wake up and you won't be sure if you woke up. You'll start to dream completely lucidly. With the full awareness of the fact that you dream and what you dream about. Humans will begin to perceive themselves too entirely consciously, which will allow them to smoothly move between those two realities as they will become equally real for them. It will occur to humans that there is more than just one true reality that they've got used to. And, in time, they will start to move appropriately in both of them, until they reach a point of full integration and perception of them as a coherent whole."

"From my point of view, it sounds fantastic," Kal gave the news, "However, I know that for people it will be difficult to understand initially."

"With absolute certainty, and you're right that it's not easy. That's why, this is so important for them to know what happens to people so that they could appropriately identify these processes. Otherwise, their mind, being used to only one space, will be thinking it's mad. And the people who are not awake yet, whom the former ones will tell about their experiences, will tell them the same, confirming the incorrect conviction that there is something not right about them. And this can result in many unpleasant incidents, which are not necessary to anyone really. On the contrary — in the process of ascension humans are supposed to help each other."

"Let's hope that this information will reach many people and they will take it to heart."

"And so it is, Smaisi. This has already happened in the future. However, there will be those who will want to cling tightly to the third density, hindering the awakening of others. Therefore, there will be gradually a different type of separation than the one that the reptile civilizations lead to. Namely, this will lead to the separation into two fractions. Those awakened and those who are still sleeping in the matrix zone that was built for centuries with the participation of Orionids. It is even now visible for more sharp eyes. Soon, many more people will see that they will be forced to make a choice who they want to follow and which reality to merge with."

"And what about the theory of perceiving time as in the fourth dimension?" Kal suddenly asked, changing the subject entirely.

"Time is, in fact, perceived as the fourth dimension. Space and time are tightly connected with each other. Many scientists have confirmed Einstein's theory according to which big objects that have mass generate gravitational fields that influence time and space, altering them. Of course, the scientists are very close to the truth. Those four of all dimensions are located in the basic spectrum of human perception. First three of them create the net in which you somewhat live, and they give dimensions and shapes. I'm talking here about the height, width, and depth. Whereas time is the fourth dimension. That's where human perception ends. What's above the fourth dimension is only a subject of speculation of many scientists, because what they don't perceive is much more difficult to confirm, and the whole scientific world is based on confirmations."

"What's above, then?" Kal would have not been himself if he had not asked.

"In accordance with the rules of mathematics it's the fifth dimension," Semjase laughed out and Kal opened his eyes wide, surprised by the way she made fun of him. "Okay, okay. I'll explain. Imagine the fourth dimension as time. The fifth dimension is the branching on the timeline, which is presented by the fourth dimension."

"I don't understand any of this," I pardoned, slightly embarrassed. I got lost at the beginning and I was afraid to think if I would understand what would be explained later.

56

"Don't worry about that, Smaisi. Gradually, the whole knowledge will become clear and bright like the sun. The human mind has its limitations and it encodes the knowledge gradually. You can't comprehend everything at once. It's simply impossible. Let me explain to you a little more and you'll be able to ask questions then."

"Alright, you calmed me down a bit. I guess Kal doesn't have such problems as I have."

"Kal is Kal. And you are you and both of you have their own capabilities at a certain time. Kal wandered into this all a bit earlier, so it is easier for him now," Semjase explained to me.

"So then... Where have we finished off?" I asked, filling myself up with a new energy.

"So, from the fifth to the ninth dimension," Semjase continued, "We deal with the spaces that can be called the medium level of creation. The fifth dimension is the dimension of the light body, this is where the restoration of consciousness takes place, which you already identify yourselves in as multidimensional beings. This is the level which the soul unites with the spirit completely on and is fully committed to it. Many beings have incarnated on Earth in this time exactly from this level. They did that to serve the world in this much important time for humanity and the whole universe."

"So have we," I said silently.

"Exactly, like you Smaisi. The fifth dimension is the first dimension of consciousness which goes beyond the limitations of time and space. In the third and fourth dimension those limitations still exist and the beings are somewhat subject to them. Basically, the beings in the fifth dimension have no mass and this results in the fact that they aren't subject to any influences of gravitational fields. Despite the fact that the fifth dimension doesn't have any physicality in the form which is known to humans it's filled with many objects. From the human point of view — the forms and objects located in the fifth dimension seem to be fleeting. They are apparent as they aren't fully a material substance. This can initially make an impression of something unreal, although that's not the case and what we can see does really exist in this fifth dimensional space."

"So, will we become apparent when entering the fifth dimension? Less real and material?" I inquired because it seemed to me that Semjase mentioned our bodily form would not change, only the body would transform from the carbon structure into silicon-crystalline.

"You remember well, Smaisi. This time, on entering the fifth dimension you will continue to experience yourselves as having a human body form — the one you have currently. This is exactly why the transformation into the silicon-carbon structure is so important, as it allows for the first time in a long time to exist in the space of the fifth dimension in a fully physical and material body. In the fifth dimension you will find the same things as the ones you got used to in lower densities. What I mean here are human bodies and solid matter that you experience now in your reality. What will change though is your experience of the space, because it will become much more fluid and time as a reference point won't exist anymore. The challenges which humanity will face, will alter completely as well. However, the possibilities that the transformation will bring and the sole ascension into the fifth dimension, will be much better. It will become this way as you won't be limited by either space, or the previously known reference of time, that was somewhat caging you. Thanks to this transformation, humans will have greater possibilities to express their creativity. What's more, the speed of manifestation of this creativity in matter. This whole process of changes can be called the dimensional evolution. It's nothing else but a gradual progress of abilities of living in full awareness of the whole existence as well as simultaneous dwelling and traveling in the multidimensionality. Reaching the place where humans achieve that, will be a long and winding way to go. It's not easy because it requires living in a specific dimensional reality — with its direct experience and simultaneous moving about other spaces and dimensions. So far, humans have had the chance to master their existence in the space of third and fourth dimension. Yet, now they have the possibility to experience higher dimensions, while dwelling in the spaces of their incarnated existence — the one that is assigned to them currently. What will happen in connection with the transformation of the planet and humanity, will rapidly accelerate the dimensional evolution of a human being. Humans have a form that can be called subhuman up to the ninth dimension, yet every subsequent level of consciousness is more subtle and less dense than the previous one. For the beings that reach to the ninth dimension and above, the bodily form regardless of the degree of its density disappears completely. They take more geometrical shapes. So that you can imagine it better I'll present it with me as an example. When I enter the tenth dimension, I become a sphere. An entirely etheric being. I'm not a ball that appears in numerous photographs that people call orbs. The real orbs, in contrast to those visible in the photomontage, are multidimensional beings that take the shape of spherical geometry."

"What does it mean? " I asked, slightly intimidated by the fact that I did not understand things constantly and was assailing Semjase with numerous questions.

Semjase did not answer, she only waved her hand and right next to her there appeared a luminous sphere.

"Take a close look. What can you see?"

I was watching the sphere very closely, it was difficult to skip the layer of light surrounding it in order to see anything else. When I finally succeeded in that, I noticed that inside of it there was something in the shape of complicated geometrical labyrinths.

"That's exactly what you were meant to see" Semjase confirmed that, reading my mind.

"That's awesome!" Kal squeezed out of himself, which seemed quite odd to me because he was in some sort of a state of lethargy. He was staring at the luminous sphere as if it was the most beautiful painting in the world.

"The spherical nature of multidimensional beings is quite common and you need to be aware of the fact that the multitude of different types of beings takes this type of geometrical form in the zone of highest dimensions. It's completely natural."

"How will it look like now then, Semjase? What humans need to prepare for? Should they know everything about the changes and processes which will take place around them and inside of them?" I asked suddenly, completely changing the subject. For a moment I forgot about the luminous sphere that was still slightly drifting above Semjase's head.

"Yes, Smaisi. It's very substantial for them that they know that. For the knowledge will allow them to understand these processes better, and, as a consequence, merge with them entirely. This will, in turn, result in fuller and faster ascension to the space of multidimensionality and better ability to move in it. This is an inevitable evolutionary change that can't be stopped in any way. Humanity has faced the so-called wall and it will either bump off or learn to fly. And this flight is equal to the ascension into the fifth dimension. The transformation that humanity will need to go through will be problematic for many. The processes taking place will often be for their minds irrational, the changes will touch not only their minds and the ways of perception, but also their physical body which a transformation will be taking place in on the DNA level.

"Could you describe more specifically how this will be taking place? What should humans pay particular attention to?" Kal asked further, "Perhaps they shouldn't pay attention to some events which will occur in their space?" He corrected himself after a moment because basically he was not sure himself what to expect and what would be the best for humans.

"Of course, I'll explain. That's where I've been heading anyway. For you need to know that in order to be able to pass this information on to others. The first and quite natural problem which will surface will be the changes in human consciousness appearing during the process of transformation. The ascensions to higher realms lead to radical differences in perception of surrounding reality. They differ considerably between beings who are fully physical, whose bodies are subject to forces of gravity, and those whom these forces don't influence at all. In other words, standing at the threshold of third and fourth-dimensional reality wanting to enter the fifth-dimensional world, humans will face the wall of different perceptions. This will disrupt everything that they knew so far. People who can connect with the fifth dimension, first they experienced a sense of loss of senses, because the way they experienced time and space, that they were used to in lower dimensions, was suspended in time. Due to the greater fluidity of perception --- in higher dimensions, people get the impression that they are outside of their own life. As if they left their body and traveled to a completely different space where time and imposed norms simply don't exist. It's felt by them as if they were totally disconnected from the reality and any earthly needs of existence. Many people receive this with a huge relief and happiness, however, it also happens that this state triggers tension and anxiety in them. What is important here is the level of consciousness of a given individual and whether he or she is ready for this kind of experience."

"What does it depend on if he or she is ready?" I asked further, wondering if I was already at the stage of being ready.

"Smaisi, don't make me laugh, please. You are right now in a completely different space than the one you got used to as a human and you move in it with a particular lightness and grace." Semjase laughed. "When human consciousness moves to the fifth dimension, the personal identity of a particular individual changes. The person is unable to identify himself or herself based on the earthly existence that he or she got used to. This is the most difficult challenge that anyone who's decided to ascend in the process of transformation of the planet needs to face and to not be left behind. Particularly when the transfer to the fifth dimension takes place for the first time and an individual is not entirely aware of the process that is occurring. The ascension from the fifth to the higher dimensions is in nature much easier considering the fact that you don't overcome the limitations connected to the perception of time and space because they were absent in the fifth dimension so it's completely normal. There is no such great transition that would pose a shock to the mind. Therefore, it can be surely stated that the transition to the fifth dimension and higher requires some sort of nicety and ability to adjust to the changing conditions of perception of reality. Humans will need to learn to continue their lives in a given density, at the same time learning to tune into the higher realms, which will allow them to see and hear more. It's like a multidimensional coexistence in which you exist in all the dimensions at the same time, taking from each of them what's best for you.

"I wonder if humans will succeed in learning that?" Kal asked with a slightly sullen face.

At that moment, I knew that he did not see any hope for many of them. In this matter, I approached the future more optimistically. I counted on myself. Perhaps, this was the reason why I was creating only positive visions for the future as a result of my own work and help to others.

"They will succeed, Kal. They need time but they will. One of the future talents of humanity, saying this collectively, so the society as a whole, will be the ability to live in the third and fourth dimension --- in such understanding of time and space that they have now - - and simultaneously in the fifth dimension, in which time and space are not considered to be limitations. This dual reality will offer humanity the possibility of deep creative insights into themselves, they will discover their talents about which they have no idea about at the present moment, even though they possess them."

"It's sad how little humans know about their own species, where they come from and what they are capable of." I summed up.

"This is all the result of the manipulation that the human race has been subject to. And this will be another problem that humans will encounter during the transition between dimensions. Even now people and beings that are in the process of transition encounter many difficulties. Others in their surroundings, who don't understand the process in which a given individual is, judge, scold, and criticize. It's happening because of the programs in which they are stuck themselves and which they still try to impose on others. Anyone who trespasses the frame of what is commonly considered to be a norm, seems to be a madman, crazy... " she interrupted for a moment and added,"You still have here on Earth plenty of synonyms that are no use mentioning. More than once, the cultural and religious factors have great influence on that, that imprison people in some ideological cages from which it is incredibly difficult to get out later on. Take a notice that from the point of view of dimensional evolution the building of the whole human civilization is built on foundations of a lie and illusion sown by the reptile species. The human got engrossed in this illusion so deeply that this swamp swallows them up. The illusion is nothing else thanks to the conviction that your world is constant and that time and space are based on reality not subject to the influences of your consciousness. And it is the consciousness that is the base of creation of your reality. Here you can clearly notice the separation and its influence on human civilization across the time. All the philosophical, religious, and political systems that are in certain spheres prey on humanity and are dependent on the maintenance of the illusion, without which they wouldn't exist. The illusion, that they feed to humans, is the fuel for existence for all the systems, for their maintenance of power and control. And, in truth, every being is free and there's no question about this freedom in accordance with the universal laws. Believe me when I tell you that this whole game created by the reptilian species together with the human hybrids that sit on the highest levels of power, is merely a wobbly house of cards called the human civilization, which will eventually fall down. It's inevitable and it's slowly taking place. The tentacles of the darkness are being bombarded by the light more and more and they can't reach as far as they could. When the curtain of illusion falls down, more and more people will come to notice and set themselves free from the life in low-dimensional reality and they will desire something more for themselves - - in accordance with all the laws that are due to them."

"Do you think... I mean, can you tell us, " I corrected myself because for a moment I forgot that Semjase knows the future of human civilization exactly, "Will it all suddenly fall down? You know, that curtain of illusion."

"No. This will be a gradual process. Humanity at this stage of programming wouldn't withhold the weight of the whole truth at once. I said that to you many times. The disclosure has to be conducted in a safe for humanity way so that it doesn't end up with a massive chaos, which would take hundreds of thousands, if not millions of innocent beings. Let me draw your attention to other factors that can influence the ascension to higher realms and which aren't less important than the first two. I know that you're interested in the future and you would like to know exactly what will take place but the time will come for that. As I promised, I'll tell you everything precisely."

Both Kal and I nodded in agreement, switching to listening and registering the most important information. In fact, all of them were important. They would not need to be sieved.

"Unfortunately, at this moment the earthly ecosystem is situated on a downward spiral, which makes it challenging for biological organisms that fight for survival. This situation triggers tremendous stress among animals and in the plant world, although many humans would be surprised by that. The human is not an exception and this influences him or her as well. Some of the dangers currently impacting the earthly ecosystem aren't dependent on humans and come from outer space. What I mean here are the changes in the sun's activity, gamma radiation, or any other types of radiation reaching Earth from deep space, which don't stay indifferent for the whole life on this planet. The following dangers come from Earth itself which is purging itself now and is at the stage of reversal of polarity, which will also have influence on all the living organisms, including humans. Nevertheless, what comes from outer space and from Gaia herself is nothing compared to the damages that the human creates. One could enumerate for hours: the emission of greenhouse gases, the increase of oceans' acidity, littering of the Earth, digging in it in order to reach the deposits of the highest quality for the human, breeding of farm animals on a mass scale. Human activity is a complete disrespect towards nature and Mother Earth. Humans in their arrogance started to destroy their own environment. The

Earth that they live on, in fact. Where will they go when everything is destroyed? When the resources of coal and oil are exhausted? What then? None is asking this question to themselves, yet the answer is simple. People are afraid of the answer which they know very well. Despite this, they still hope it won't happen in either their or their kids' lifetime. Oh, how egotistically they approach the matter of life and the survival of human species on this planet. Anyone who believes that everything is alright with the health of the planet is hugely mistaken. There are many huge firms and corporations that deal with the distribution of false information about the ecosystem. They inform how good it is, when in reality Mother Earth is on the verge of breakdown. Thanks to these lies, they maintain high profit and salaries - - - at the expense of other life forms on this planet. Again, they put themselves higher because they feel they're the most important species on Earth. What happens now is an intelligence test. If humanity doesn't wake up and the need for change isn't stirred up in them, it will lead to further degradation of the ecosystem and finally to the confrontation with the future in which there will be no point living. Depriving themselves of the change for a better future, humans take it away from millions of other lives dwelling on this planet, whose quiet voice begging for a better tomorrow is not audible for them at all. Another obstacle for humans while ascending to higher realms will be overt or covert intervene of foreign civilizations. The majority of nations assist humanity in this process and observe with hope their ascension. However, as you are already perfectly aware, extraterrestrial civilizations and their genetic modifications reach far into the past. Some of them still have a huge impact on what's happening on Earth. I'm talking about reptile civilizations, of course. As you surely remember very well, foreign species created for themselves a long time ago the race of slaves who were used for gold mining. These nations desperately needed metal to strengthen the disappearing atmosphere of their planet. That was when the experiment was conducted on a group of earthly beings in order to create a race of subordinate workers who were used for work in the mines. These were the beginnings of something that is commonly called slavery on Earth and the seeds of lack of freedom of every being. In this way, it was encoded a long time ago in the system of human consciousness, the tendency to be subordinate to the other and to worship other, self-proclaimed gods and putting them above themselves. Human mind and the technology that it then possessed, was far backwards when compared with the ones of these gods. In the eyes of the human race, they became something more than that, a more powerful race, to which worshiping and paying respects was due. That was the way in which humanity lost the honor, freedom, and independence becoming the element of an enormous slave system in which they have unconsciously been stuck till this day, being sure about their freedom which has been merely an illusion."

"Ascension will be difficult for humans. I can see that very clearly." Kal said out loud. "There are many reasons for that. They will feel disorientated, they won't know what's going on and if what they're experiencing is real."

"You're right Kal. It's never easy. Remember that it's a jump into higher spaces, rather than climbing onto another floor of the building during which you'd only slightly gasp if you had a bad physical condition. The moment of transfer from the limitations of the third and fourth dimension of existence into the greater freedom of the fifth dimension and higher can be a reason for an emotional challenge which a given individual will need to face. Let's don't forget either about how many traumas will need to heal a given individual and how much to understand about oneself so that such a transition is even possible. And you're right. The great freedom of experiencing that the fifth dimension offers can lead to a temporary disorientation. It's caused by the disappearance of the perception of time and space as a point of reference, which the human is so used to. Manipulations pose another problem. If a given individual won't clear oneself from the programs of servitude and cults that were installed in their consciousness, his or her experiences in higher realms can be deformed. Even over there, the dark side can impose an illusion which will make the human jump from one illusion into another one. There are plenty of entities only waiting for the opportunity, looking for a gap which will allow them to create a cult to subordinate others. What the choice of humans will be, that's how their reality will look like. For they forget how enormous their force of creation is inside of them and how much they influence what happens around them. They don't understand how little effort it requires for their dreams about a new, better world to become real. Before humanity enters the higher realms, they need to get rid of the programmes of slavery and worship. In the whole universe, there aren't such beings that it's needed to offer low bows to. The respect among races, if they deserved that, is required but there are no such who stand higher or lower. We're are all equal. One should never place foreign civilizations on pedestals. For each and every, I repeat, each and every being stands on the same ground and on the same level. The fact that some groups are more or less evolved, either civilizationally or technologically, doesn't matter here at all. Every being has been created by the Creator of All that Is and every one of them is love and light and they are equal. The moment the human realizes it's true and merges with it, everything that he or she knew so far will fall down like a house of cards. Simultaneously, this will be the beginning of a new world filled with harmony and cooperation among all the beings dwelling on Earth and the whole Solar system of this galaxy."

" What about death? " Kal inquired suddenly.

I was slightly surprised by his question. I did not know, taking into consideration his level of consciousness, that he was bothered by that at all.

" Don't worry, I want to know how to explain to others that they are immortal, that there's no end, only the end of a certain stage, after which another one comes and another" he explained as if he read my mind.

"Death is for humans a difficult subject because they simply don't understand it. Until they don't wake their consciousness up, the fact that they're immortal beings will be simply surreal for them. Despite the fact that religion tells them about the resurrection and life after death, it's shown completely differently -

- it's said, they'll go to heaven. What is heaven then? Heaven is nothing else but higher realms, the river from which the souls watching the Source come out and where they wait for next incarnations. Partly, you can call the transition into the fifth dimension death. Who said that death has a meaning solely biological and physical? I'm referring to the physical shell in a given incarnation, of course. Take a notice that when you move your point of reference to the fifth dimension, your personal history of this life and the way you start to perceive it becomes a dream. It happens like that because you rise above the anchor of physical senses of an incarnated life. In some states of deeply broadened consciousness this dreamy nature of life can be experienced directly and during a specific incarnation. We're talking about life in multidimensionality. But for the majority of human beings, this experience is possible via the transition, which you call death. And here we come to a point where death has more than one meaning. There are two types of the transition that is called death. The first one is the psychological and spiritual metamorphosis appearing while transitioning into the reality of the fifth dimension. This can be often perceived as a type of a transition — death. Why is that? It happens because you get to know new you and what's old somewhat expires. You are reborn, with new knowledge, new consciousness, new possibilities of perception. You die to be reborn like a Phoenix from ashes. Your whole orientation and perception of reality based on the senses. You begin to wonder and you look in yourself for deeper answers. Who are you? What's the meaning of your life? What are you doing here? These basic existential questions are under a great influence and need to be asked during the ascension to the higher dimensions. Without an answer, the ascension wouldn't be possible. The sole moment of ascending as a state of consciousness can be perceived as death. You don't need to be anxious about it, it's only a change of perception which has nothing to do with the death of a physical body. With this, there is the second type of transition—the death of biological reality, that is the physical body, in which dwells the soul. Many wonder how this process takes place. Therefore, I'd like to tell you about it. At the final stage you stop receiving the sensory signals from the outside world, and your experience of time and space, that you were familiar with and that you got used to, is completely shattered. This feeling can be disorientating if you're not ready for it. The majority of humans aren't because they're afraid of death, not knowing that it's only a stage. This event can be also joyous, if we understand in fullness of your consciousness that this is the nature of the process. The way the process of our death depends on the state of our consciousness and wisdom that we hold in that moment. If you fully identify yourself as a biological organism and if you forget about the immortality of the soul, the moment of transition can be indeed terrifying. You perceive it then as a complete end of your path. It's different when you tasted the freedom of the fifth dimension, you have the awareness of infinite existence, you know who you are and where you are from, what was and what will be. Thanks to this awareness and thanks to the experience of altered perception from the life in multidimensionality — your transition will be easier as it won't be filled with a sense of fear. When the moment of transition is complete and the death of the biological body occurs, there is a confrontation with three portals, in front of which the soul is placed. The first one of them is a light tunnel created from the prana tube running through the central part of your body, starting from the crotch up to the crown. At the time of transition, your consciousness moves upward via this tunnel which via the symbiote and crown chakra opens to another dimension of consciousness which is without the limitations of matter. At the other side of the tunnel the bright light is shining and it was many times described in the testimonies of those who managed to return. On entering this light, you may have an impression that you are on a bridge above the stream or a river. Behind this bridge, there will wait for you your nearest and dearest from your life, which has just ended. You'll be able to sense those who walked across, meaning died before you. There will also be animals which you had because the souls of animals dwell in this space as well. Therefore, it's not true that animals don't go to the so-called heaven. This is a realm for every existence and it belongs equally to everyone. There are no separation or restrictions. And that's where you can encounter a trap. That's why, you need to choose consciously and well. Very often humans get attached to the life they've just departed, to the people that they shared it with. If it turns out that any unfinished relationships, relations or unfinished businesses are connected to those beings, they may need to feel the need to enter this light. However, by doing so, they will enter a new cycle; the beginning and end and the end and beginning, and they will incarnate again on Earth, despite the fact that there are many universes and a multitude of galaxies."

"And this is the trap and the quarantine about which so much have been talked about recently?" asked Kal.

Recently he had been even telling me about it and the wisdom passed at that time was resonating with me fully.

"Yes, Kal. There was a blockage placed on Earth that forced humans to reincarnate here again, without the possibility of an informed choice. However, as you probably think, it was connected with the level of human consciousness. If they knew, would they like to reincarnate on Earth every time? I'm certain that many luminous beings would prefer to return home, to their realms they originate from."

"And what are the other two portals? As I understand, by consciously not choosing the first one, we have to choose between the following two," I put in the conversation.

"You're right, Smaisi. The second portal is created by the central glow. When you walk into it, you'll enter a vibrational field in which you'll immensely feel your personal connection. Those who choose this portal will find themselves in the place which is nothing else but a fulfillment of deep desire to merge with the essence of the light ether. This road will take you to the place called existentiality, which is defined not only by the evolutionary possibilities, but also by the lack of limitation of the being. The last of the portals is the one which opens to the darkness. Walking through it leads to the void of existence from which everything is created. If you choose this portal and you earlier prepared for the

70

way to act in such a level of freedom, you'll be able to explore other dimensions of the cosmos and even go beyond them on a scale that is unimaginable for you at the moment. There will be no physical barrier for you. This portal gives you an opportunity of existence in realms in which you'll become the discoverers of anything you desire. I wanted you to know this so that you could choose according to your will and on the basis of your acquired wisdom which portal you'd enter after you finish your earthly existence. What is death then? Definitely not what everyone believes it to be. Death is not the end of anything. It's the fulfillment of the journey in time and space and the end of a stage in the evolution of the soul. Death takes you to new realities that you create yourself. It's the end only on this plane and in this dimension of your existentiality. There's no death. This is the time of transition and that's the only correct term. The body only dies, that you took on for a particular incarnation. The container that was holding your soul, allowing you to experience physicality. Your consciousness is, on the other hand, infinitely alive. You need to understand that it has neither the beginning nor the end, it's eternal and completely independent of the physical bodies put on a particular incarnation. Despite this knowing, fear of death can be present in you. You usually don't remember your previous stages of transition, therefore, you don't know what to expect, you don't want to leave your nearest and dearest more than once. The human species is full of emotion. So beautiful emotionally. However, this makes it not only attach strongly and love deeply, but also hate the most. This array of emotions, the greatest in the whole universe, is a blessing for humans, but used inappropriately becomes a curse. But this always depended on humans how they use their emotions and this will never change. At this moment, humanity doesn't know that it's possible to live without fear and concerns. But the time will come, and it's not that distant, when they will learn and nothing will be the same as before."

"It is because, when we descend into incarnations, we pass through the curtain of oblivion, or at least that's how it is called. Human beings are largely unaware of their origin, and their

71

continuum of consciousness is disturbed," Kal summarized.

His words apparently gave Semjase the possibility of a fuller development of his thoughts because immediately after that she continued her lecture:

"You're correct, Kal. This is how it looks like at the moment. This is a barrier which gives a soul possibility to experience, let's call it - - fresh, but it has its downsides too. It's totally different in higher dimensions."

"How is it then?" I asked further. I started to catch myself wishing there was no gap in my knowledge. Perhaps I was afraid of what I would say if someone asked me about something I did not know.

"That's so sweet, Smaisi, " Semjase laughed softly but I knew she would answer soon. "On the higher level the eternal consciousness is connected with everything and everyone, similarly the past, present and future which are merged. For it, the concepts of time, transience, and place where it could belong more than to others do not exist. The eternal consciousness is in the higher dimension, inaccessible for physical beings. Intuition is the message from the consciousness of your soul. These pieces of information are not transmitted by your senses or body, rather by sensitivity to certain vibrations, which your consciousness wants to pass on to you so as to warn you or call you to certain positive actions. Often, these signals turn you back on track of the soul plan."

"So the soul is constantly trying to communicate with us despite the programs and limitations imposed by reptilian beings?" asked Kal, surprised.

This was obvious to me.

"Of course, yes. At one time the soul chose the earthly incarnation, but many souls fell into the loop and reincarnated on Earth by entering the first of the portals, that is straight j to the trap left by reptilian beings. Some people called what has been happening so far the quarantine of the planet Earth. Although, to me, a much better term, and certainly more accurate, is the prison of souls. Consciousness keeps always in touch with every even the smallest part of the soul. Thanks to this connection, which is not limited by either time or space, the consciousness of the soul can give signals and try to guide in reality itself in the direction of truth. You should know, Kal, that if you weren't here with Smaisi on Earth now, you would be in nearby realms to assist and protect her. For, all in all, you are one and you want the best for each other — for your soul, for its growth and evolution. Pseudo quarantine has made the souls relive the same experiences completely unnecessarily, not being able to break free from the karmic circle created by the Orion races among others."

"Humans need to learn how to freely enter the higher dimensional spaces. We need to find a way to prepare them for that, teach them that. Is it possible at all?"

I needed to know that. Anything that could help humanity was worth its weight in gold. Knowledge is one thing, and practice… Exactly, is it not what makes a master? If humans knew what awaited them and knew what to do — that would be halfway home. To a new home, on a new Earth free of darkness.

"Of course, you can prepare them. That's why you're here. Exactly you, star children."

"What if we don't know how?" Kal spoke timidly.

"To show you how I'm here for and other luminous beings supporting you and with a similar mission as yours in this unusual time," she replied and a beautiful smile poured onto our faces. "But first, theory," she added and our faces fell. "Entering into higher realms and gaining freedom in a transcendental reality is not that difficult to achieve when you accept the lack of limitations in perception of time and space. To check how freely you move in higher dimensions, you should try out a simple sound meditation. With its help, you move into higher spaces and get used to no limitations in perception. In time, this will be much easier for you. It's enough to imagine that you are in the space or in the garden of your soul and there are no barriers. You can do literally anything. Having the ability to penetrate into higher realms in connection with your biological existence on Earth gives to humankind enormous possibilities of multidimensional evolution. Entering the higher realms is a feeling, an inner experience, which is possible via the activation of the right hemisphere of the brain that is responsible for space management. That's where the change in perception and release of the blockages, which has been withholding humanity, takes place. When you enter the expanded feeling of spaciousness via direct experience, there occurs a sudden shift in your consciousness. You somehow become heroes of the dreamy nature of your current life, your stories which happen around regardless of the time they started and you merge with every phenomenon surrounding you. This gives you a sense of freedom. Thanks to the possibility of creating — stepping into higher realms and creation from that level is reflected on the earthly plane of your physicality. You can, thanks to the multidimensional creation, influence reality in a way that is unbelievable for you at the moment. Humanity is not aware of the fact how much they are capable of."

"Let's hope that when they finally get to know how to do this, they will use this knowledge in a good way," I made a remark.

"If their intention is different, they won't be able to ascend to this level. It's vibrationally impossible then," Semjase explained.

"What do higher dimensions present then, what possibilities do they give?" Kal asked a question, seemingly knowing already everything about the fifth dimension.

I sensed even a slight boredom with this layer of multidimensional space in him, which together with the excitement to know more and more created a small bomb of impatience. Semjase probably sensed that too because she laughed cheerfully. She took a deep breath to continue, however, one of the crabs was so brave in its trip that it appeared at the top of her head. Semjase only fixed it so that it did not pull her hair, after which she focused on higher dimensions.

"When we talk about the sixth dimension, we need to emphasize from the onset that this space contains the patterns of DNA of all the species that exist in the universe. A human one too. There are encoded all the languages of light built mainly from colors and sounds. It's the level in which the creation of

74

consciousness is manifested by thought. Many people travel to this space while dreaming. There isn't any body on that level, unless we create it via thought. The being that can exist sixth-dimensionally becomes something like a living thought. Consciousness is creative, yet it's not necessary for it to have any sort of vehicle in a sense of a physical body. You can just be, without enclosing yourself in the barriers of any body. This is the pure essence of existence. You are, even though you are not there physically. While you're dreaming, sometimes you look at something to the side. You can't see yourself or how you look. You can see what surrounds you though and you actively take part in that dream, being only a thought at the same time. The following, seventh level is a plane full of creativity filled with pure light, pure geometry and pure expression. It's the level of endless sublime, in which the power of creation is so flawless that it permeates everything around. You become the creation yourself. You create from love and light. This is also the last level where one can experience oneself as an individual."

"So we now move to the areas where we haven't been yet," Kal got excited and rubbed his hands in order to physically manifest his deep willingness to learn about things hadn't known yet.

"Ha, ha!" Semjase laughed out, "Soon there won't be many places where you haven't been yet!" she added.

"That's what we count on, although we are aware that we will never get to know everything," I confessed.

"You already know everything, your soul does. And you, here, it's indeed something different. It will require plenty of work from you to reach the majority of information. However, you don't need to know absolutely everything. Yet, about the next dimension, definitely. So, the eighth level is the dimension which can be called the realm of a group spirit or a collective soul. It's a place where everyone meets the greater part of oneself. There's no individualized consciousness here. If you reach that level, the greatest difficulty will be to maintain your own consciousness because in this realm you become a part of a collective and you work together with others to achieve the collective goals. At the beginning, it can seem for you that your consciousness is suddenly erased or dimmed. The following level, that is the ninth, is the level of collective consciousness of the planets, stars, galaxies, and dimensions of realities. If you succeed in reaching it, you'll have a really huge problem to maintain your individual consciousness for it almost doesn't exist here. You will feel everything as you, because everything will be in you and you will become everything.it can be compared to becoming the consciousness of the whole galaxy."

"Now I don't know myself what to expect of higher dimensions," I sighed, feeling like a galactic consciousness for a moment. I was a star, the sun, the planet and the whole universe simultaneously. I could feel anything that happened there, the energies were running through me like waves and I forgot who I was for a moment and felt inside me a huge unstoppable willingness to create anything that is beautiful, good, and harmonious. Kal either felt the same or was influenced by my emotions because I saw he was melting in his own imaginations.

"Beautiful!" Semjase shouted out, "That's exactly how you feel in this dimension. Be cautious though, for it's hard to return to reality and much heavier matter. And you will be needed for humans on Earth for a longer period of time, Smaisi."

"I understand, I understand. I was just… You know. Okay, I'm going back and focusing on the next dimensions."

"Kal!" Semjase shouted because he was far from returning.

One of the crabs, probably upon Semjase's request, pinched one of his buttocks. Kal jumped up and I felt a slight pinch too. I remembered how Mommy had told me that twin flames can feel ailments and pleasures of a physical nature together. Kal and I had never tried it out before though. There was no time for that and our minds were occupied with worrying how to save humanity. And so I received first evidence of the fact that our connection gave us such experiences together.

"I'm back," Kal stumbled, massaging his buttock. He snapped a finger at the crab to give it back, which was met with an angry look of Semjase. He grabbed it quickly from the ground and began to stroke it like a teddy from childhood. It looked like the crab enjoyed that, for when Kal stopped, the crab demanded more tenderness with a slight pinch.

"Very well, let us continue," Semjase distracted me from the twin flame thoughts and Kal managed to put the little crab away. "The tenth and eleventh dimensions constitute the higher level of creation. The tenth level is the source of rays. Here are the new plans of creation designed, so the whole architecture. Next, they're sent to the medium level of creation, which carries them out. On this level there can exist the 'I' consciousness but not in the same way as in the third dimension. The eleventh dimension is the level of slightly formed light. It's the point right before the creator, the condition of exquisite expectation for the creation. That's the level of creation of the whole system of the source. The twelfth dimension is the level in which the whole consciousness recognizes itself as oneness with All-That-Is. There's no separation here. When you enter this level you consider yourself as perfect oneness with All-That-Is, with the creative force. You become it. If you enter this level once and experience it, you'll never be the same as you were before. That's because if you at least once experience the perfection which oneness is, it's not possible to return to the level of separation again."

"This is incredible," I summed up.

Semjase was right by saying that the information she passed onto us was only a supplement to what we had already known.

"You'll learn even more, Smaisi. But every subsequent level of knowledge depends on the understanding of what was below. I'll give you an example. How do you want to learn addition without knowing the numbers? Or read without knowing the alphabet? Knowledge has a wide spectrum of structure. You won't notice what's above until you fully see the foundations. Similarly, you won't see higher dimensions until you fully accept and comprehend its existence. Another example is your physical body. Until you fully understand what its function is and how many layers it has, you won't know how to properly take care of it so that it becomes the container of your soul for longer. "

" I have a feeling you're about to tell us about that, " Kal interrupted.

"It couldn't be otherwise. And it's because as a human species you possess a physical body in this world and it's very important for you to have a vast and deep knowledge about it. Medicine is evolving but too slow and you don't even know a fraction of what you really should know, especially about yourself. Doctors forget about the structures of the body that have influence on what's outside its physical barrier and about how much you can do for the body from this perspective. The biofield and aura as well as what their condition is, have a great influence on the physical body and vice versa. The former impacts the latter one for they are one — only defined and separated into layers so that it's easier to comprehend how they are built and what they are responsible for."

"Humans can see only the bodily shell. Additionally, many times they don't accept it. Does this have an impact on their health?" I asked. At school I had many friends who were not pleased with their looks. They hid from the others and I perceived it as an escape from yourself.

"Yes, Smaisi. It has an impact, and a tremendous one, for acceptance is the key to loving yourself fully. Without it, there's no way to ascend to higher realms, therefore it's key."

"That's what I thought," I only added and started to wonder if I accepted myself in one hundred percent.

"You're perfect, Smaisi," said Kal, "don't search for nothing bad or ugly in yourself, because you won't find it anyway. It's only a waste of time which, in fact, does not exist. Thus, it multiplies the nonsense of your thoughts."

Semjase choked at Kal's utterance. I was amused by it too. Little crabs hugged me softly stroked me at the sign I lacked nothing. I felt that they tried to pass on a thought that I was beauty in itself — inside and outside.

" Tune into their wisdom, Smaisi. They don't judge you by the looks. Humans do on the contrary. Many people treat their bodies like their worst enemy. For they believe that because of it they're forced to experience karmic limitations. You would be surprised if you knew how many people think: "If I didn't have a body I wouldn't experience all those limitations". The body has a purpose. You have it for a specific reason. It possesses its own consciousness and the purpose of its consciousness is to serve the soul which chose to dwell in it. The lack of acceptance towards your body makes the consciousness of the physical body begin to sense that and the body starts to feel tired and rejected. You shouldn't be surprised by this. When you don't like someone and you begin to show that, this is how they feel. The same perception is manifested by the consciousness of your body. This can influence its physical condition and result in diseases. People don't listen to their bodies and the body together with the consciousness of the soul can teach you a lot. The majority of the human population ignores the whispers of the physical body. They ignore what the body wants to eat, how much exercise and movement it needs and many many other things that the body says. Instead, they have their bodies in their so-called four letters because there's something they don't like about it. There is always "but" and the lack of acceptance only leads in one direction — to problems with health."

"I have a friend at school. Since she was a child she's been overweight. I really didn't notice that she eats a lot. She walks to school on foot and it's far so her body is active. What's the reason that she can't even slightly lose weight?"

"I suppose it's a complex problem, Smaisi. The first factor is usually the pattern of feeding from her childhood, when she wasn't aware what and how much she ate. The second one — it's the lack of acceptance resulting from the lack of consciousness, which makes the body feel rejected and it doesn't want to cooperate. If she fully accepts her body and listens to it, in time it will return to its best divine form. But this requires a lot of work and, most of all, lots of self-love. So what, if you say that you love your body and yourself if you fill yourself up with meat and fast foods in the evenings. You're in denial of yourself. It's enough when some part of the organism is not happy with what you eat and it will have a direct effect on your whole physical body. Many teenagers have problems with breakouts on their faces. And do they pay attention to what their diet looks like? What they eat and in what quantities? The organism, especially a young one, still wants to fight and tries to cleanse itself, it alarms that something harms it and that it has to be let out. But nobody listens to that and the problems layer up."

"What layers does our body have then? Is it like an onion?" I joked, remembering the comparison from the 'Shrek' movie.

"Partly, you can say that." Semjase replied with a smile. "The human species possesses something that is its etheric template. Those who have formed a higher level of etheric perception can see it about one centimeter from the skin."

"Aura" I whispered.

"Yes, Smaisi. This is an interchangeable name for this layer of the human body. It fills the whole body up and goes beyond its edges. This etheric body maintains the seventh, sixth, fifth, and fourth dimensional structures. I'll explain that to you on the basis of the dimensional model that you've already learnt. Currently you're in a third dimension. The fourth dimension is the astral plane. Over there, in the astral body, the majority of your patterns are written. These patterns cause the movements, which come through other energetic bodies and trigger karmic experiences that bind you to others. They also make your DNA work in a very limited way that is directed at having a specific experience. It happens so due to the reduction of light that can be absorbed by your body. Apart from the etheric shell, humans also have another shell that has been dormant until now. I'm talking about the fifth dimensional structure of the light body, which is currently under the process of slow activation. This structure has something inside that resembles etheric crystals. These crystals block specific energy threads, preventing a too fast activation of the body. This fifth-dimensional etheric template consists of an axiatonal meridian system. It's a bit complicated to describe. A drawing would present it much better. I think that Nju-en will do a great job if you ask him. However, to make it simple, it can be said that your light body is responsible for your direct connection to your Higher self and other star nations. By blocking this coating, the reptilian races effectively make this impossible for humanity. This resulted in a partial brain atrophy as well as the appearance of aging processes of the physical body and, finally, death of the physical shell. The body, by the use of these currently dormant axiatonal lines, can connect with the Symbiote Oversoul and resonating star systems. It is those lines that allow that the human body can be reprogrammed by its Higher self and enter into a new body of light. The axiatonal lines exist independently of all the physical shells and biological forms. They come from various star systems and the galactic body controls its renewal mechanism by the use of it."

"I must admit that it's quite complicated even for me" Kal got sad. "Is there any easier way of explaining this? Do you get it?" He prompted me.

"Not really. Perhaps in fifty percent," I replied l, although that number was surely overstated.

"Hmmm... How to illustrate that to you?" Semjase pondered, "How about you try to imagine the Milky Way. It's like the body of a living organism. Different species inhabiting the stars and planets are the organs of this organism, their task is to renew the energy of its cells. So that the separation could continue as planned by the Orionids, the Earth and her inhabitants have been cut off from the galactic body and from their Oversoul of the Symbiote and, at the same time, from the possibility of regeneration of the physical body. Now the time has come, however, when this blockade has been removed and humanity will be able to reconnect with it. However, in order for this to occur, there are changes needed in the human body, which will react to the influence of axiatonal lines and will be synchronized with them. These lines are made out of sound and light. When the body will be again adjusted to the intake of them, the Higher self will be able to naturally send suitable frequencies of light, thanks to which the physical body will transform into the light body and the process of an accelerated regeneration will be activated."

"What exactly are these axiatonal lines?" Kal was breaking

down the topic into parts to understand it better.

"The axiatonal lines run along the meridians known to humans in acupuncture and they connect with them through the axles, points of spinning. The points of spinning can be illustrated as small swirls of the electromagnetic energy in the shape of a ball that are located on the surface of the human skin and inside of every cell too. The human body is entirely filled with them. These intracellular swirling points emit certain frequencies of light and sound, which makes the atoms of cells move faster. Through the increased molecular turnover of these atoms, threads of light are created which build a sort of an energetic net which contributes to the faster regeneration of the cells. This stops their aging process and eventually prolongs human existence. Due to the way of the dimension line running so far, those lines haven't been connected with anything. This has resulted in a complete disappearance of the axiatonal system of swirling of the human species and has considerably lowered the quality of life on this beautiful planet. As you already know, humans used to live even thousand years, Lemurians — tens of thousands. After the renewal of the connection that has been slowly taking place, human life will be longer and will be again gradually reaching hundreds of years or even more. At present, the points of swirling on the surface of the skin are gradually being connected by the energies of the fifth dimension with the points of swirling in every cell. This has a huge impact on the transformation of the human DNA. The axiatonal system works similarly to the human neurological system, yet it has a more electrical nature. The energy pulsates in it in a way the blood pulsates in a human blood circulatory system. The impulses sent from the Higher self are responsible for the whole."

"Are we somewhat steering this on our own? Propelling it?" Kal kept asking.

"You can say that. Your Higher self sends the energy to the axiatonal lines. This energy in turn flows to the point of swirling on the surface as well as meridians. In this way, the whole axiatonal system of the organism is being nourished. When the organism in cooperation with this system receives energy supplies from its

Higher self, color and sound are being processed. Adequate frequencies of color and sound form the blood, lymphatic and neurological system, strengthening and regenerating them. That's not all though. The axiatonal system also transports energy of Higher self to the swirling points in the cells. This stimulates them to emit light and sound and contributes in this way to the creation of new nets for human evolution. Human bodies depending on the origin of its Higher self, that is its main essence, will be transformed in a slightly different way and this can take place either faster or slower."

"What does this depend on?" Kal kept asking.

"On the structure of their DNA and the dimension which the axiatonal line strands come from."

"Can you explain?" Kal was not giving up.

"It's not that important at the moment, but if you want I'll try to simplify this for you."

"Well, since we're already on this subject..." Kal suggested.

I needed to admit that he was annoying but since I benefited from this annoyance, it suited me.

"Okay," Semjase continued, "The structure of the sixth dimension contains templates and patterns which are used to form matter and luminous bodies. It's in this structure that all the information from human DNA code is stored. It's the templates from the sixth dimension which decide what the DNA contains and how the body of a given human is formed. And here, for example, humans who serve light — who are often called star children or the lightworkers on Earth — carry in their DNA parts and fragments of genetic origin of many species from three hundred eighty three other planets. Here the strands, depending on their origin and roots of space they come from, can have influence on the acceleration of the process of transformation into the light body.

"This means that someone can have in their DNA the genes of many star species at once?" I asked out of curiosity.

"Yes, Smaisi. The majority has them. DNA is a mixture of genotypes of various species, similarly to the human who originated from five star families, every being possesses a compilation of various genetic fragments inside. Thanks to this, the universe is filled with millions of different species of beings despite the fact that the roots of many of them are similar and come from the same spaces. I would like us to return to our onion and another body that the human being has. Okay?"

"Ah yes, I completely forgot that we were talking about that," I said slightly intimidated. If I did not remember then how would I be able to pass this on to anyone?

"You need to understand, Smaisi, that the knowledge I've been passing on to you is only an impulse of consciousness for your own soul. You already know all of that. But due to the processes and blockages imposed on the human species you have to remember. I only unblock these memories for you. In the flood of information it can seem to you that you don't remember what I've told you, but when you need this information, it will return to you on its own."

" I hope so, " I responded and I had to admit that Semjase lifted my spirits up. I trusted her and I knew that if she told me that that was how it would be and I would not let anyone down.

"Let's return to the subject of the layers of the human body which are intertwined — another one is the emotional body. Looking from the perspective of the fifth dimension, the emotional, mental, and spiritual bodies are built of double tetrads, that is of the elements that consist of four parts. Tetrads rotate at a particular speed. In the emotional body there are all the wonderful, almost fairy-tale blocked places which are nothing else but inconsistently moving geometric figures. The movement of these figures is conditioned by their ethereal pattern of a four-dimensional structure in self-expression. The human as a result of the imposed programs has learnt that self-expression is dangerous because it is under the evaluation of the external, and since the evaluation is not always positive, it's not worth putting yourself at risk. There is little openness to the other person in this world, not to mention a different species from unknown stars. When humans can't express themselves, they close inside those beautiful geometric forms, creating a block at their own wish. And live with this blockade until the time they encounter blockades similar to theirs. Suddenly, everything starts to match. These little geometric forms mesh repeatedly creating karmic relationships. And now you're still blocked but as if together. You walk the path together until the moment the block is released and then you start to wonder why you are here, what are you doing here and whether, in fact, this is what you want to do. Another layer of the aforementioned is the mental body and it as well — similarly to the emotional body — consists entirely of the geometric structures. The function of this human body is deciding over what is your reality. The mental body believes that it has control over everything that surrounds it. That it's a so-called boss. However, the truth is that it's only function is to decide what is real in the surroundings. It's the mental body that decides how the universe matches your plans. Because it's the body that decides about what is real and what is not, humans get caught up in the karmic cycles. The mental body doesn't like changes a lot, it hates them. If it sees the risk of any change, it straightaway sees it as a threat and danger to life. It's a huge block in the human potential. The mental body maintains the vision of reality all the time, in which as it states, your life is not threatened by any danger. Regardless of the fact if it's true in a particular situation or not, the mental body is indifferent and doesn't care about the fact that its decision will make you happy or not. To the mental body the most important thing is to keep your present state at all costs."

"This part of the onion is bothering a bit," I summarized.

"It's only because you're not aware of the fact what it's actually capable of, how it can control and that what counts for it is only its own point of view," Semjase replied. "The awareness of all your bodies and what each of them is responsible for makes it possible for you to merge all of them in one and use each of these layers in the best and most optimal way. You need to understand that being united in yourself is a natural state for All-That-Is. It's a perfect state in harmony of the spirit, soul, body, and mind."

"How to do it then? How to merge with all your bodies?" Kal's analytical mind flashed again even though this question came to my mind immediately too. This time he was simply fast.

"First, you need to understand that the amount of energy needed for the maintenance of the illusion of being in separation is enormous — much greater than the one needed for the liberation of it. That's the reason why the mental body developed such a power to control. In order to maintain the illusion of being in separation, it was easiest to impose on the mental body that it should perceive as unreal everything that it's unable to notice. Again, we return to the idea of the barrier in perceiving. Because it can see only things that are tangible, it doesn't want to hear, see, or feel the impulses from the symbiote, as a result of which the connection with the soul is blocked."

"And what about the spirit? Is it also a layer of our body? I read about it once and in many articles the spirit was distinguished from the soul. Can you explain the difference?" I was very curious what Semjase would say as many people were wondering about it.

"The spiritual body is built from the same geometric structures as the previously mentioned two bodies. It's not subject to any karma. It's role is mainly and in fact only to make the connection with the Symbiote Oversoul, your consciousness, and the I Am consciousness happen. The spiritual body is not subject to any laws, it's above them and it's not bound by any ties. But the emotional body because of the separation makes the noise on the connection, let's say it this way. And this all complicates a lot l because the information passed one by one onto the individual layers of the body are distorted and, as a result, manipulated. It looks like this: the emotional body emits and transmits the informational impulses to the spiritual body and then, in turn, the information is sent to the mental layer. The mental body tells you that what you see or feel is not true because it doesn't notice as a result of the programmed perception. This, unfortunately, makes a human close up instead of start to express himself or herself and perceive everything without limits of the time and space which the mental layer considers as the only right and real. And this is exactly the way that the cycle of the limitation and separation from the soul consciousness and source of humanity has been repeating itself for hundreds of years. Now you more or less know how all of this works. This should help you understand how the control over humanity has been taking place and on how many bodies of the human the reptilian races have had influence for such a long time. When something gets programmed, it's difficult to reverse the program, the only chance for a complete elimination is a destruction of it. And this is exactly what humans need to do — cut off the old programs and start anew in agreement with the soul and spirit, which do their best to guide humanity all the time."

"I have to admit that today's lecture has shed a lot of light on matters which humans have no idea about. A lot of them don't even know what chakras are," Kal summed up.

"About chakras you'll learn soon too. That's all for today though. I sense your tiredness with the amount of the assumed knowledge. I don't want it to be too much. And I immediately anticipated your question, " Semjase winked at us in a friendly way. "The fact that you had a break and time for rest doesn't change anything," she added seriously.

Kal laughed out and we accompanied him.

"And now, go home!" she only added and everything around suddenly blurred.

I was convinced that I would wake up in my bed. However, that was not the case...

Chapter 4

"Letting go, letting go, acceptance… Like light shone through a prism, it is one of the vibrations of love. It becomes a constant part of life in the evolution of consciousness in the moment when we become more vulnerable, we touch our divine essence deeper, the level in which we can perceive the dark side hidden in us so far is rising too. Often after a long fight, letting go becomes like a soothing balm for a sensitive and wounded skin. It opens the path to even greater self-discovery."

Damian Buczniewicz

Chakras — the energetic whirls of the human

I found myself in the garden of my soul. I looked around. I did not know what I was looking for. Then I saw him. In front of me there was an enormous Draco being. I was surprised a bit, but the vision of it did not frighten me at all.

"What are you doing in my garden?" I asked. I knew he could not harm me here, just as I could not harm him. I did not know though how he managed to enter the garden without any invitation and what the purpose of this visit was.

"This is not your garden. This is only an illusion which I created in the astral realm to lower the level of your potential fear."

"What do you want?" I asked straightaway. Gray got me familiar with this type of abduction. I was not touched by that.

"Help," he replied so quietly that I almost did not hear it.

"If it is about Shiru code, I don't know anything, I don't and I won't have any knowledge of it," I confessed briefly and concisely. I did not feel like repeating again what I had already said to Gray.

"I don't look for the code. I only want to get to the source. To the light," he said again so quietly as if he was afraid to be heard. As if he was afraid that anyone could stop him.

"How could I help you with that according to you?" I inquired because I was really curious about what he would reply.

"I ask you to open the portal for me through which I can get to light. I'm looking for an escape." He confessed slightly louder.

"Since when do the Draco beings escape to the light?" I was surprised but soon after that I remembered what Majka and Mariusz were saying. Many beings who until then were on the dark side were shifting and joining the light.

"I know you have already found the answer to that question. Would you help me then?" He asked and I sensed that he really cared about that.

"I have no idea how to do it." I confessed sincerely. "Besides, can't you open the portal for yourself?" I tried to find out.

"Only the being that belongs to light can do that. When I express my willingness to change and you give me a chance—the portal will open because our intentions will connect. There is no limit in this space for you. You already know that. Simply, open the portal to the light", he explained.

"Why me? Why do you ask me?" I asked further.

"To show you out of gratitude for my freedom the power that you carry inside you. If I didn't ask you for that you wouldn't know you're capable of that. And this is crucial for you to be fully aware of that." He replied and he was right in fact.

I had nothing to lose. I saw too much already. I decided to let my soul guide me. I focused and swirling my finger, I imagined how the portal to the light appeared in front of me. A huge hole opened in front of me that looked like a luminous tornado swirling horizontally. The view was incredible. Almost hypnotizing.

"Thank you, my star sister" said to me the Draco being and, probably worried that the portal could close, he quickly jumped inside.

I was left alone. The portal closed and disappeared as fast as it appeared. And I immediately landed in my bed and opened my eyes.

For a moment I was coming round, I could not entirely believe in what had just happened. Was it true? Perhaps I was simply dreaming? This did happen—I heard Semjase's voice in my head. It sounded as if it was coming from far away.

Without even having a wash, I ran downstairs in my pajamas to my parents to tell them all about what had happened. They were not in the living room though. It was only then that I looked at the clock. It was five in the morning. I realized that they must have been sound asleep. Daddy slept as much as he could and it was difficult to drag him out of the bed. The energies coming down from the space were affecting him more and more. Mommy decided that Daddy was going through some sort of a bodily transformation and he needed more sleep. I did not feel any hunger that would have stopped me in the kitchen so I went upstairs again and lied down in bed. I was staring at the ceiling trying to relax and suddenly everything started to blur. I felt I was flying upward, pierced through the ceiling that suddenly became a translucent matter. I flew high up in the sky, I was getting higher and higher. I passed the clouds and shooted in the infinite vastness of the cosmos. I speeded farther. I had a goal, but I did not know what it was yet. I felt blissful and safe as if I was returning home. I fell into a child's euphoria waiting for where I would get and what I would see. Before I got the chance to see all that though I heard the voice calling me back to Earth.

"Smaisi! Smaisi! Come back! Now!" Mommy's voice was not heralding anything good. It was sharp and commanding.

I submitted to it and returned to bed so fast as if I was rushing with the speed of light. I looked at Mommy and noticed terror in her eyes. I was trembling from the cold. I was ice cold and my body had a faded blue tint. I got scared by that although I somehow knew what that meant.

"Mommy! Mommy, what has happened? What have I

done?" I was disoriented and it was only then that I looked at the clock hanging in my room. The hands were at eight o'clock. How did it happen that I was away for three hours?

"Time doesn't exist there, Smaisi." Mommy replied and started to vigorously massage my legs and arms. She tucked me in the blanket and Daddy appeared at the doorstep with a mug of hot chocolate. He did not look happy either.

"Can anyone explain to me what has just happened?" I requested. That was when the telephone rang. I looked at the screen. It was Kal. "Have you called him?"

"We didn't have to. He must have sensed this. Pick it up. Otherwise he'll be worried." Mommy said and left the room, making it clear that she would be back soon to explain everything.

"Kal" I whispered to the receiver.

"Smaisi, are you okay?" He asked. He sounded as serious as Mommy.

"It's alright now. Mommy brought me back. But don't ask me what has happened. I'm not sure myself…"

"I sensed fear…" he whispered, "Such enormous fear and emptiness. As if you were moving away farther and farther, completely out of control. Suddenly, I stopped feeling you and panicked even more. But now you're back. I can feel you. Don't do it again, please!" he said almost with a begging but firm tone of voice.

"I need to only get to know what I've done and how to avoid that again. " I replied. I had a few words with Kal and then we said goodbyes as I wanted to speak with my parents as quickly as possible. I did not need to call them. They sensed perfectly when I was ready.

"So, what has happened to me?" I asked when I again appeared in the room. My body became pinkish already and the sensation of coldness was slowly leaving me. However, I still felt as though I had been sleeping all night outside in the frost only in pajamas on.

"You left your body, Smaisi. Completely. In addition, without any control over what you were doing. That's why you shooted out so far in the cosmos. Your soul started to unconsciously return to where she came from. To home" Mommy answered in a few words. She reckoned they would be enough for me to get what had occurred.

"How's that possible? I didn't want to do that," I continued explaining, "I simply floated away suddenly. The space started to blur and… And that's when it hit me. Completely unconsciously I did it to myself. I was even more unconscious to stop it. I had no idea what was going on."

"And you've answered, as always, your own question" said Mommy.

There was a grain of truth in what she said. I always had my own conclusions after the analysis that I was fully resonating with. The day dragged on forever. Kal promised to his mother to help her with the household chores, therefore, we did not make an appointment. Even though we were constantly in touch and I felt when he was thinking of me, putting the previously dusted off books and albums on the shelf, I was missing his presence. He got me used to the fact he was always around. This caused the fact that a day without him was a wasted day. But it was not wasted completely because I was writing all day tucked in a warm blanket. I still felt the need of constantly warming myself up, as if I was freezing up from the inside. Yet, my fingers were dancing on the keyboard with such grace. As if my uncontrolled travel gave me inspiration to write. In the evening, when I clasped the back of the chair completely exhausted, I cheerfully realized that I had written above forty pages. I went downstairs for dinner. To my surprise, Kal was sitting at the table.

"Why didn't you say that you're here?" I asked, although I knew that I should have sensed his presence.

"But you haven't sensed it because you were so engrossed in writing. I didn't want to disturb you and decided to wait in a place which you sooner or later would get to" He laughed.

"Ah, yes, the fridge," I joked. I ate much more than before. The vegetables and fruits were finishing in a blink of an eye. It was only then that I realized that I had eaten about two kilograms of green grapes. Essentially, I needed more hydration. I was absorbing everything that had large amounts of juices inside. The intuition was telling me that this was the effect of the processes of awakening and changes occurring in my body.

"Do you feel like eating anything specific?" Kal asked.

"I'd love to eat a watermelon but I guess it's not the season for that, " I said with sadness in my voice.

"Definitely. Although it should be available because they import them the whole year. I can go to the shops and buy you some, if you really want it," he offered with care.

"We can go together. I would love to get some fresh air."

I grabbed my coat and a thick woolen scarf which Mommy knitted for me and we left home. The shop was almost a kilometer away. We did not hurry. We were walking slowly, I felt freezing air filling my lungs up. I did not miss the sensations of cold on that day.

"Can you feel it?" I asked Kal. I was wondering if it was the effect of my sudden travel or perhaps it was...

"As if it was about to snow," Kal replied who perfectly read my feelings.

"It's high time," I stated.

It was the end of November, snow would not have been a surprise to anyone. The temperature was around zero degrees. Anything was possible then.

At the shop it was crowded as always. People were strolling along the alleys, packing their baskets in mainly with conserves and tons of meat filled with fear and suffering of which they were probably not aware. Our basket was quite usual in this respect— filled with fruits and vegetables to the rim. It was weird because the people seemed not to notice this phenomenon. Perhaps it was because they were so focused on themselves and absorbed by the pursuit of life which is in fact not possible to be caught up without stopping even for a minute. They did not know that. I felt the emotions that were tearing them up. The feeling of this was not pleasant for me at all. Fear, suffering and constant analysis of their problems were dominating. There was no love in them. How to wake up in them something that was not there? Was there at least a tiny spark that could turn into a beautifully blazing fire?

We packed our shopping into bags and headed back. We were halfway back when the first snowflake fell to the very tip of my nose from the sky. The warmth of my body melted this wonderful and unique geometrical shape in the blink of an eye. I looked up and from there were already rushing hundreds, thousands, and millions of them. Tiny particles, each of them unique, were dancing in the wind, wrapping the entire space with themselves.

"I love the first snow. It's always so magical" I uttered quietly but Kal heard me saying that.

"Enjoy yourself. Soon this whole magic will disappear for a long time" he replicd.

After a moment I only realized the meaning of his words. Semjase mentioned to us that after the reversal of Earth's polarity there will be a change of the climate on Earth to a truly heavenly one. From one point of view, it was good news, from the other though I knew that I would miss snow.

"I wonder if Semjase will take us somewhere tonight?" Kal asked as we were entering home slightly chilled.

"I hope that yes," I responded because I had never enough of her company.

We found my parents hugging each other lovingly, looking out the window with delight. We did not want to disturb them and interrupt that magical moment in which they both were hidden. We went hurriedly upstairs in search of our own magical moment. I knew that, as always, we would find it too.

Kal stayed almost until midnight. I was tired. I was glad that our nightly trips did not badly influence the quality of my sleep and the rest that the body needed. After Kal had left, I quickly took a hot shower so as to warm up properly before sleep and I went to bed. I could not fall asleep for some time. I was still thinking of the climate changes which humans would need to face during the switch of Earth's polarity. I needed to admit that I was slightly worried about what the icebergs were hiding and what they would release when the whole ice mass would melt. I pushed away those thoughts though and focused on a slow and steady breathing which slowly put me to sleep.

When I opened my eyes, I was in a blue space. The blue color that was surrounding me was extremely beautiful, it did not resemble the sky though — it was like a fog. I looked around and I saw dozens, hundreds, or even thousands of planets. Some of them were closer, the others were farther — all of them were spectacular. Soon after that I noticed Kal who with a similar delight was watching the place we landed in.

"Where are we?" he asked, astonished by the sudden change of localization by Semjase.

"I have no idea but I'm staying here," I confessed, remaining under the influence of the beauty of this place. It was magical. That was how it could be defined precisely.

"You'd better be careful with those travels in the cosmos of yours or you won't ever come back again to me one day." Kal suggested and he was somehow right. I definitely needed to be more careful and avoid this type of situation.

"You're in the area of Saturia. In my home," a beautiful vibrant voice spoke to us. I did not need to see Yriah to know it belonged to her. She appeared to us after a while, floating in the air on her shimmering white and gold wings.

"Today you kidnap us?" I asked, satisfied.

"Yes, Smaisi. It's me today," she smiled radiantly and waved her hand. On our backs there appeared white wings which we already knew. "It will be easier for you to move about," she added and flew away leaving us slightly baffled. We looked at each other questioningly. "Well, what are you waiting for? For an invitation? So I invite you then!" she said to us from a distance.

Kal, guided by her voice, set off first and I followed him immediately. I already forgot after those few weeks how amazing it is to fly and how free you can feel when floating in the air. The blue fog was becoming thinner and we finally landed on one of the planets. It was almost entirely covered with crystals and in the distance we could see an enormous crystal castle.

"Is this your home?" Kal inquired.

"One of the many. My roots, just like the roots of the majority of other winged beings, come from the space of Saturia," she replied and I remembered the story that Mariusz told us about Yriah's incarnation on Earth. "Yes, Smaisi. Even the winged luminous beings need help from time to time. Especially those incarnated ones", she clarified, having read my thoughts.

"What are you going to tell us about today?" Kal never wasted time. He was always impatient.

"I would like to tell you about your energetic centers. I know that Semjase was telling you about the human layered bodies. Now, let's dive deeper into that — into the world of energetic meridians that are called chakras too."

"That's an incredibly interesting subject," I admitted. I had been reading a lot about it. Even before Semjase appeared in my life. I was certain that I knew at least the basics of this knowledge.

"We're about to find out," she replied to my thoughts. "Humans are familiar with seven basic chakras inside the human body. Little is said about the rest of the energy points which are located outside of the human body yet they belong to it as well. We'll start with the well known ones though. Are you ready?" she asked.

Of course, we were. We always were. I did not even know why anyone would ask us that.

"Good upbringing requires that, Smaisi, " Yriah responded to me and started her lecture. "Let's start from the root chakra, which is marked with red color from where the kundalini energy comes from. This chakra is responsible for your life force, survival, and the quality of your existence on Earth. It's always been responsible for the survival of the human species. That's the reason why the reproductive organs are located there and of which the main task is the perseverance of the species. The kundalini is an energy that is mainly considered as sexual. But when properly used it has great power of regulating the energy in the whole body, healing, and regenerating of the body cells. Next to every chakra and the blocks on them, there are physical ailments in the human

96

body. The more closed the chakra is, the greater the issues are with the emotions which the particular chakra is responsible for and the physical organs that this chakra is supposed to regulate and keep in good condition. We won't get into such details though because this has been described perfectly in the earthly world and these pieces of information are easily accessible. I would like to mention though that the root chakra is so important because it opens the way to the energy of the Earth and allows for the flow of energy upward through the rest of the human chakras — up to the crown chakra and, extending above it, it gives access to the connection to the Source. The second chakra is the sacral chakra which is coded with orange color. It's responsible for the joy of life, vitality, it's also the center of sexuality. What's most important — it's the most important center of creation. It lets create the new and, at this stage, this is the task of humanity — to create the New Earth and the Golden Age. Many people think that this will just happen, that nothing needs to be done, one can just be. Nothing is more misleading. Unaware of the power of their own creation, humans completely forget that these are their thoughts shapes which by turning into energy create the reality of the planet. Humanity has received help from the above that is beyond their imagination. They will never be able to count how many galactic families have been taking part in this grand ascension process of humanity. How many spaceships have been hovering above their heads for decades, making sure that everything goes smoothly. How many wars have been played out in other realms so that humanity can be free again. They won't get to know that because nobody will boast about that. Every nation does that out of love and nothing more. This huge assistance won't matter though if the human won't get down to work and start creating for the benefit of humanity. For the benefit of the self."

"What do you mean by that?" I asked because I sensed that there was a bottom line to this statement.

"Look, Smaisi. Humans wake up and are literally flooded with the news about the processes on Earth. They trust them but at the same time they are afraid of them because it's the unknown.

They're not sure if this all will take place or not and how this process will unfold, how hard the Earth will shake humanity up during those changes. And instead of creating what's beautiful — they wait for it in fear and are filled with various thoughts. Not always positive. Many of them ask questions: Will I shift into another dimension? Will I survive? Has my soul chosen to transform in this lifetime? They wait for the answers from the heavens instead of taking action so as to what they desire can come to fruition. The shift starts from the inside. From your own self. If they want to change the surrounding reality, humans need to start from changing themselves. It's that simple. When the human changes, when creates beauty and goodness, everything that surrounds him or her becomes the same — high vibrational and perfect. What do you think — what reality would you live in if the majority of humans understood that?"

"Definitely not the one we are currently stuck in," I said with certainty. It did not take a philosopher to draw the correct conclusions.

"Precisely. Humanity needs to remember about the power which they possess and which is hidden from them. There is no god that humans know and worship like hypnotized. Everyone, I repeat, everyone is the spark of the Creator and is god inside. They create for themselves and for others because they are in the space of the collective to which they are in a way subordinate but also make it subordinate to them. If you're afraid of something, if it lowers your vibration and you feel bad about it, you don't give attention to that. Simply. You walk past it, focusing only on the positive thoughts. A wanted or unwanted thought is always information that is sent out into space where it has the power to manifest in matter. The quicker humans understand that they are the change and they will sow the golden age thread by thread, the quicker this moment will come and none will need to keep waiting for the beautiful event. It will simply take place, because this will be the will and creation of the people. The universe gives us exactly what we want. It's wonderful but you need to be careful with that. Now we shall move to the solar plexus chakra of the beautiful yellow color. It's responsible for the joy, the power of our will, drive and assertiveness in the expression of opinion and emotions. Take notice how crucial it is, especially nowadays. How many humans that are awake sit under the broomstick, avoiding the subjects connected with the awakening. There are two worlds in one yet neither of them know anything about the other. Kal, let's assume you would take part in the conversation and try to explain to someone what you believe in and know and this person would attack you — would you suddenly change your mind? I don't claim that you need to fight with words with such an opponent but there are plenty of such people who start to doubt themselves. They doubt what they know and what they believe in. They regress again instead of moving forward. People need to feel the truth with their heart and intuition. For them, it's the truth even though it seems like a lie for thousands. But this lie doesn't belong to you, Kal, but to someone else. You've finally found the truth. Why would you go back into the lie again? Only for convenience, in order to become part of a blindly moving forward herd which the faster goes the more backwards becomes?"

Yriah could accurately assess the situation and perfectly put it all into words. That was what humans needed. The truth that was spoken out with no bullshit and saying only about how beautiful that event would be. Indeed, it would be so and we would reach the golden age but it would be hard work and the shift that would need to take place in many. Nothing happens on its own, although seemingly everything happens so.

"Do you think that humans will really comprehend that?" Kal inquired further, as always with a pessimistic approach. "Actually, they don't have much choice," he added.

"Stop there, young man!" Yriah growled menacingly, "What are you creating now? What have I just said about creation and doubts and you've just reinforced them with your thoughts and energy. Don't ask if humans will understand that and don't let this bother you. They will comprehend. They've already had. Full stop. Think in a present time that is accomplished, and the matter will follow, " she almost ordered.

Kal cringed in shame. I felt sorry for him slightly but someone had to smooth out his aspirations of doubting his own mission, in a sense.

What Yriah said was very logical. Since you think that something will not happen and you doubt yourself, you have not applied yourself to it as sufficiently as you should have. If you are certain that you will not pass the exam, you neglect the studies then because you know you will fail. What would be the effect of such actions? Such obviousness but not so obvious for many. I laughed inwardly at the thought I created. Yriah smiled as well.

"Let's move to one of the most important chakras for humans," she continued, "Beautifully glowing green heart chakra is a place of unconditional love to all existence, where altruism, compassion, and empathy reside. It's the center of your inner light because as souls you're love and light. The heart chakra is the center of your connection to the soul. That's where you feel the energy when the soul wants to contact you — it's your intuition. It's said that you can hear something with your heart. That you're drawn to something or that intuition through the accelerated heart beat tells you not to do something. That's the way your soul speaks to you because other means of communication have been blocked for you. Sometimes it's worth listening to it, but first you need to learn about the other ways of communicating with the soul, beside the best way, which is the direct one. This chakra will be also very crucial for without self-love you won't be able to love anyone else fully. There will always be something missing. One element won't fit in and this will spoil the whole picture. You've chosen how you look in this lifetime and who you are. You'd loved yourself like this before you were born on Earth. Fall in love with yourself again for only then will unconditional love return to your life, allowing the most beautiful creations. Love is the most powerful energy in the whole universe and is equal to gratitude. In this way, we reach the fifth chakra — the throat chakra, which perfectly fits the color of Saturia in which we currently are, for it's blue. This chakra has always a lot to do with creativity, especially the spoken one, with the sense of worthiness, and self-confidence. I guess I don't need to add that this chakra also plays an important part in the ascension process. The next chakra on your way is the third eye chakra. And here it's getting more interesting. While the first three chakras are responsible for maintaining and experiencing life on Earth and its biological shell, these chakras — from the heart and above — are connected to your Higher self and the whole universe. Your indigo, that is your pineal gland, is responsible for your intuition and seeing what is difficult to perceive. What is completely unperceivable in this space. It is responsible for focus and the reception of stimulus from the other dimensions. It opens the connection to them. It simply allows you to perceive the truth in the crowd of lies. It finds it intuitively. Finally, we will put a crown on our head," Yriah laughed out brilliantly. It was clear she was making an effort to put some humor into these serious topics," The crown chakra is the last energetic meridian in the human body and it allows the flow of energy into space. It's violet color is considered to be the color of the spiritual awakening for a reason. It can be related to great common sense, the understanding, and openness to comprehending of all that is. There are no limits to it. When this chakra is unblocked and a given person is open to their journey of ascension, the connection to the source will be retrieved and such a being starts to remember the long forgotten abilities and develop them. So as you see, all the chakras are important, especially now when such changes occur on Earth. It's essential as well taking into consideration the transformation of the human form from a carbon to silicon-crystalline based. The chakras are taking an active part in this process. The more effectively they work and are not blocked, the milder and faster the process is taking place. You need to know that during this transformation of the physical body, the chakra system is also going through a transformation and changing its function. Every human has fourteen energetic meridians. We distinguish seven chakras of the physical body that we have already enumerated and another seven that are located outside of the human body. There are also the alpha chakra and omega chakra which humans know a little less about."

"How can people feel their meridians?" I asked. I knew how

I could perceive them myself—as whirling points in my body. Perhaps, however, their perception was different for others.

"The majority of people perceive their chakras as radiant, rotating energy sources. Not many people know that chakras have a six-dimensional internal structure too. In the karmic cycles, the structure of seven chakras of the physical body was intentionally limited in a way that it could transmit the energy only from the astral level. It can be said that the chakras were somewhat sealed. According to this limited template, the chakra resembles two cones, with one of them opening to the front of the body and the second one opening in the opposite direction, that is in the direction of the back. The place of contact of these two cones is sealed so that they remain motionless. This block is the effect of the residue of the emotional and mental structures. Their influence is that the cones rotate with a declining speed which results in the energy shortages in the whole chakra system. Such blockages in the meridian system trigger the fact that the energy is transmitted only to the front and back of the body which, in turn, results in the fact that the system has no possibility and is not predisposed to receive vibrations from the higher dimensions and realms. This, in turn, can lead to many illnesses in the human body, and the complete stopping of the meridian movements can even cause death."

"And the majority of humans have such blockages, unfortunately," I summed up, "How to change that then? How to remove the seal?"

"There are many ways to do that. Many sounds with suitable frequencies support human energetic chakras, help in cleansing as well as slow and safe opening of them. Meditation and yoga are other methods, which to a great degree can improve the quality of energy in the chakras. From now on, though, everything will start to change slowly. The karmic cycle has been stopped. When humanity enters the activation process of their light body, the blockages in their meridians will be removed. Thanks to that, chakras will start to slowly open and will be doing so up to the point they morph into the form and shape of a sphere. This will allow them to receive and send again the energies and frequencies to higher dimensions. Thanks to that, the energetic limitations which have been a problem until now, will cease to exist."

"Could you describe in greater detail how exactly this transformation of energetic whirls will take place?" Kal requested.

"Of course. I enjoy it when someone absorbs the knowledge so willingly like you. It's a pleasure for me to pass on the truth to you. My heart is overjoyed when I sense your inner desire to get to the truth. And so, the following chakras, namely the eighth and the eleventh one, contain flat crystal templates through which pass galactic axiatonal lines which Semjase has already told you about. When the connection of meridians via these lines takes place again, the symbiotic soul will retrieve the possibility to regulate the influence of stars on the human biological body. Then, axiatonal meridians and the axiatonal system of the human body will be again matched and joined with each other by the eighth chakras. Thanks to this join, the eighth chakra will again take control over the mutation of the human body and over the fusion of all the energetic bodies of the human, creating a coherent and ideally working energetic wholeness that is deprived of any blockages."

"This is quite complicated," I summarized Yriah's utterance.

"You're right, Smaisi, but everything that is unknown to humans seems to be more complicated than it actually is. Until now, the alpha chakra and the omega chakra have been almost completely dormant in the human body. And although these chakras are energetic centers as well, they are built according to a completely different template than the ones that are known to humans the most. The alpha and omega chakras are like very sensitive regulators that are capable of absorbing all the various energy waves. Yet this is not all. They are the anchor for the seventh-dimensional etheric template, to which humanity will consequently seek."

"Where exactly are these chakras since it was not easy for humans to locate them?" Kal inquired.

"The alpha chakra is located about fifteen to twenty centimeters over the human head, however, not in the center — it's moved five centimeters forward, towards the forehead. It connects you directly to the immortal light body of the fifth dimension. Whereas the second chakra — the omega chakra — is situated more or less twenty centimeters below your tailbone. This chakra is responsible for the connection with the holographic level of planet Earth and with the whole incarnation web of a particular soul. This connection is completely different from the karmic structure of the fourth-dimensional matrix. When all the chakras are opened and the energies inside them join together in an unhindered flow, the chakras will connect with the axiatonal lines. This will allow for the merging of the emotional, mental, and spiritual body into one. Into a united field of energy. Thanks to that, it will be possible to receive impulses from the Symbiote of the Oversoul. Because of this merging, there will be many changes triggered that will be strictly of a biological nature, for example, a completely new system of liquid circulation in the human organism."

"At this point, though, humans are still limited, right? The energetic unification, that you're talking about, hasn't taken place yet?" I asked.

"No, it hasn't happened yet. It's a process, nothing happens instantly. But you're right. At present, humanity is still in the zone of some limitations. Living in the state of separation as well as having such an attitude towards their biological body, humans are actually not present in the body. It probably sounds quite odd, but that's the truth. People can't fully merge with their bodies, they don't care for it or listen to what it says. They're not an integral whole with it, instead they just only coexist close to each other. But it's not enough though, as it means to some extent a lack of self-respect. It's not enough though. Not being fully in their bodies, humans have no possibility to activate the heart chakra and when it's no active, the root and solar plexus chakras dominate which leads to the fact that the interactions with the external are based on instinctual vibrations, that is constant worries, dwelling in imposed programmes and patterns. People focus on power, lust, and jealousy. They play egocentric games of power and superiority with others. And this leads them to their downfall only. Not being fully in his or her body, a human is not capable of experiencing higher states of consciousness or even interacting with them. These states are not available for him or her, not to mention the fact that the chakras that are outside of the body are not activated either. The circle closes and the human is trapped inside it. By saying that the transformation is a longer process I meant that some of the DNA activations and changes have been already sown so that in time they can be harvested and have influence on the ascension of the human species."

"What do you mean sown?" Kal asked hesitantly.

"In order for you to understand, let's go back in time until March of nineteen eighty-eight. That was the time when the majority of humans whose mission is to carry the light on this planet were activated to the first level of their light body. In April nineteen eighty-nine, the whole crystalline grid of matter and all of the inhabitants of the planet were activated to the third level of the light body. This occurred collectively. Humans had no right to choose whether they want this change or not. Many of them will soon leave this planet because they won't like to undergo the transformation in their current incarnation. Every soul can decide in which lifetime and which parallel reality they want to undergo this process in the journey of the evolution of their soul. Those who decided not to do it now are simply not ready yet, therefore, it cannot happen in this particular incarnation. During the first stage of activation of their light body many people started to feel weird, as if a light bulb was lit in the DNA that was sending the message that it's time to go home. The body was feeling that in a similar way. It was bursting with enthusiasm and energy at the same time it was reacting with a decreased density which in many cases resulted in the appearances of flu symptoms. The illness that was well-known by many people back then was nothing else but a symptom of a DNA mutation and the changes occurring in the body. When the body loses its density, it has a tendency to show symptoms such as headaches, muscles and bone pains, nausea and diarrhea. It was easy, therefore, to confuse some of these symptoms with a commonly known disease like flu. That was the reason why in March nineteen eighty-eight there was allegedly a flu epidemic, which in fact wasn't the flu epidemic, it was the epidemic of light that was spreading in human bodies."

"Indeed, there was such an epidemic. Mommy told me about it. Many people were ill then. Many for real. But if there was an epidemic no research was made which would have confirmed that the reason was indeed the flu virus? I asked slightly astonished.

"Even the contemporary knowledge about human genetics is not able to determine the real purpose of almost ninety nine percent of human DNA, which makes this topic completely disregarded by the scientists. They skip something they have no idea about and this leads to many mistakes of medical and scientific nature. Human DNA contains the elements of genetic material of all the species living on Earth. On top of that, there is a genetic fragment that is a holographic record of all the experiences of humanity at the turn of millennia and a web of data about the incarnations — those from the past as well as the present. But that's not all. You'll see for yourself how little humans know about their bodies and DNA structures which they are in reality made of. DNA contains genetic fragments of as many as three hundred eighty three species of beings inhabiting five neighboring universes; there are hidden codes in it that allow mutations and the transformation of the human body into the light body. Before the flu epidemic merely seven percent of these codes were active. It was only after the epidemic that symbiotes which had been working based on the previous mutation could activate further series of codes, letting through the body more appropriate frequencies of light and sound — this was due to the decrease in body density during the alleged pandemic. When the new codes became active again they gave the sign to further DNA mutations of the human body and lead to many changes connected with the processing of energy in human cells. "

"Can you measure the level of the light body in the human body? I mean, can you check at what the stage of transformation into the luminous body a given person is?" Kal got particularly interested in this matter.

"The first stage of the light body can be measured based on the ability of human cells to process light. The determinant of this new activity of cells after mutation is the amount of ATP, that is adenosine triphosphate, in the human body. Let me explain in short how it works. Before the activations of the light body, the whole energy that the human cells need to function properly was derived from food and the resources accumulated in the body, which resulted in some energy fluctuations between ADP, that adenosine diphosphate, and ATP. ATP is a way of binding energy previously stored in cells. And now a bit of chemistry. Food is converted into energy in the mitochondria of the human body. This energy is accumulated in the body as ATP, which is made up of a chain of three phosphate groups. When ATP loses its outer group, the phosphate becomes an ADP molecule. Breaking this chemical structure causes the production of energy, thanks to which the cell can correctly fulfill its functions, such as building proteins. By absorbing the extra energy — ADP can turn again into ATP. In this way, ATP and ADP interchangeably either lose or gain a phosphate group so that cells could have energy when needed that is indispensable to fulfill their functions in the body. It's a closed system of biological energy that leads to the aging and death of the human biological body due to the diminishing metabolic capacity of cells."

"It's a bit complicated. I don't know why but I never liked chemistry," I confessed.

"None said it's easy. That's the reason why we won't delve into this any further. The biochemistry of the human body is very complicated and many people don't understand it, even the scientists who devote their whole lives to this subject don't know everything because there is no such technology on Earth that would allow us to study certain DNA functions and cells of the human body. But I was heading to tell you that during the initiation of the mutation process, a series of genetic codes of human DNA was illuminated, which gave new commands to the body's cell. One of the first commands was giving a sign to a cell that it should accept light as its new source of energy."

"Turning from food to light. It's like photosynthesis." I laughed.

"Not entirely but indeed — plants need light to grow. Yet, it doesn't mean that humans will turn into plants." Yriah laughed out so loud that her laughter echoed in the space. "And not a complete change because humans still need to eat but the light has become a kind of an additional pillar from which humans can draw energy."

"What was the reaction of the human body to this change and the new commands for the cells?"

"Good question, Kal. Initially, the cells didn't know what to do with such information. They were lost. But when they were flooded with light their mitochondria, which are in fact very sensitive to light, surrendered to this new light and sound activation and started to produce huge amounts of ATP. Thanks to that the body became saturated with the energy it needed to function properly. In most people, however, cells have failed to absorb enough light to stabilize this change. This led to the next reduction of ATP in relation to ADP, as a result of which the cell metabolism of the human body accelerated. Any deposits of toxins, pollution in the body, and psychosomatic traumas, thoughts, emotions which were not aligned with light started to be released from the body. Hence, the human body had to throw them out in some way, which it did and that triggered symptoms that were flu-like. That's the truth about the alleged pandemic of a flu. You can observe that the longer you're in the sun, your hunger decreases and you have more energy than on cloudy days when the body does not absorb enough light."

"Was the adding of the new ability to absorb energy the only change at the first stage of the transformation into the light body?" Kal asked. He was inquisitive and I was not surprised. "If humanity will still go through these transformations shouldn't they be informed about what can happen to them in the process of mutation? Especially, since these mutations will eventually contribute to the improvement of health and the prolonging of life of human species. However, during these mutations humans will experience some inconveniences of a biological nature which can frighten them and make them visit a doctor unnecessarily."

"No, not only. At that time, humans distinguished functions of the left and right hemisphere. The pineal gland and the pituitary gland were the size of an orange instead of a walnut. The first stage of light body activation changed the chemistry of the brain and started to create new synapses containing codes of survival. And so these changes were gradually introduced too. As you probably know from Semjase, there is a code of a human Shiru matrix in the synapse. Such a synapse was not too long ago given to a female human being. This synapse contains a code of survival for the new human generation. In the future, this woman will conceive and give birth to a child that will be a representative of a new human generation. It's the seed of a new Earth. The beginning of a completely new human civilization. This girl is the first child of a new era."

"Who is she?" I asked out of pure curiosity.

"I can't tell anyone. She's too precious and any information about her and her whereabouts would threaten her and the future of a new human species," Yriah explained, counting on our understanding.

"I understand. I won't ask any further then," I smiled, "Changing the subject then, what is the second stage of the transformation into the luminous body? Perhaps it's Covid? Or is it still ahead of us, or perhaps people have already gone through it?"

"Not everyone, naturally. This takes place, as I've already mentioned, in stages and it depends on humans if they are actually ready for the next one. It's also dependent on their level of consciousness. In the second stage of transitioning into the light body the six-dimensional etheric pattern is flooded with light, which breaks all four-dimensional structures that link people with karmic experiences. It causes a breakdown and a feeling of some disorientation. It is also possible to get sick more often with flu-like viruses, during which the body cleans itself more and more and reduces its density. It's also a time when your mind starts to sense that there is something more, something you never thought of before. You can feel some sort of integration with the soul but you still not entirely grasp this connection. Hence the disorientation and fighting with yourself and the top-imposed programs. All these changes lead to exhaustion of the body. People often need much more sleep and rest then and they shouldn't be denied this."

"Ah yes, do humans feel soul or spirit then? Are these two concepts the same?" I asked for confirmation so that I knew how to describe it in my book.

"No, they aren't. I'll explain. Under the concept of soul there is a varied part of the spirit that experiences through incarnations into the physical body. On the other hand, the spirit is an unvaried part that is completely connected to the source. The symbiote, that is the soul, is therefore, as it were, an intermediary between the spirit and experience on the physical plane."

"I guess I understand now..." I stated unsurely and Yriah laughed out, "And what's next? What are the following stages? There are some, right?"

"Of course, there are. This is not the end of the transformation. The next phase of the mutation is the third phase of transitioning into the light body. At this stage, the physical senses become incredibly strong. Smell, taste, and hearing sharpen up. The scents can initially be downright annoying. Everything felt much stronger. You can hear and see better. You can even sense the objects that you sit on or the clothes you're wearing. You can feel their constant presence on your skin. You're more aware of them. It is not until the third light body transformation that many people begin to feel the pleasure of sex again. The latter change was the direct cause of the increase in births after 1989. Human body was created in a way that it was possible for it to decode and make use of higher energies of light and be able to pass it on to the planet, however, during the separation this ability was lost. The sharpening of the senses is the first sign of changes that are occurring and the entering into a third phase of a light body. In the previous stages the body was as if bathed in light, whereas, in the next stage, via the

111

activated axional system, light enters directly each and every cell of the body. This is a phase in which mitochondria recognize light as a new source of energy and under the influence of light new ATP cells start to create. Thanks to the fact that cells receive energy from light that they can make use of, less ATP is forced to convert into ADP. The axional system feeds the points of whirling in cells with the energy that comes from the Oversoul and, as a result, they begin to produce light and sound frequencies that alter the frequency of atomic movements, particularly of hydrogen atoms. As the mobility of ATP molecules increases, they begin to play a new role in the body. The three groups of phosphate that make up the ATP molecules become like antennas that receive homogeneous light. The symmetrical tip of these molecules becomes a kind of prism that splits pure light, producing a full, colorful spectrum. Then, it can be used by still dormant DNA codes. Before activating the luminous body, ribonucleic acid, or RNA, functioned as a messenger in the body, but only in one direction. It carried the active command of seven percent of the DNA to other parts of the cell. These commands contained information, for example, on what type of protein was to be synthesized. On the third level of the luminous body this changes and the RNA becomes the messenger in both directions. It can now deliver the light — refracted by the ATP antenna prism into usable frequencies — back to the DNA strands. With each successive level, dormant genetic codes wake up and transmit information to the RNA that supplies them to the entire cell."

"This is already very complicated. I don't understand this at all" I admitted.

"That's true. The processes taking place in the human body during the transformation into the luminous body are difficult to understand. The easiest way to describe it is in a few words: changing the way the body receives energy affects the activation of new DNA codes, which in turn affect changes in the human biological body. This allows a dialogue to develop between the physical body and the symbiote. After crossing the third stage of the light body conversion, it is no longer possible to go back. The mutation is permanent and cannot be stopped anymore."

"What was the purpose of activating human bodies since there is already a new species of a human on Earth?" Kal kept asking.

"The activation to the third level of the light body was conducted because of a simple reason — so that none could interfere with the process of ascension of humanity and the planet. The synapse is inviolable. During this activation there was created a connection between Gaia and other planets that head towards this transformation. This connection maintains them in synchronicity. Because it's not only this planet that ascends to a higher level, but the whole dimension and the whole astral plane. The whole process is called the inhale of the source."

"What do you mean exactly by saying the inhale of the source?" I got intrigued.

"The Source — everything that exists, that is the point of oneness, manifests through inhaling and exhaling of the creative force. It manifests as a very slow exhalation and a very fast inhalation. As if the exhalation lasted millions of years, whereas the inhalation only lasted several dozen. This is because as one you choose to experience a billion possible nuances and experiences that you can only achieve through the levels of progressive individualization. It can be illustrated by the example of a stretching elastic band. It stretches and experiences to the point it's stretched to maximum. It is at this point that you move further and further away from your oneness, entering ever greater duality and separation. The tension caused by this is tremendous and finally there comes a point where you just turn around and let go of the rubber band. It makes you come back to your oneness very quickly. And that's what's happening right now. The rubber band has been released. On this planet, the separation phase is complete as humanity has gone through all possible role changes and interactions. Any karmic relationship that could be explored is already known. There are no more opportunities and room for new experiences for souls. This is the reason why the new inhalation is slowly taking place. This is the time of return to home and oneness.

There have incarnated on Earth many advanced light beings that have descended here of their own accord so as to assist humanity during this transition. They're here to help and show the right way. They've incarnated here as humans and similarly to them, they've passed through the veil of oblivion. They wake up first though. Like you, for example. The star children, because it's mainly about them, will pave the way for the whole of humanity in the direction of a new golden era, which is right behind the corner."

"Then, we have to believe that we will do our job well" Kal summed everything up.

"It's not faith but certainty that will lead you to a point you want to be at. Remember about the power of your creation" said Yriah and I felt that suddenly the whole space of Saturia was withdrawing, "See you later, dear ones."

Kal and I were quite shocked that the netting with Yriah was over. The only thing I registered was her last words. These were the key words which suggested that it was not the end of meetings with her, which made me very pleased.

Chapter 5

"Silence like a surface of water in a lake, at sunset ... It allows you to see what only your eyes are looking at..."

Damian Buczniewicz

Water always remembers...

The following days were passing and Semjase was absent at night. I even had a strange impression that maybe something happened. Kal was not worried by that. He was focused very much on his matters and was searching for as much reliable information as possible about extraterrestrial races, as well as those living right under our noses. I had a weird impression that our mission got somewhat split. He has his own part and I had mine. I did not know at that time if it was good or bad and I followed the blow, with every day writing down the next pages of my book.

I woke up this morning exceptionally rested. Outside, white powder enveloped everything and the beautiful sun shone through the delicate and thin clouds. Beautiful weather. The weekend was going to be extremely fun with the prospect of numerous winter walks. Kal promised me that if enough snow fell, and it happened that night, he would take me to a certain place where there is the perfect hill for a sledge ride. I did not remember when was the last time I rode the sledge and I was excited by the upcoming possibility. I went downstairs in a perfect mood. My vibrations were increasing at the very sight of fluffy snow and sun rays — for some time I felt that they were rising in me more and more. I was ascending. Slowly yet successively. I did not need any confirmation of that fact, I could feel it with my whole being. I knew that many people felt at that time the symptoms of descending on Earth energies. Unfortunately, for many they were initially problematic, not infrequently even painful. It was a process though, which every being currently inhabiting Earth needed to go through. There was no other way but to synchronize with the upcoming changes in order to fully merge with the frequencies of new Earth.

My parents were sitting in the living room, looking at the TV. The pandemic was harvesting its crops. The Orionids were feasting so loudly that their ears were shaking from the excess energy of fear drawn from humanity. I knew very well that these were their last moments on this planet and that soon the time of a great turnaround would come and everything would change. I saw in this alleged pandemic some positives though. People were afraid but simultaneously a lot of them woke up thanks to that. They could see the falsity of the pandemic as well as strange behaviour of world governments. Every country was reacting differently to newer and newer restrictions. I started to consider if the rulers were not using the knowledge of changes in human DNA during the transformation into a luminous body and the symptoms accompanying it to create a false pandemic. I was not certain, though, and I was aware of the fact that they were capable of anything to stop the ascension of humanity and the planet or at least to delay it. They had little influence on the planet itself. It was successively getting closer to the central sun of the galaxy. But humanity... Humanity could still be held back in some way. They did what they could to make it happen.

"How's the daily gibberish?" I asked my parents, entering the living room with a cheerful stride.

"No changes. As idiotic as yesterday or the day before," Daddy replied and laughed out. He changed the channel as well. He knew that I did not like watching the news. Especially when the same things were said all the time. This is called the programming of the mind. "I can see you got up in a good mood," he added after a moment and glanced at me questioningly.

"Yes, in an excellent mood. Kal promised we will go

sledging, when there is lots of snow. Aaw, what a beautiful, white fluff!" I shouted out and almost jumped out of happiness. I danced to the kitchen. I poured a full glass of fresh juice and returned to the living room.

"Oh, the snow has fallen, indeed. Who's gonna clear the driveway now, then?" Daddy was wondering and Mommy laughed out.

"Semjase has been gone for a long time" I said, counting on the fact that my parents might have had any knowledge of her whereabouts.

"She's busy, Smaisi. There are many important things happening at present of which Semjase is taking care so that the time's up. It's more important than your little lectures. The right time will come for them. Anyway, you know well that you can ask us at any moment about some matters. It's not only Semjase that has such a vast knowledge. I'm certain that we could help you equally, although we know how much joy it brings for you to meet with her, " Mommy responded.

"Alright. I must consider what I would like to ask about. Perhaps it will turn out that you indeed know the answer" I laughed and winked at them.

It was then that Kal entered the house. He was not even knocking anymore, he was just entering as if it was his home too. One day Daddy, who did not want to get up from the couch to open the door, simply suggested to Kal that since he visits us so often there is no point in him knocking at the door every time. It is true that he did not get his set of keys, but the door remained usually unlocked during the day.

"Are you ready for sledging?" he asked at the threshold.

He was dressed as if he was heading to Antarctica. I laughed at the sight of him. He was wearing a ski suit and a large hat with ear flaps. The scarf was almost covering his whole face and he was wearing gloves that were so thick that I was sure he had difficulty bending his hands.

"Is it really so cold?" I asked, still unable to believe what I was seeing.

117

"If you can't believe it, check it for yourself. What do you think, why, despite the sun that looks from behind the clouds from the very morning, the snow is still in perfect condition? It hasn't melted at all".

Perhaps he was indeed right and I myself need a proper outfit? I did not even know if I had one. I approached the back door and opened it a little to stick my nose out of the door frame. As soon as a freezing cold blow of wind hit my face it fell and I stopped being amazed by what Kal looked like.

"Indeed, it's cold," I admitted, "And now we have a tiny problem. I really want to go sledging but it seems I have no outfit for that. My jeans will soak straightaway. I have a warm jacket but is it enough? Not to mention the boots. Snow boots are not part of my wardrobe equipment."

This time Kal's face fell.

"I must say you have prepared yourself for the sledge on average." He was not angry. I felt though that he was wondering how to solve the situation.

Before I had time to say anything, he disappeared behind the front door leaving me with my mouth wide open in surprise.

"What are you doing?" I asked, connecting with him telepathically.

"You'll see, " he replied, "go and eat. And get ready for a sledge adventure of your life."

I felt that he had a plan so I trusted him and following his recommendation, I ate a nutritious breakfast.

"What are you up to today?" I asked my parents. Since I spent most of my free time with Kal, I had little interest in my parents. Many times they left the house together and came back laughing. I did not invade their privacy and did not ask where they are when they are not around.

"Maybe we will go sledging too" Daddy suggested and poked Mommy to the side. This triggered a burst of laughter that I did not understand.

"Eeh.." I sighed only because I understood I would rather not find out anything.

They did not even ask me where and with whom I went out. Anyway, it was logical that each and every free time I would spend with Kal. They did not worry about my safety then. With the increase of awareness in the package, I was given full liberty and freedom in decisions made by me. And even though I was not 18 years old that was how I felt for some time.

"This so-called adulthood is only a time norm that is imposed from the top. It is not dictated by age but the mind and consciousness of a being. Many times even a ten-year-old has more decency and judgment than an adult male. People can't be measured with one standard. In fact, they can't be measured at all. Everyone is individual and unique and has their own life path which none should interfere with. We know your path and we know exactly that it's time we set you free so that you can spread your wings entirely" Mommy turned to me in all seriousness.

Sometimes I wonder if I like it or maybe if it irritates me more that most of the people I spend time with freely read my mind.

"I've just remembered an anecdote," Daddy giggled and I was sure that he was about to reveal it, "Some time ago there was a cartoon meme on the Internet. In the picture there were two gray beings sitting on the Moon and looking at Earth. One of them asked the other one: "Why don't humans have the ability to communicate in their minds?". The other one replied: "Because humans have too much to hide from one another". And even though this may sound funny, it's unbelievably true too. For only pure hearts and conscious souls have nothing to hide because they are oneness and they have a high level of forgiveness toward themselves and others. Whereas humans and non-humans, because there are plenty of them here too undercovered, the only thing they do is lie and manipulate on such a scale that the retrieval of their ability to read minds would end up with an immediate downfall of the whole civilization. Among the people who would not be on a sufficiently high level of consciousness there would be many conflicts triggered. For many of them it would be a shock the mere concept of free will and life in complete freedom and in harmony

119

with their own heart. Initially, they wouldn't be able to grasp it, what's more, they would resort to norms and programs that are well known to them because this freedom will seem too surrealistic to them". In this way, Daddy was able to change a small funny anecdote into a mini lecture about humanity.

Suddenly Kal burst into the house with a huge bag full to the brim.

"What's that? Are you moving in?" I laughed under my breath.

"Unlike you, my mom is skiing. So I've borrowed from her an outfit for you for today's winter craze."

He pulled out from the bag a ski suit, a really thick jacket, a woolen balaclava, ski goggles, a scarf that could be used to tie around the neck of a giraffe, and, in the end, proper winter boots.

"Up to minus forty Celsius degrees," he added with pride, "Your feet won't freeze for sure."

The last sentence triggered a loud burst of laughter in me. I did not notice any gloves, nevertheless.

"Mon did not give me any. She is very attached to hers. I gave in because I assumed you have your own. Because you do, right?" he asked unsurely.

"Yes, I do," I replied. It seemed that the clothes Kal borrowed from his mom should fit me perfectly. Anyway, she had a figure similar to mine. She was only slightly taller than me. "And the boots, will they fit me?" I asked, looking at them. My feet were quite tiny.

"A size bigger but I have thought about it too," he reached to the bag, "Look. We'll make your feet bigger with these wool socks."

I couldn't help but laugh. Besides, not only me. My parents were laughing their socks off and so was I. Kal was looking at us surprised but after a minute he joined us having realized how funny the scene of sledge trip rescue was.

It took a while until he managed to shove me into so many thick clothes. Even the trick with too big boots turned out successful. In the end I looked like a tiny snowman disguised as a ninja. I was ready. My bodily movements were slightly restricted, but the most important thing was that I would not freeze. Kal was not looking any better.

"Two little snowmen are going sledging", he said as we were walking to the place he had told me about.

It was cold but I did not know if we were dressed too warm. During the walk I sweated out the meals from at least a few days before. In addition, Kal was dragging quite a large old-style sled with metal boards. I was sure that even though they glided smoothly over the snow, they were certainly not the lightest.

"Going? I would rather say rolling" I laughed out.

"It's not far," said Kal.

We entered the forest. For a moment I was considering the fact that trees as the obstacles in the way would have ensured a lot of fun time for us filled with adrenaline, but they would also have posed a real threat.

"You are so wrapped up that you would be okay anyway. Besides we're going over there," he pointed at a meadow with a steep hill. Fortunately, there were no wooden obstacles on the way down.

It was only when I looked closer that I noticed that the descent continued far down and ran along a forest path. The very climb up the hill was quite a challenge. I felt that after a few climbs I would be taken home by a rescue helicopter.

"Stop inventing pessimistic and scary visions. You'll see, you'll love it!" Kal decided to cheer me up a bit because my enthusiasm for the sledge trip slightly subsided as we were walking.

When we managed to climb to the top of the hill it appeared that the hill seemed much smaller from this perspective.

"Wow!" I only got a word out.

"Yeah! It's gonna be fun! Sit at the front!" Kal perched on the sledge and left space for me at the front. "Don't worry yourself, I will hold you. I did this a thousand times!"

I sat down and waited for what was about to happen. My heart was beating so hard that I was afraid that it would jump out in a moment. That was when Kal pushed off with his feet and the sledge started to ride downhill at a dizzying speed. My initial terror soon changed into a squeak of satisfaction. I squealed so loud that the nearby birds soared into the sky scared by the wild sounds of an unknown origin. While the descent itself was wonderful, the re-climbing to the top was not so much. I even had an idea to sit comfortably on the sledge and ask Kal to pull me up the hill, but before I said anything he pierced me through with such a look that I only swallowed loudly. After a few descents we both had enough. We needed to rest a bit. The clothes turned out to be way too warm for such an amount of activity. To catch a breather we sat down on the clearing right next to the hill. I removed my gloves and gently uncovered the scarf to let more fresh air reach my face. I took a snowball in my hand and played with it for a while. The snow was melting very quickly in my hands. I watched with delight the drops of water falling to the ground which cut small tunnels in the snow. Suddenly I noticed in one of the drops a reflection of a silhouette standing behind me. I turned around and grabbed Kal's arm pulling him to look in that direction. Kal intuitively turned around and when I saw his content expression I knew that I was not the only one to notice that.

"Hello" said the being that looked like an Arcturian. Kal confirmed my assumption.

The entity was very tall. Much taller than we were. It definitely measured more than two meters. A slim figure and blue-violet color of the skin were drawing attention. The being had big eyes and a little nose and narrow lips, its head was slightly contoured to the back and in the middle of the forehead there was a diadem that added majesty and charm. A long cloak ideally exhibited a long slender neck.

"Hello" we replied, synchronized as always. I had no idea why it turned up.

"You are probably surprised at my sudden visit" it said after a moment, smiling at us.

It did not have to read our minds. We saw it for the first time so it was natural that its appearance was a surprise for us.

"Well, maybe slightly, although, there is not much that can

122

surprise us besides the fact you showed up in our density in a complete physical form. We usually travel to higher dimensions," Kal responded.

"The spaces begin to penetrate more and more. The Earth is ascending, which makes it easier for us to enter its physical level. Semjase does that very often too. She uses mimicry for that."

"What brings you here?" I asked, as I was more surprised by the fact it appeared right now, during our sleigh trip rather than the very appearance of it.

"You called me, Smaisi" it replied and this surprised me even more because I did not remember anything like that. "Your quick and fleeting thought of water was enough to initiate the meeting."

"Water?" Kal was astonished.

"That's right. And what you need to know about it. Perhaps Smaisi is not aware of this but she has created with her desire for a sledge excursion such a huge snowfall. The energy that you've put into this thought form and the fact that the willingness to experience came from your heart space made the manifestation of energy very fast. And snow is water after all. You've called in water. And water, in turn, called me in so that I can tell you about it — about what it actually is and how many hidden powers it has."

"It's amazing how it all actually works" I responded.

I was not aware of the fact that I was on such a level of consciousness that my thoughts could manifest so quickly. I decided I would try manifesting something different, but for now it was to give us a lecture on water. Even if I was not conscious of that, my soul knew very well what I needed on my journey and I trusted it immensely. It guided me and I followed its signs and my heart.

"For sure, a lot of things will surprise you, despite the fact you know quite a lot about water. Water is not respected on Earth and it should be totally opposite."

"What does water have to say to us?" I asked as curiosity took over. I knew the abilities of water from my previous trips with Semjase and from the expedition to the bottom of the ocean when

I was honoured to meet the Dag Aquaticus beings. So what else could the water surprise me with?

"Oh, with many things, Smaisi. Water has to say to you more than you expect. Even if everyone forgets, water will always remember. For water has an incredible memory which you already know about, and you, Smaisi, have experienced this during your trips with Semjase. You've learned quite a lot about it from Algaton as well. But it's a drop in the ocean of truths and it's these truths that I'm about to reveal to you now. Humanity has no idea how important water is even though their biological bodies consist of seventy, or sometimes even up to ninety percent of water. It's a matter that they need to get familiar with so that they can be more conscious of its influence on them and on the whole life on Earth."

"It's a pity that I don't have any notepad on me" I confessed because I had a feeling that what water wanted to tell us was not that easy to grasp.

"Don't worry yourself. I'm always ready" said Kal and he pulled a phone out of his pocket and turned the recorder on.

I had no idea why I did not think of that myself. Anyway, I left my phone on the bedside table at home. The last thing I could have thought of was that it would be needed when sledging.

"Are you ready for a bit of knowledge?" it asked.

"I have a feeling that it won't be a bit" I laughed out.

"Your hunch doesn't disappoint as always. I don't know where to start. There is so much of it and nothing is more important."

"And could you tell us your name?" asked Kal and that was a perfect question as I did not notice she had not mentioned that before.

"Call me Arkana," she replied shortly and started her story straightaway. "You can call water a liquid crystal. As it's as valuable for life on Earth as crystals which can be used to obtain renewable energy. It's the foundation of all life on this planet — in the seas, oceans, rivers, and in all the layers of atmosphere as well. Even inside the Earth where the sight can't reach. Water is everywhere, it surrounds you all the time in the form of steam that is present in

124

ARCTURIAN

your surroundings. How much of it there is depends on the degree of air humidity. Not to mention the fact, as you already know, it is the main building block of the human biological body and of all creatures and plants. Water has a perfect memory. It exists in a constant state of dynamic harmony with everything that surrounds it. It has the ability to recognize, remember, and take over the properties of other substances, although its own composition does not change. The structure of the water molecule is very simple. It consists of two hydrogen atoms and one oxygen atom. Its formula is H_2O. Despite the simplicity in construction, water in a liquid state is a much more uncanny substance for people than they think. They are not aware of the fact that they have a treasure that is at hand. Water has peculiar physical and chemical properties. There are no such molecules on the planet that would contain so much energetic vitality and which could be called the root of life. Literally every property of water — and it has a multitude of them — is unique. Water is made of molecules that combine to form a variety of patterns. These complex structures are called clusters. They're in a continuous stable thermodynamic equilibrium. These structures hide encoded information, which are stored in specific memory cells. This is the characteristic that is responsible for the water memory and is used by people in homeopathy. And although the memory of water can be perceived as a positive feature, it also has some negative sides. As it is said, there are things about which it is not worth remembering."

"What do you mean by that? " I asked just in case the answer to my question was not planned for this transmission.

"Imagine a situation in which a drinking water intake is located in a place where it is in contact with various chemicals among other things which are often toxic, in sewage. The water from the sewage is being purified and after that it's considered to be drinkable. Nothing more misleading. The chemical purification of such water is useless because this water simply remembers and encodes in its structures everything it gets in contact with. It doesn't matter how many times it will be purified, it's memory won't change and people will drink water with all the assortment of

additives that the water encountered in sewage. It doesn't sound good, right? "

"Now I know why Mommy from my early ages has been telling me that if I drink tap water again she'll have me sit in the corner", I laughed out. Our house has always been dominated by fresh juices squeezed from vegetables and fruits. We rarely drank pure water.

"Exactly. She didn't want you to absorb substances that were energetically contaminated", Arkana replied to me and continued her lecture. "Another example of a situation in which water gets in contact with what it shouldn't is an inhuman slaughter of animals. Shortly before they die, their bodies produce a great deal of stress hormones, and the animals feel pain and suffer tremendously. Animals instinctively feel the danger and it's present in their bodies long before death. What's worse, many times they see other animals being taken and not returned to the herd. There are also such cases when the slaughter takes place in the same place where the animals are held. Put yourself in their position at least for a moment. Feel inside you the reactions and emotions it would trigger in you. So the emotions of these poor animals fill up every cell of their body of a given animal with chemical substances of low vibrations. The mental state of an animal is precisely encoded in the water structures of its body. In the muscles, fat, and blood. There is water everywhere and it remembers perfectly well what it came in contact with. As a result of this process, that can be called murder, humans eat meat that is permanently stuffed with traces of agony and horror. And they mistakenly believe that it has no effect on them. The codes of these emotions influence the water structures of a human organism which receives information that is encoded in water about the emotional state of an animal that they've just eaten."

"Semjase told us about it," I interrupted, "She said that humans indulge in fear and suffering on their own wish and they are surprised later on why their fate is the way it is and why they are consumed by diseases."

"Exactly, Smaisi. That's why it's so important to understand the process of remembering information by water. Perhaps people will finally start to think over what they do before it will be too late for them. Eating meat that is soaked in fear and suffering has a huge effect on the structure of the pineal gland which is a very important organ of the human body — it's the connector between body and soul. And I confirm what Semjase has already told you. The codes transmitted into the water structures of a human after drinking contaminated water or eating meat of another being, influence the human and create various diseases. People are surprised why they are ill on such a big scale while the answer is right under their nose, on their plate."

"But how does water remember such things and how is it possible for it to transmit such information further?" — it's good that Kal asked that question, otherwise people would give it some magical properties and I felt that it has nothing to do with magic.

"The water molecule is a dipole, i.e. a polar molecule that is asymmetric, which is influenced by the fact that the centers of the positive charges do not coincide with the centers of the negative charges. This contributes to the fact that water molecules associate very easily, i.e. in colloquial language — they combine into larger aggregates surrounded by ions and cations of toxic substances, which include chemical pollutants and hormones, including the stress hormone. Such substances get attached to them. These aggregates have their own resonant frequency, which makes them able to break up. It happens through delicate breaks of hydrogen and proton bonds, which result in the release of harmful substances from the cell. They can also capture these toxic substances and release them later on, but we will get to that later. And so these water aggregates, even if the molecules which they were created around are removed, will still exist. That's how water memory works. The removal, or rather the attempt to remove a given pollutant from a water molecule does nothing. Even after multiple chemical cleaning, removal of bacteria and distillation, water will still send electromagnetic waves with lengths characteristic for the removed substances that were contaminated with, for example, lead, mercury, cadmium or aluminum, which are very harmful to the human body."

"And what about osmosis or distillation treatment? I also heard about carbon-ceramic filters. Are these methods more effective?"

Kal surprised me, I did not know that he knew such terms.

"The ways of purifying water that you've mentioned make it clean but dead at the same time. There's no life in it, therefore, it's neither its transmitter or creator. If you were to freeze such water and look under the microscope, you wouldn't see any beautiful various structures, instead you would see an awful shapeless compact mass."

"Is it possible then to bring it back to its initial state? To the full purity?" I asked because I suddenly started to feel sad.

"It is, but only by restoring it to the correct electromagnetic information it has in nature. In order to do that, there needs to be removed the whole information that water obtained on the way and it is necessary to restore its memory of the water matrix. This can be done with devices that use the laws of nature to restore water to its original shape. As a result, purified and revitalized water regains its spring water properties. Such living water — the source of life — resonates with the human body and accelerates human development as it has a crystalline structure. If you decided to freeze it, it would create beautiful shapes on a hexagonal basis that would resemble snowflakes. Look! "

She took a bit of snow in her hand and I don't know how she brought it closer to us like under a microscope. This was like a completely different, beautiful world. Suddenly, we found ourselves in the middle of this snowball. Crystal snowflakes with unique patterns connected with each other creating ice labyrinths. I was about to run into them when we returned to the snowy clearing right under the slope. I felt slightly disappointed.

"Where can we find such living water?" I asked. I suddenly started to feel like freezing it and purchasing a microscope so as to observe it endlessly.

"Living water with a natural primitive structure can be found in glaciers, virgin rivers, or really clean lakes. In its natural environment, it is subject to numerous effects of the Earth's magnetic fields, it is heated by the Sun's rays and it succumbs to the influence of the cosmic field of the Moon. In nature it's free. It flows through the rocks of various types, it resonates with the surroundings and with the elements of Mother Earth. With the wind, the current of the river, it foams and whirls. Constant movement and the intentions of Earth influence its renewal. It carries lots of information and energy that it passes to all the living organisms on this planet. For water it's enough to just touch another substance — it immediately encodes in memory its properties. It is thanks to the crystalline structures in the water. By remembering information, water seems to acquire different properties, but this does not change its composition in any way."

"If water can retrieve information, can it also convey it? If it can release substances, it looks like it can" contemplated Kal. His dynamic mind continued to amaze me.

"Of course. Water emits the information that it contains in the form of electromagnetic vibrations. Upon contact with water, it fuses and resonates, resulting in changes in the molecular structure. It is thanks to this characteristic that it is used to build interdimensional portals. Thanks to the structural changeability water energizes with its vitality every living organism. Its memory encodes all signals coming from the environment it is or was. For every living organism the contact with water is needed if not indispensable for survival. Water encodes not only everything that it comes in contact with. This is a curiosity, but it also reacts to electromagnetic frequencies in sound impulses — in music and words. Water, although it may surprise you, shows feelings too."

"It looks like tap water is not friendly for us", Kal summed up. "Then it's better not to drink it at all than to drink it."

"You summarized it very well. It's structure is distorted and for the human harmful is not so much the substance which the water came into contact with, but the harmful electromagnetic frequencies of the substances that once polluted it. The memory of water is in reality the ability to remember and store the vibrations that are characteristic for substances that water has ever

131

come in contact with. Therefore, it is best for the human to consume spring water because its structure hasn't been changed and it is fully living water which can pass the spark of life on, which positively influences human health."

"Without water, life on this planet would not exist. This should be enough for humans to understand how important it is, " I added. I was surprised by the fact it was not respected that much until then. I was also certain that the elites knew the properties of water very well but they were not bothered by watering humanity with its contaminated version.

"Of course they know, Smaisi. They use it for their own purposes as everything. In order for the water to function properly on the immunology of the human body, it must be alive and clean. And only like that. A different one is harmful instead of helpful. Water adjusts to human blood, carries over memory and an electric charge that allows cells to regenerate, multiply and nourish themselves. Cells under its influence restore their electric charge and they start to push away one another which allows them to freely transport oxygen in the body. A properly oxygenated body is, firstly, healthier and, secondly, it regenerates faster. For example, the water contained in freshly squeezed juices has a healing effect, but also a rejuvenating one. It is not hard to wonder how much it influences the human body. For millennia humans have been settling near natural water reservoirs, digging wells so that the water extracted by them was as clean as possible and as close as possible to its natural source. Even a lot of rituals were performed in the past by tribes of various nations incorporating water. They used to sing to it and chanting mantras was practiced to give water an intention, that is healing properties. Yet, humanity was gradually cutting off the resonance and properties of a living, pure water. It's time to change that. People have no idea that spring water can prevent or even heal a malignant tumor. It has an amazing effect on cell regeneration and their reconstruction. It's a living structure. It's a spark of life that is not appreciated by humans ".

"And what about rain? Taking into consideration how contaminated the air is at the moment, can we trust that rain water is alive? " I asked. At the tip of my tongue I had a question about the sensitive topic of chemtrails sprayed in the atmosphere, but I came to my senses in time because it was probably not the right time for such topics.

"Water that after evaporating from the soil comes down in the form of rain, freezes, in turn, and then melts again filling up the rivers, has a fully harmonious and natural structure. The elements shape it and it's a natural process for it. When it comes to air pollution, well, it's another subject and it won't be skipped for sure. You need to remember though that water has a memory of matrix which means that it can be restored to its original living state. It's not an easy process but it's feasible. It is enough to use the usual electrolysis. Thanks to it, water will be vitalized. There are devices on Earth that can restore the water to its original form. Even the mere freezing of water and its unfreezing changes its structure. And such water has a much better effect on the human body than tap water. Humans need to remember that every cell in the human body needs a suitable amount of water of a certain structure and frequency for proper functioning. When this balance is disturbed, it affects the state of the organs, vibrations, alternation, vitality and emotions, up to energy resonance along with the magnetic field and torsion field in the human body. Water is the source of life. The purer it is, the purer the life and healthier the body becomes. It gives the human body a high frequency of energy. Water is a gift from Mother Earth. Humans should always remember that. The waking up of humanity is taking place now and is escalating. Everything will slowly start to change and humanity will see the truth, also the one that concerns water."

"Can you tell me how your nation perceives the waking up of humanity? What threatens us and how will this unfold?" I inquired. I was still persistently looking for an answer to my own question: Will I manage?

"Humans will define with their own creation how exactly the process of waking up will look like. The external factors and supportive energies are one thing, but the inner being of the human and the creation from the heart level is another thing and a more important one. Humanity has been deceived for a long time almost at every step. The informational manipulation exists on such a great scale that it can be easily called a programmed control of human minds. People won't find on the media any true information as such are blocked, instead they are programmed in such a way that the system could function properly and so that humans were obedient. The world elites will do anything and what I mean is really anything that is in their power so that the systems of infiltration, financial, religious, and military control is maintained in the old model that serves only them. And the fact that on Earth there are more good things happening than the bad ones is not published anywhere. However, none can stop the awakening process now. Many changes will occur. People will start to discover them and create with their own desire to change. By setting an intention, they will generate energy that will contribute to the creation of the surrounding reality. The global shift of consciousness is manifesting more and more clearly, although it may seem that it is taking place slowly. These are the struggles of consciousness immersed in fear with the new energy of change in which love and forgiveness are key and only the right thing. By forgiving, humans change the potential of energy. New energy that is approaching teaches how to forgive and feel love for yourself. Many people need to forgive themselves and wrap their old programs in which they have been stuck for decades with love. Fear, helplessness, constant judgment of others — all of this needs to be worked through and forgiven, so that the energy of change could spread first in the reality of a given individual and then could successively influence the reality of the whole collective. All of those old feelings of low vibrations need to be dissolved in the breath of love. This is the future of humanity. It will be beautiful if humans decide to follow it and create it. What is really happening is the global reprogramming of human minds. Until now, vibrations have been imposed on the Earth, keeping humanity in fear and helplessness. Fear has become your home and the mere thought of leaning your head out of the window created a next wave of discomfort. Humanity, by choosing the ascension and connection with the consciousness of their soul with the assistance of supportive surrounding energies, will permanently split up with old paradigms. They will come to experience oneness with themselves and the whole creation. Creation out of love will allow mankind to see the world as they want it to be, and you cannot let anyone be distracted by the propaganda of fear, which is still led by the elite. People must cut themselves off from what they have known so far and boldly start changing themselves, starting from their inside. Thanks to that they will finally be able to be for themselves and the others. Their conscious action will change the reality. The thought is the energy of creation. And what is birthed in love, returns in the same form. It's always been like that and will always be. Humans need to define their desires and create in accordance with them, regardless of what is happening around them, because even though they are unaware of it, their environment is them and their own creation and thought forms, which they fill up their individual space with. The energy doesn't go away. Never. Humans have forgotten that they are the greatest creators. Perhaps when they remember and believe in themselves — instead of giving their energy to self-proclaimed gods — the change that they so long for will come."

I was about to ask another question when suddenly beautiful Arcturian disappeared, leaving us alone again.

"That was so cool!" Kal exclaimed, having realized that she was gone. "Did you feel how I was fighting off the enthusiasm when she appeared? Just not to let her know how great a shock and honor it is for me."

"I wasn't focused on you, but I'm quite sure she felt that too," I replied amused by the way he tried to hide his emotions at all cost. To me, completely unnecessary.

"I need to cool off," he said and threw himself face down into a thick, fresh layer of snow.

I did not wait long and I did exactly the same thing. Laughing, we slowly began to feel hungry. It was time to return home. As soon as I thought of the journey we had ahead of us, I started to feel weak.

"Perhaps I'll call Daddy to pick us up?" I suggested.

"Seriously? You're that tired?" Kal inquired.

"Yes, quite seriously. Since you already have this phone, why would it go to waste" I joked and sat on a tiny hill waiting for a cab home.

Talking to Daddy, I played beautifully that I was barely on my feet and urgently needed a portion of fresh fruit juice. Dad, of course, sensed that I was distorting reality and that I was just lazy, but when I added that an Arcturian female had visited us and that we had all of her messages recorded, he rushed into the car instantly.

Chapter 6

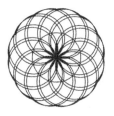

"Every time you throw responsibility on external factors, you take away the opportunity to change."

Damian Buczniewicz

The Moon

Since our meeting with the Arcturian female a few weeks have passed. December started frosty and windy. However, only a few days after our sledge trip, the snow melted completely, and then it did not snow anymore. Semjase did not show up. I was slightly worried by that. I tried to focus on my task and I was doing quite well. It seemed to me that I can safely assume that I am already in the middle of the book. Kal helped me from time to time, but his words were not as beautiful as mine. He told me so one day and this compliment made me blush. He pointed out that it was not accidental that I was to write that book and he was to technically describe the races. One day I reached a point in the book where I described the Moon, what it is and how the Ancients used it to escape their planet of Maldek. Even though Semjase mentioned that humans were on the Moon and were banned from visiting it again, I wanted to learn more about this escapade and what happened there. I resolved that as per Mommy's proposal, I would ask her if she knew anything more about this topic. Perhaps she would shed some light onto this occurrence.

Mommy was sitting in the kitchen and was peeling vegetables for the soup, humming under her breath. She did not need to look at me to know that I was creeping in.

"What's up daughter? Is something bothering you?" she

asked openly.

"I would like to know more about the Moon and about how the mission went. But you know—the truth rather than the food for the masses," I explained although I did not need to.

"Do you want to describe it in a book?" she asked though she knew the answer well.

"That's my plan. Why? Is it bad?" I wanted to be sure that by writing about this, I would not go on too brittle ice. Perhaps Mommy knew something I did not know.

"None of these things. It's one of the elements of the hidden truth. Another puzzle, which needs to be first faced up, then watched carefully and matched to the rest. What would you like to know then?"

"Everything that you know." I did not choose the questions. I wanted Mommy to tell me all her knowledge.

"Very well. I hope that it will not bother you that I will keep peeling the vegetables".

"Of course not. I can even help you with that," I offered. Mommy handed me a knife and a whole heap of potatoes.

"My dear, this is a portion for the whole army!" I joked.

"Almost. You have no idea how much Nju-en and Kal can eat for the whole week," she laughed. "As you probably know, the Moon is an artificial creation, the ark that was built by the Ancients that was anchored next to the Earth as a satellite and it influenced the terraformation of the planet and its better adjustment to sustain life. The Ancients used their best technology to create it. The Moon consists of two thick shells between which there's an atmosphere. The inner shell is thirty kilometers thick and made of extremely hard metal, while the outer one is four kilometers thick and is made of materials that protect its coating from temperature changes. These are very resistant and non-oxidizing rocks containing chromium, zirconium and titanium. As you know, craters on the Moon that are astonishingly shallow for the circumstances of their formation, were formed when rock fragments from the crumbling planet Maldek glided through space and crashed into the Moon. The outer shell, thanks to its construction, perfectly absorbed the tremors and rock fragments that were crashing against the surface and moving to the sides, unable to penetrate deep into this great structure. Hence the large size of the craters and their extremely disproportionate shallowness. The Moon, similarly to the Earth and tones of other planets, is not completely empty inside. Gravity is based on the relative masses of objects and distances, which the Ancients knew very well when constructing their ark. At present, there are many active bases of many civilizations. Those positive ones as well as those that are not so positive. It's a neutral zone though where the respect for the laws of the universe must be respected by all races. At the beginning of the fifties of the last century, the human bases were under construction. At that time there was a breakthrough in negations with Americans and it allowed for the transformation of nazi into an industrial powerhouse, which was to compensate for the expenses incurred in the conduct of a war.

"Hmm, and what do Nazi have to do with that?" I was surprised.

"Oh, my dearest — they built this base. They used their power and built A multi-level base in the shape of a bell, which reached deep under the Moon's surface. They made first attempts in the thirties of the last century, yet they encountered an issue. They discovered there an old building built by the beings much older — the Ancients that you already know. During the construction of their underground target base, they strengthened the buildings that they found so that they would serve them until their own project was completed. They tried to hide it so that it was as little visible as possible in the structure of the Moon. It couldn't be observed by the telescopes that could even then reveal to the world the whole truth about their secret project. One of the structures on the Moon even has the shape of a swastika. The surface structures of the base were built around the old structures and became what is called these days LOC, that is, Lunar Operations Command. There are many bases on the Moon, not only one. In fact, it's not only the Moon. Mars, which is only now being mentioned, has long since been sealed by humanity. Nazi and

Americans even have joined bases and they work together on the project that is called Black Project, of which purpose is to extend the structures of the Moon and Mars. There is a Secret Space Program, under which control this all takes place."

"Well, but what about other beings? Humans just like that received a land to build on?" I was surprised.

"Humans created their bases far away from the bases of other beings on the Moon as well as on Mars. Other civilizations had their bases there for a long time, therefore, they have the majority of territories and lavatories needed to maintain the operational system of the bases. These bases are so vast and extensive that they could hold millions of inhabitants."

"What about the landing on the Moon? Was it just to show off while in reality they fly there all the time?" I asked. Taking into consideration the information that Mommy just passed onto me, the one-time landing on the moon that people were shown was simply a mockery. Confusion for the entire population and nothing else.

"You're right to think it was made for public display. Why do you think the astronauts, after landing on the moon in 1969 did not notice any signs of alien life or any other life, since the moon was already so densely inhabited even by humans?"

"I have no idea, Mommy. I don't even want to guess," I confessed, still slightly confused by the pieces of information I received.

"Do you think that Neil Armstrong knew that there was more going on and that the Moon was the place of secret projects of American and Nazi governments? Or did he go there with all seriousness knowing that in fact he will be the first person in the history of mankind who will put his foot on the Moon?"

"Again, I don't know," I replied truthfully, having no idea what to expect.

"I know that you don't know, my dearest. But sometimes, when you ask the right question, the answers start to arrange into logical wholeness. In reality, nobody knows what knowledge was possessed by those astronauts during the trip to the Moon. It's

known though that erasing astronaut's memory is a common practice. In the past, memory erasing procedures consisted of administering special chemicals to a given individual, but over the years this technology has changed and today electric fields that affect memory are used to do so. The images are uploaded into their memory that are identified by the brain as true. And how much they really know and remember depends on them. However, it is quite known that just after his return, Neil Armstrong did not want to appear, let alone speak in public. After the analysis of his statements, it could be inferred that he was used and deceived. After the whole incident, Armstrong fell into deep alcoholism and one can say he drank himself to death. From his authentic reports it appears that he saw a convex circular ship nestled on the edge of one of the craters and that he was definitely not the first creature to walk on the lunar surface. He repeatedly said that someone had already been there before him. The truth is that the astronauts then only moved along the satellite and did not walk on the moon at all. Due to the fact that the moon is divided into zones belonging to given nations, their appearance there was not welcomed. All the more, it did not help them at all when they dropped the command module or something like a rocket to the surface. They were asked then not to return ever again. Still, they continued their journey around the moon, took a few pictures and made a report about what they saw on the surface. The astronauts used a code in which the password "Santa Claus" meant an observed activity of extraterrestrials. When, during their trip, they went to the dark side of the Moon and then the range of radio waves was updated again on the bright side, they announced in a live transmission "Ladies and gentlemen of the whole of America, we're honoured to announce that Santa Claus is real". The transmission triggered many mixed feelings in people as they completely didn't understand the message."

"So where do the pictures from their landing on the moon come from? Are they entirely fabricated?"

"Yes, Smaisi. While the journey itself was real, the landing was staged because they did not get off their ship. On Earth, lunar-like scenes have been set up and ready for use so — in case the mission fails — everything is ready to be recorded in real time. Hollywood is still involved in these types of scams. It was similar then. In the race to the moon, the Americans did not want to lose with the Russians. Of course in the media, for the crowd show. So the plan was to fabricate the mission, even if it wasn't successful in reality, only in order not to lose the propaganda war between America and Russia. Another fact is that the radiation on the moon then was too intense and the attempt to catch anything on the tape would have ended up overexposed. So, in the argument whether the lunar mission took place or not — both sides are right. The mission did take place and the ship did land on the moon, however, no astronaut did set a foot on it. And only this fact was directed and passed onto people all over the world."

"Not bad. I wonder if anyone will believe in that?" I wondered.

"The theory of the truth of the flight to the moon has many supporters and opponents. None assumes though that everyone is correct to some extent. And that everyone got fooled a little. Basically, everything that people know about the Moon is a lie. After the US government spent billions of dollars on the unfinished Tesla research, the doorway to the moon flung open. The Moon has been a home for decades for many people and alien civilizations among which there are also grays. There are ruins of lunar cities, translucent pyramids and domes, which are currently deeply hidden in NASA vaults. Everything is documented yet available to a selected few."

"And what happened next?" I inquired.

"In 1974, soon after the Apollo program was officially canceled, the cosmic agency sent three astronauts on a secret mission. Its aim was to research the north pole of the Moon and odd events connected to the presence of alien civilizations on the surface of the Moon. This presence was confirmed by previous Apollo missions. So... Officially, none flies to the moon, yet unofficially the Apollo program still exists and has never been finished. The missions that were before Apollo 14 were always

143

shrouded in mystery. Astronauts flew unknowingly, not knowing what exactly they were flying for and what was the research goal of a given project. Their families were not informed about the missions. Everything was kept strictly secret even from thousands of NASA employees. However, when the amount of information that could have leaked into public opinion and the risk of that were too big — the whole flight project was taken over by the Pentagon."

"They play people so much. It's unbelievable," I could not believe that the world governments were capable of hiding from humanity so much and for so long. "Thank you, Mommy," I said and ran quickly upstairs to meticulously describe it all.

Chapter 7

"If the system was built on truth, would it censor any information? The truth is undeniable. If one can undermine the system, it means that the system is false. In fact, every system is an illusion..."

Damian Buczniewicz

Free energy is omnipresent

Kal showed up at my place in the late afternoon, excited by his new discoveries. He was researching the subject of free energy lately. A few words about Tesla thrown by the Arcturian during the conversation with her triggered in him a huge seeker of truth in this matter. He was persistent in his pursuits so I knew very well that he managed to gather a lot of information.

"Would you mind if I ask your Dad about it?" he asked in the doorway, "I'm sure he knows a lot about this subject. Generally, he knows a lot yet this subject is of men's interest in particular."

"Sure, no problem. I would love to learn more about it too and Daddy, as I assume, will be delighted to tell us more. And when you ask him about the orgonites later on... Oh, that will be a lecture."

"Orgone energy. I've read about it. Great! OK, shall I call him then?" he asked, not being sure if that was the right moment.

"Yep, you can. The element of surprise will allow us to avoid charts and boards, " I laughed, remembering the lecture about the Earth's densities.

"Very well, I'm going to get him," Kal disappeared behind the door.

I was not sure if I should feel saddened or neglected because I didn't even receive a greeting kiss. He was so excited about the free energy. Oh well…

After a while, I heard them going up the stairs and lively discussing the topics that our lecture was to be related to. I'm not sure if lecture was the right word — for sure it was a presentation of truth yet this term was associated with a very school-like way, almost university-like.

"I'm so glad. I didn't expect such an exciting afternoon," Dad stuttered out, comfortably sitting down in the armchair. I was right that he would derive joy from this. He knew from Mom that I asked her about the Moon expedition and he felt slightly ignored. Now, he had his chance to give a lecture that he had been dreaming of for a long time.

"Neither did I," I added ironically, but I didn't need to explain to anyone that it was a joke. They knew that very well. I was not — similarly to Kal — resistant to new knowledge. Quite the opposite, we were equally absorbing it like a sponge. "So, Daddy, what can you tell us about free energy?" I asked and sensed that Kal did not say a word that the next issue to be discussed were orgones which Daddy just loved. He created a few of them too and they were arranged in the whole house.

"I have a lot to say about that. A few things you already know as I assume. Semjase has surely mentioned to you already about the energy obtained from the crystals and about the energetic grid of the Earth, which, once activated, would become an inexhaustible source of energy. I would like to focus on more earthly matters though, of which knowledge is being blocked, because if all the information on free energy was shared — overnight, the entire economic system would simply collapse. The elites don't want to allow that. This is one of the elements of the shackles in which humanity is chained to."

"The amount of the shackles sometimes brings me to high fever. It's incredible how they organized everything to serve themselves. It's good that it's the beginning of their end and that humanity will be free again," I said and tried to wrap in love the

146

irritation that I started to feel.

"Imagine that the whole human population has access to free energy. The truth is that the machine that produces free energy already exists and anyone can build it. There's more. There are even devices that change the energy into another kind. Unfortunately, if that happened it would lead to the disturbance of the still existing structures and completely destroy their Babylonian system of control over people based on money. Money is their magic trick, however, coming from dark magic. If one could approach it from a less materialistic perspective... Free energy has always existed, but those in power hijacked it for their own benefit. How cleaner the Earth would be if this beautiful technology that is safe for the environment and all beings of this planet wasn't blocked. Air, water — all of that would be much more natural and harmonious. Humans would feel much better too, and would be healthier. But another shackles are being placed on them instead, because they need to be sick and get medicine produced by the same elites that hold free energy in their hands."

"Is it why Tesla's inventions have been confiscated?" Kal asked.

"Of course, yes. Nicola Tesla knew very well about the fusion and possibilities of obtaining energy from space. He was given that knowledge by light beings with which he came to contact. Tesla was, like you, a star child and he very quickly awakened his connection to the consciousness of the soul which gave him access to not only the wisdom encoded in the space, but also the possibility to communicate with the beings from higher dimensions. He wanted to reveal that to everyone and make this knowledge universal that there are energy sources in the surrounding space of which humans have had no idea of. People who are used to their surrounding reality wouldn't even suspect that any energy could emerge literally from ether. It would be too surrealistic for them, although they don't see the electric current either but it has been told that it's there. And this changes the situation and their own perspective."

"How did Tesla achieve that?" this time I asked the

question. Perhaps Kal already knew the answer but he did not say anything, he only listened carefully to everything that Daddy had to say.

"Thanks to the insights that Tesla had, he designed a machine which, simply, saying, was getting energy from the steaming water in the air. All the inventions of free energy that have amazed the world so far have focused on producing more energy instead of on how much energy is needed to generate new energy. However, all that time humans have been afraid to break the laws of physics which surround space, because physics was seen only in a narrow field, it was not known how much of it remained invisible. The truth is that you can get energy from air. And to say it more precisely: from the energy gained from the differences in humidity."

"Water," I said quietly, "the source of life. That's another evidence of how much we underestimate it."

"That's true. However, it's not only water that we need to appreciate. For example — as a curiosity — our whole surroundings are filled with bacteria with the graceful name of hay sticks. This bacterium has a certain physiological relationship. When it dries, it shrinks in order to form its own spores, but if it is in a humid environment it rapidly reverts back to its former shape and size. The power of this metamorphosis is very great. Imagine that with only half a kilogram of such spores, water would generate energy that could lift a small passenger car up to a meter. Spores of this bacteria would be an ideal base material for the production of engines of which workings would be based on getting the energy from the water processing, which already happens in the surroundings all the time, even at room temperature. People mistakenly believe that free energy is linked with breaking the laws of physics. On the contrary, it's a genius way of using these laws. This bacterium is one of the many examples and evidence that there are many sources of energy surrounding us that people have no idea about or they just don't try to use them. The knowledge and multi-tone unconventional thinking and ingenuity allow you to obtain energy from the proverbial air and from the surrounding

148

space, and some processes take place in this way, whether they are used or not. The elites have had knowledge of how to obtain free energy for over a hundred years. Until now, they've managed to block it but soon it's about to change. And when it changes the first block of the domino row will fall and the reality that is ahead of us will be completely different. Think about it, how much money from the household itself goes to energy consumption, how much is used to produce food. All of this suddenly becomes free. Not to mention, the food cultivation technology that you know from Telos will also be introduced. Both of these things will change the world beyond recognition. Of course, for the benefit of mankind, everyone will be fully independent. In other words, free! And the elites will lose control over humans forever."

"Daddy, I have an impression that you know more than you've been telling us up to now. What do you mean by saying: fully sovereign?" I continued asking because I felt in that word the key to understanding how our future would change.

"First, you need to understand that energetic sovereignty is connected with food self-sufficiency. I'll tell you what the future will bring. Anyway, Semjase will soon take you there. But we're focusing now on the subject, that is, free energy."

"Okay," Kal and I agreed together and I started fidgeting in my chair. Naughty Daddy. He knew so much and he didn't want to share.

"You know very well, my daughter, that sometimes by knowing too much about the future you can get lost even more than if you knew nothing at all. And so, I'll tell you what I reckon can be said at this moment, so that it doesn't influence the events on the timeline. The incoming changes are imminent. This is a process that cannot be stopped. In the next few years, the entire oil-carbon-nuclear lobby will simply disappear and will be replaced with free energy instead. This will also apply to the automotive industry. Drives based on new technologies using free energy and anti-gravity energy will be introduced. Pharmacy and medicine will also undergo many transformations. Suddenly, devices that can cure people of all diseases will be given away with excellent results.

150

The future has only beautiful and bright colors. In order to serve the planet, many modern technologies will also be based on the anti-gravity energy that I've already mentioned."

"What will this energy be used for? I know that there are anti-gravity phones, although the information about them was swept under the carpet very quickly, because the connections between them are free of charge and they don't lose reception. I know as well that spaceships and ancient civilizations used this technology when constructing the pyramids," Kal interrupted, "Yet, I don't know how it can be used for the planet's benefit. Is it only about the reduction of pollution which is the result of harvesting energy in accordance with the old patterns?"

"You're right. And as for Earth — and what I mean here is that this energy will be used to influence the weather conditions as well, which — as you know — due to the reversal of polarity can pose a problem for humans. It will be widely used in many fields of human life and science. The anti-gravitational energy is called, in other words, the energy of a rotating mercury plasma."

"Wow! What an amazing name! Well, well!" Kal howled out. With Daddy we didn't need to use the tricks as with Semjase. Daddy loved to tell stories — the more, the better.

"I don't know if you understand anything at all of what I will say as I read your reaction as an expression of desire to get to know the subject more broadly," Daddy preferred to make sure if he could continue speaking.

"Oh yes, at least a little bit more. I have a very technical mind," Kal boasted, adding to this his pleading eyes of the cat from the Shrek movie.

"So be it. In this technology, due to the rotation of the vortex disks, plasma is produced, mainly from mercury. This happens at the pressure of two hundred thousand atmospheres. By cooling it down to one hundred and fifty Kelvin (K) and reducing its rotation up to fifty thousand rotations per minute, a superconductor is obtained. The superconductor, rotating in a variable field, causes the lifting of the field by as much as eighty-nine percent. Thanks to this, each object becomes so much lighter.

151

It is precisely because of this that spaceships on anti-gravity drive can make rapid and fast turns in the atmosphere, and reach speeds of up to nine Mach more. There is another way to achieve anti-gravity — it is by the use of discs with mono-atomic elements, which include gold, iridium, rhodium, platinum, silver, palladium, and several others. When the elements are in mono-atomic form, i.e. in the state of white powder — they are heated or subject to the play of lights."

"Yes, but part of the green energy was introduced some time ago. I mean the wind, geothermal and water power plants. There are even solar collectors," Kal suggested, "Why were they allowed?"

"They had no other choice. Coal and oil resources are becoming increasingly unavailable and the costs of their extraction are rising. Governments know that such energy cannot be taxed and so they only allow a small percentage of it, while still retaining most of the energy production from the old systems that they benefit from. People need to open their eyes. Everything is blocked for them. The fuel reaches really high prices because of the taxes that are getting higher and higher. Because the money in the elite's wallet needs to be correct. Imagine that in every household there would be a generator of free electricity which would provide electricity, light, central heating, and air-conditioning. Humans would become self-sufficient. And this is exactly what's blocked; not energy but the independence and freedom of humans. They feed us more and more contaminated food, which is allegedly not cleansed so as to minimize the expenses of the production, and yet food is still getting more and more expensive. What do people pay for then? Look at it really. If free energy was in every household that none needed to pay for and everyone had their own house without any rent or a repayment of a high-interest loan, the only thing that people would spend their money on is food and clothes. The living costs would drastically drop. People would be able to spend their hard-earned money on their development and passions. They would start to expand because they wouldn't have fear of survival. By cutting people off from better living conditions, the elites not only derive energy from human fear, but they also do billions of dollars by exploiting their hard-earned money. The treadmill is working but only one side wins. And it's always the elites. It's never the average man."

"I would like to ask about one more thing, if you have time, of course," Kal started off timidly.

"Ask!" Daddy replied with a smile on his face. He was pleased that his mentoring role was not finished yet.

"Orgones" Kal only uttered.

The sun seemed to shine up on my father's face. He beamed to such an extent that flushing showed on his cheeks.

"Etheric energy — one of my favorite topics. I'm happy to tell you about it!" he shouted out in excitement. I could almost see how he floats on a small cloud called happiness.

"Yes, please" Kal responded and lay comfortably on the bed. I did the same.

I knew quite a lot about the orgones — one could not walk past this subject indifferently — I was sure though that Dad would surprise me with something that day.

"The etheric energy fills up the space in places where there is almost a void. It's a living cosmic energy of nature. Orgone energy fills the whole universe up. It's a spontaneously pulsating energy that doesn't possess any mass. Humans know very little about it. Science hasn't been officially interested that much in this matter, although, unofficially it has been researched by many pseudo-scientists. Scientists do not visit these areas because they haven't found any evidence of the existence of this energy and they can't explain its resources. It doesn't possess matter that is measured by its mass. The etheric energy is in other words called the life force. And I need to make it clear that it's not always connected with the force that it's usually identified with."

"How can you identify it then?"

I was ready for the fact that Kal was about to squeeze Dad out like a lemon of the whole knowledge that he has in this matter.

"Energy has four complementary states. These states and the energy they contain are designed to give life energy to a given biological organism. It is not said, however, that it only exists there. It can accumulate in plastics with an organic structure. It is also perfectly assimilated in the aquatic environment. Therefore, it has such a positive effect on the human body that mainly consists of water. Ether for many scientists is still a taboo subject because it's something they don't comprehend. Though, this energy prevails in space in a complete balance. It balances from the Eastern perspective of two states of nature — the positive Yang and the negative Yin."

"So scientists haven't proven the existence of this energy yet?" I asked.

"Some of them have but they're not perceived as scientists. Even our military technicians noticed long time ago that when two energy fields with the same power are overlapped, the water vapor that is subject to high condensation will begin to condense. I'm talking here about the Orgone energy that was discovered in 1929 by the psychiatrist Dr Wilhelm Reich — Austrian born in Lewisburg, who managed to detect and measure the existence of etheric energy. He used a modified Geiger meter for this purpose, and based on his discovery, the first orgone emitters were constructed to trigger rains. Orgon is an opponent of some chemical elements and bodies containing a given element in their structure.These are mainly elements from the halogen group, i.e. chlorine, fluorine and iodine. Whether they are pure or in compounds, they destroy the orgone, destroying the life energy."

"Yet they're commonly used in our daily lives", I replied, slightly scared.

"That's true, Smaisi. Again, the lack of knowledge contributes to not only the deterioration of human health, but also it has a huge influence on the planet itself and its life."

"In what way?" I asked further.

"Let's have a freon as an example of a fluorine compound which is contained in the compressor gas in refrigerators. Freon breaks down triatomic oxygen in the upper atmosphere, increasing the ozone hole and endangering the existence of life on Earth. So, as you can see, a seemingly harmless refrigerator standing in every

154

kitchen and improving the quality of life has consequences for the natural environment and for humans. People, being unaware of life on other planets, should take care of their planet more, the one they live on. As they know, it's not possible to just take a train to another planet that they haven't destroyed yet. This all comes from the lack of knowledge of the majority rather than planned actions. Although, I need to mention that fluorine is added to the drinking water intentionally in order to calcify the pinhead gland and block the retrieval of consciousness and soul memory. But this is a completely different matter."

"Can you gather etheric energy?", Kal asked suddenly, "By accumulating it in one place in space?", he added to clarify.

"Yes. This can be done and many are already doing so. To gather up the etheric energy one needs to lay the glass fibers of the organic substance alternately with steel wool which is an inorganic substance. This will cause the etheric energy to be attracted and accumulated in that place. Boxes commonly called orgone accumulators or oraks can also be constructed. By using the method of alternating layering, a space is created in which the orgone energy is concentrated. People can be healed of multiple ailments, even cancer, just by being in this energy space for extended periods of time. Only thirty minutes in such an accumulator triggers positive psychophysiological effects. When humanity learns about the new ways of using energy, medicine and its technology will unrecognizably change. People need to experience that the invisible to them energies really exist and can be practically used."

"I saw orgonites in the form of a cone with crystals inside and resin around them. Are they the source of orgone energy?" Kal asked. "I suppose so, if you have a few of them in your house."

"Yes. I made them myself. Orgones are an invisible medium of energy. It is made up of the existence of dark matter, the vacuum flux, and the zero point energy. The monoliths of small quartz crystals are always included in the composition of orgonites and are one of the most important elements in their creation. They have the ability to gather and transform the etheric energy. They're also ideal for emission of this energy in space. In contrast, resin acts here as a self-energizing and permanently working matrix of energy transmutation. Organic resin has a tendency to shrink during the hardening process. This causes it to compress the quartz crystals in its interior, creating a piezoelectric effect inside the crystals and influencing the electrical polarization of its endpoints. Thus, orgones work perfectly as energy generators. They're able to clear space during a year, that is, heal the surroundings and etheric space. Enthusiasts of orgones know very well how to build a more advanced generator of energy, which is called chembuster."

"Do you know how to build it? Do you have one?" Kal was intrigued. I could feel he was intensely scanning the images of memories from our house in search of this device.

"No, I don't, but I know how to build one. I guess you would like to know that too, right?" Daddy asked Kal a question.

"Yes, of course. I would like to even propose for us to build one together", Kal inquired timidly, not being sure if Daddy would agree.

"It's a great idea, son," Daddy answered.

After these words, something as I'd cracked inside Kal. I could feel it. Love flooded his entire being. Yet, it was not connected with either the chembuster or its construction, but with the way Daddy called him. Kal had never felt love from his father before and it could be noticed how he missed that.

Daddy reacted very fast and started to describe how to construct the chembuster so that Kal could get hold of his emotions and stop the tears from welling up in his eyes.

"A typical and the most popular chembuster consists of six copper pipes, each of them 6 feet long. They are embedded in the orgone base. At the base of every pipe there are two-pointed quartz crystals so as to create the effect of an etheric energy vacuum. It works in a way that all the negative energy from the sky within a radiance of a few miles of such a base is literally being sucked in by the orgonite. Then it is purified and transformed into positive energy. Unlike cloud absorbers — chembusters can be safely left unattended to continuously generate and purify energy.

156

Thanks to this, the appropriate energy balance in a given area will be restored very quickly. Chembusters are extremely useful in those regions of the world where there is drought."

"How does it work exactly?" I asked the question this time, because it was not that clear to me.

"Chembuster with the orgone base transforms literally every energy that is being pulled in from the atmosphere. The rest of the device is responsible for active balancing of energy between the sky and earth, working as an electric generator of whirls. Such devices eliminate air pollution and negatively charged artificial cloud formations or chemtrails. After their elimination one can see a beautiful clear sky with small, purely natural clouds. There are many instructions on the Internet that clarify step by step how to build an orgone pyramid as well as a chembuster. These days, if such a technology was spread out on a greater scale it would be very useful. However, people don't entirely believe in its workings, until they don't try it out. The multitude of digital cell connectivity contributes to the creation of a thick layer of negative energy in space, which saturates people and the environment with low vibrations, which badly affects their mental well-being and health as well. Orgones effectively eliminate this electric smog by cleansing our living space. Usually, small pyramids operate in a field with a radius of several to several meters. That is why it is worth setting up such pyramids in the house where you spend the majority of time. However, there are also mini orgonites that you can carry with you anywhere. They then reflect negative energy within a radius of several meters. I was thinking of making one for Smaisi. But a mini pyramid was too big and heavy to wear it on a chain. Finally, I enlarged it slightly in my project and it has been standing there for years. " Daddy pointed at a small shelf located above my bed.

There was a small pyramid on the shelf. It was gorgeous. Daddy gave it to me a long time ago. I was little back then and I was afraid of beings that were visiting me at night. Daddy said then that this tiny pyramid would protect my space. And even though it was working only on the level of etheric energy — the fact of having it and Daddy's words influenced my subconscious and fear disappeared entirely. This, in turn, made it difficult for the low vibrations to come near me.

"So how to fight these antennas that appear as if after the rain?" Kal asked.

"You can try to fight, although, at this stage the system is still stronger. Many people though are not idle in their endeavors. Some people throw small pieces of orgonite in the vicinity of such towers. They often bury them in the ground. This alone reduces the harmful effects of a given tower. This movement even has a name — Tower-busters, and has become very popular recently. Many people already know about the great and positive effect that the orgone energy has on the human body. Many will soon find out, and this knowledge will soon become commonplace. Everything we are flooded with by our wonderful world governments has a detrimental effect on the human body. They just poison us in many ways, a little on each side. And then people die. Do you know that the human genome is anti-cancerous? People shouldn't get cancer. So why do they get sick? Just look at what we breathe, eat and treat ourselves with. Everything is filled with chemistry that affects the errors of human DNA coding and drastically reduces the body's immunity."

"What do you mean anti-cancerous?" I was surprised, "Daddy, could you tell us a little more about it?" — while Kal didn't seem to be interested in that, I had an enormous willingness to listen to this subject. Every year the statistics among adults and children dying from cancer were staggering. From what Daddy said it could be inferred that the human served himself such a fate, or rather a self-proclaimed god.

"The human genome and molecules are designed to eliminate cancer cells from the body. It's a self-destructive mechanism. The human genome contains fragments of the RNA chain which are responsible for inhibiting the growth of cancer cells. Remember that cells have memories and can reform themselves in order to survive. In the human body, molecules of ribonucleic acid — siRNA — are formed, which interacts with

158

genes that determine the rapid multiplication of cells dangerous for the human body. This acid has a little influence on healthy cells because it has a code of survival and this is what it's pursuing. This ability can be activated in the human body by the use of a sequence of six nucleotides to activate genes and initiate the process of protein formation in RNA — their task is to activate a dormant gene. In this genotype sequence, a process of forming multicellular proteins of organisms that eliminate cancer was encoded, even before the immune system had been developed in the human body. This is a system that is five hundred million year old — it has been encoded in the genetic sequence of the human matrix and forces cancer cells to self-destruct. It is active in every single cell and its job is to protect the biological body against cancer. The human body creates free siRNA structures that destroy cancer cells by cutting open a large RNA strand. This process activates the formation of a protein structure responsible for fighting cancer cells in the body. This is quite a complicated topic for someone who is not familiar with genetics. Such a process can also be triggered in the body — without the use of dangerous chemotherapy, which, instead of curing, kills."

"The question is how to do it?" Kal, as always, approached the subject very technically.

"This is already in the field of molecular medicine. By using molecules, the siRNA containing the code for the destruction of cancer cells can be directly transferred into a life-threatening cell. SiRNA kills cancerous cells with a brutal and simultaneous attack, during which these cells cannot acquire immunity and adapt, so they cannot develop any further. There is even a way to create artificial microRNAs that will be more effective in fighting cancer than implanting siRNAs into the human genome. This method will dominate oncological treatment in the future. There is also another way to fight cancer. Namely, taking monatomic gold."

"Gold is always at a premium," I said with a slight smirk.

"That's true. What do you think, why is this element so wanted by all nations in the universe? It is invaluable in many aspects of life, from health to technology."

"How does it work then?" Kal asked, again. He was like a child in a car who constantly kept asking how far the destination was.

"Thanks to the consumption of gold, human DNA regenerates after some time, and the cancerous cells disappear. Taking these monoatomic elements has other positive effects as well. One of them is the enlargement of the human aura, which develops the ability to sense other people's intentions and — attention — allows influencing their choices by developing the ability to read their minds and transmit their suggestions telepathically."

It was getting late. I knew that that day we probably would have not been able to get anything else out of Daddy. And I was right. A moment ago after he stopped talking, Mommy entered the room and called us for dinner. During dinner, Daddy was fiercely discussing the subject of chembuster with Kal that they were planning to build together. They searched for parts for the construction on the Internet and they ordered so many of them and Mommy and I were wondering if they would start a mass production or not.

Chapter 8

"Like a mountain stream flowing in the crevices of a mighty rock. Protected by Him so that it flows uninterrupted giving life and new beginning...
Like the air that let's Him fly.
Carries His wings so that He can reach his destination...
Like the Earth digested by fire,
She gives herself to him to give birth to a new life from the ashes... Like an apple tree that bears fruit to sweeten his forthcoming journey... "

Damian Buczniewicz

The element of life and its protection
The role of feminine and masculine energy

After dinner, we returned with Kal upstairs to spend some time together. We were slightly tired from Daddy's lecture. These were not simple topics. I started to slowly understand that the topics concerning awakening are not simple as a rule, and this is because they do not merge with what our learned mind can assimilate as new. The increasing connection with the soul lets people open to the truth and feel it inwardly more and more.

We sat with Kal on the bed in front of each other. We sometimes enjoyed staring into our eyes. Magical things were happening then and it was sucking us into past and future incarnations on various timelines. Every time, it was an amazing experience, even though we had a lot of time to get used to that. Our memory of past lives was improving and there were fewer and fewer missing pieces in the puzzle of our common soul evolution path. We were happy because of that, yet saddened as well, because

161

we wanted to discover it again and again. There were many incarnations that we were not on an earthly plane at the same time, and these were the most foggy for both of us. Those we shared—connected with a mutual energy—appeared to us most clearly. Holding hands, we were sending light and energy of love to the whole planet Earth. We enveloped her in this light and erased all the grays on her. We did this almost every day. It was an amazing feeling of creating love and light, that was filling us up to the brim. Every time we were done, Kal used to look at me with love and say:

"I am you and you are me."

He used to confess that with a great affection and I used to reply:

"And our love always was, is and will be eternal."

After this confession, Kal used to kiss me tenderly and we were lying, hugging each other for some time, accumulating the energy sent to the Earth and multiplying it with the power of our unconditional love.

There were incarnations that were showing us in a twisted way. I was in a male body while Kal was a female. That was rare though. We were wondering what the purpose of that was and if it was about learning to feel in a different body and from a different perspective. For sure, the energetic perspective was of huge importance here. It was clear to us that female energy was responsible for creating while the masculine energy was protective of the feminine so that she could create. And so the man was the protector of the, in fact, vulnerable woman of which power exceeded thousands of her protectors. But that's how it worked or at least that was how I understood that. When Kal left, I was dwelling on that for a long time. I remembered that before there was no division of energies into two separate bodies. Beings were self-born and had only one sex. Why did it change then? I could not remember if Semjase mentioned anything about that. Perhaps it didn't concern human species but another one that inhabited Earth and I totally confused it all? With this little confusion in my head that I was responsible for myself, I fell asleep.

"Wake up," I heard in my head Semjase's voice and I stood up.

I was in my favorite place. On this beautiful sandy beach. I looked around in search of Kal. I could not locate Semjase either. First, Kal appeared. He was walking down the beach and the water was gently washing his bare feet. He couldn't see me yet. I took the advantage of that moment to scrutinize him. He was a walking ideal to me. The only thing I felt for him when looking at him was love that was filling me up to the brim. He sensed that I was thinking of him and our eyes met. He smiled at me and, having approached me, he hugged me in greeting.

"Where's Semjase?" he asked, slightly surprised, "I thought I heard her voice."

"Yes, it was hers. I can't see her either" , I admitted, looking around.

"You need to be taught patience, dear ones", we heard her voice in our heads and we laughed out, recognizing a slightly punishing tone of her utterance. She appeared soon after. She was marching in our direction, as always wearing a beautiful airy dress. She sat on the sand, patted the place next to her and smiled brightly — "You're invited to join me. We haven't seen each other for a while."

"We missed you", I uttered, knowing that by saying it for both of us, it was true.

"I know. However, there's a lot going on and I'm needed. That's why I didn't have so much time for you. But I've been sending to you beautiful beings of light to assist you in your journey. I think that the diversity of messages and forms in which you receive your knowledge has a positive impact on you. I heard that you've seen the realm of Saturia. It's amazing, isn't it? " she said, being dreamy.

"Yes, that's very true. Yriah took us there", I responded, reminding myself of this wonderful blue space.

"She enjoys spending time with you very much. She admires your willingness to absorb knowledge in almost limitless quantities. She said that she would like to have students only like you and she asked if she can borrow you from time to time. I agreed to that willingly. It makes it easier for me in the face of so many responsibilities, especially those that I will take on in the coming months when there will be really a lot of changes on an energetic level. A lot has already happened too, which, I assume, you feel too."

"Yes. We can feel it," Kal admitted. "Transformations into the light body and the descending on Earth energies are more and more intense."

"And that's how it will continue. This will be intensifying. The human body needs time to adjust so it's a process. I've already told you that anyway, and today I would like to speak of the subject that has been tormenting Smaisi for some time."

I suspected what Semjase was about, especially since I was so intensely thinking of it before falling asleep.

"I can see that my creation manifests almost immediately," I laughed out.

"If it's coming from your heart space, it will always be like that. Almost immediately. This time, however, I worked for you. This topic was to be mentioned anyway. For me, there's no difference if it's today or in a week's time. Since time doesn't exist, it doesn't matter that much to me, " she laughed out.

"Okay, okay. You're chatting here and I have completely no idea what about, " Kal got slightly offended.

Semjase glanced at me and both of us burst into laughter.

"You're about to get to know that," she replied, still smiling. "Female energy will always have secrets that the male energy doesn't get", Semjase tried to guide him through.

"Don't use the fact that there are two of you and I'm only one," Kal was still grumpy.

"Okay, then. Don't get offended, it doesn't suit you, "Semjase expressed that in such a way that I needed to hold back so as not to burst out laughing again. "We will take both of you under a microscope. Who are you, Kal?" she asked and he froze up. He completely didn't know what to reply. "How do you differ from Smaisi?" — she kept asking so as to direct him into the right track

164

of thoughts.

"A man," he responded, "And Smaisi is a woman. And this is the only thing that differentiates us since we have the same soul."

"And this only difference is what I would like to explain to you specifically. As you already know, everything is energy, and so are you — only with a contrasting polarity and different tasks. The inner female energy is an element of life, whereas masculine energy's task is to protect it. But before we get to the gist I would like to say something. Are you ready? I know I don't need to ask you that but it's an act out of kindness."

"Of course, yes!" we replied, as always in agreement.

"Humanity currently lives in a three-dimensional world, right in the middle of very important events that are not noticeable to the eye, because you haven't been given permission. There is a constant war over DNA and energetic frequencies. You can call it a soul war in which the battles are over energy. However, you need to understand that it has a greater and deeper goal, it's a fight for survival on a certain energy level. Mother Earth, also called Gaia, is the heart and the cradle of many events. Humanity hasn't gained knowledge yet on many levels. As you know, the manipulation over human kind has been taking place successfully for millennia, yet it's not that easy for the elites since the human being created from the Shiru matrix code isn't so easily manipulated anymore. The codes need to be purged and unblocked in order to unleash the full human potential, which is happening right now. However, everything that the human has had and what has never been taken away — it's heart. The feeling with heart and following it was always pure, free from ego and imposed programs. The human though has rarely listened to his or her heart and intuition, not being aware of the fact that it was the soul speaking to them. The heart is also the symbol of planet Earth, to which the human being was assigned to energetically together with the vibrational frequency which connects with the human vibrations. Therefore, you need to always vibrate at the same frequencies as planet Earth. Even being tens of light years from Earth, the human is still in constant connection with Mother Earth's frequencies. And here we slowly come to the point. The earth will change its frequencies and the human will be forced to adapt to them. Otherwise the body will stop to be in alignment with the surrounding reality. And, as you know, the body is the only vessel for the soul which can be changed at any moment."

"Gaia is a woman," I said suddenly, not knowing why.

"Yes, Smaisi. Gaia is a woman and she carries feminine energy. She is the center of this part of the galaxy. Women are her reflections, therefore, they are the symbols of the divine creative element. They're the inner energy that takes care of the planet. Every energy point represents planet Earth. That's why, there was a male counterpart of the outer energy created which is responsible for protection of the inner energy that is the heart of creation in this galaxy. The male population has an external factor that protects the female energy, which is women. If this equilibrium was disturbed, the planet would not have the energy factor that covers the Earth. Male energy is an armor that protects the heart. Except that excess male energy is also not good, as we are dealing with this nowadays. There have been many attempts to restore the harmony of these two energies, which was probably missed by some people. A perfect example of this is the feminist movement that humanity dealt with in the 1980s. This movement's purpose was to weaken the outer energy that the male energy possesses. It was only an illusion though and a wrong direction. Feminizing males would be counterproductive. If the protection of the female energy was taken and redirected inward, the struggle for survival would be lost."

"Hmmm... I don't fully understand what this redirection of energy is all about," said Kal.

"It's simple, Kal. Smaisi is the heart and you're the armor. The truth is that the more of your energy the greater the protection, but also willingness to fight and compete increases. However, if the whole outward energy was taken, so in this instance you, Smaisi, that is the heart of creation, the energy of life — will be left with no protection. This makes their survival very questionable. Both energies are very important but they must be in

166

balance. Do you understand now?"

"A bit more," he confessed.

"Women should be independent and I totally agree with that but the elites' plan has been deprivation of the inner protection of the planet's female energy by taking the masculine energy away. Women are the divine element of Mother Earth, but without protection, the survival of the human species will be in great jeopardy. If the external energy created by the alpha male population is redirected, the entire planet will be subjugated and enslaved, and the female element will be subjected to molecular combination to give birth to alien nations. That is why the male external energy function is so important. The feminine element must be protected! It is not known why nobody wants to disclose to the male part of the population what their mission is here on Earth. Maybe if they were aware of this, the reality in which humanity is now would be much better. The female energy multiplies and transforms everything it receives."

"I have a feeling Semjase that women don't know entirely what their mission is on Earth either. Everything is so confused," I said, with a slight sadness.

"You're right. They forgot why they are here as well. Women possess great power but they're not aware of it. The majority of women don't use their power at all and only a few use it to a small degree. It's not an accident that the woman gives birth to a new life. However, the female is not only a spark to their children — for the masculine energy it's the energy of life. The man is powered by female energy — just like a car must have gasoline to drive, a man needs a woman's strength. A woman is like water — it powers a man, gives him energy and strength to achieve any goals. She helps him with her creation."

"Where does the woman take her energy from then?" Kal asked, curious about this relationship. It sounded a bit as if men were energetically addicted to women.

"The woman gets her energy from the Earth. In fact, she can download it from whatever she wants. From nature, nice emotions, even from shopping or practicing favorite sport. From

everywhere, really. Men do not have such abilities and take their energy precisely from a woman. Thus, they create external energy, protecting the planet on the astral plane as the cradle of female energy and a spark of life. It is really a common dependency. The woman offers the man life energy, in return the man protects her. It is a symbiosis and the creation of this symbiosis is only beautiful in balance."

"This is truly a beautiful dependency. So knightly," I didn't know why this word came to my mind. Perhaps because of the armor protecting my heart that was mentioned by Semjase.

"So the elites want to eliminate masculine energy, yes?" Kal kept asking to have a certainty, "So as to deprive the feminine energy of protection and destroy everything or use it for their purposes, as they always do."

"Exactly. You put it in words perfectly. The majority of parasitic beings and nations that are not friendly for humanity — including the human hybrids among the elites that rule the Earth as well — they all want to divide these energies and separate them from each other. They do this so that they have access to them on an energetic level. They are strongly connected. Therefore, the first point of the plan is the extermination of the male species that leads to depriving the planet of the energetic protection without which the feminine energy will be served on a plate. The male population constantly needs to be energetically charged up. Men confirm that — they desire women. This desire comes from their heart space and from the energetic dependency on the feminine element of life. A woman, by powering a man, gives him the energy of high spiritual and energetic potential that a man can use. The elite take advantage of the energy overload of the male element and manipulate energy to trigger wars and fratricidal fights. They do this so that the energy can be reprogrammed and, in turn, destroyed. If any nation wants to conquer a planet, at first it's forced to remove the masculine element that protects the planet. Only then can it deal with the annihilation of the female element which, without the protection of men weakens and with it the internal energy of the planet itself, of which women are the source, weakens as well."

"Was it always like that there was a division between masculine and feminine?" I asked because it was on my mind too. I couldn't remember exactly what Semjase told us before about this topic.

"Men and women are the biggest opposites on this planet. So let's go back and see what it looked like at the turn of billions of years of life on Earth. What the Earth looked like before humans appeared on it. Eager for a bit of history?" Semjase asked but it was visible on our faces that the answer to the question wasn't necessary. There were two wide smiles on our faces and in our eyes there were sparks of anticipation. — "And so… A man as a male (because we will talk about many species) was brought to life as a being responsible for the transfer of genes, he was supposed to defend them and protect them with himself. However, it wasn't like that from the very beginning. For the first billion years, life had gone without males and somehow functioned.

Single-celled organisms used to copy, divide and multiply themselves. About a billion years ago, two cells entered into symbiosis, and when they joined together, genetic material was exchanged. As a result, a new gene was created, the rate of spread of which has doubled. The mutation of this gene was responsible for the creation of new cell strains, that by their natural ability to form, reform and transform, they create new structures, and the genetic information in cells is passed down from generation to generation depending on the conditions. If the conditions for the development of a cell are favorable, it multiplies, but if it encounters unfavorable conditions for its development, it does not reproduce but goes into a survival state. It is immortal. Nature and creation hate the void, and their goal is always to exist in any possible form. That was the beginning of the emergence of two sexes. But as it usually goes, one of the sides wants to be better and starts to deceive. And that's how it happened. Big cells were more precious and the process of their division was more effective because they had greater food supplies. The production of small cells doesn't require such a high input of nutrients. However, they could not divide. The only chance, therefore, for the smaller cell was to fuse with a larger cell. Thus, much of evolution has been driven by the tension between the sperm and the egg. It is impossible to avoid differences in genetics between a man and a woman. The female core of the genetic code is the prototype of life. It contains two nearly identical vital X chromosomes. They're doubled in case one of them is damaged. It's for security. So, when two different cells joined together and a genetic mutation took place a billion years ago, the Y chromosome was created. It is the one that decides about the sex of the offspring. In the cell nucleus of the male element, instead of the second X chromosome, there is a Y chromosome, which is very short. This chromosome, which represents the male identity, only makes up one fifty of the entire genome. This makes it less strong and resistant, and it lacks regenerative abilities. Male offspring with a Y chromosome, due to the weakness of this chromosome, are born as if with a defect. With each generation, weak genes mutate more and more, and errors creep into the genotype. Over time, the male chromosome accumulates many harmful mutations due to the inability to regenerate. Each subsequent generation has more and more defects in the genetic code. If this problem accumulates in the future, the evolutionary equilibrium of the universe will only restore the female genome to nature. The genetic core code will be re-inserted into the cell without a nucleus for the survival of the species."

"Does it mean that there will be only females?" Kal asked with irritation in his voice. He was a man after all. For sure it wasn't pleasant for him to hear about a possible annihilation of male species in the future.

"There will be a new human species in the future — we can call it ONO — that will have the name "homo novus". Males as carriers of a weakening chromosome Y will be deteriorating in health more and more. Even now they statistically live shorter by six years than women, they have more cardiovascular disorders. Heart diseases and the circulatory system disorders constitute over half of all male deaths before retirement age. This is because men don't have the protective shield of estrogen that protects women's hearts. Estrogen releases nitric oxide and widens the blood vessels. It would be possible to enumerate for a long time the weaknesses of the so-called strong sex, which owes its name rather to the physical strength, with which, due to the physique, men outweigh women."

"I am happy to hear about these relationships," said Kal. There were no negative emotions hidden in this utterance. He was just inquisitive.

"Very well, I'm explaining further. Men are three times more likely to have speech impediments, be color-blind, suffer from hemophilia and are more likely to develop cancer. They go bald completely at a younger and younger age. Women are not affected by this problem. Males are weaker from birth — in the first year of life, there are one hundred and twenty-six male deaths per 100 girls deaths, although they have greater chances at the fertilization stage, where there are one hundred and twenty males per 100 female embryos. This is because the Y chromosome is lighter, making the sperm that contain it faster and more likely to fertilize the egg. The male fetus, however, is weaker and much more energy dependent. He is heavily influenced by his mother's health problems or stress. That is why economic crises and wars contributed to the decline in boys' births, in proportion to the years when external stress factors did not affect the mother's emotional state. It's a similar situation with the ecological and natural disasters. When the boy is born, he is more prone to various diseases. Especially to the brain damage, cerebral palsy and numerous birth defects. Boys develop in a slower way as well —even in their fetal life they lag behind girls by four to six weeks. In time, these differences become more and more visible. Boys perform at school much worse and statistically they read much less books. Men also have weaker psychic stamina than women. They handle stress much worse. In comparison to women, men also have worse reflexes and motor coordination. This triggers the fact that they mistakenly judge a potential risk, which, in turn, results in the fact that more men than women die in accidents — not only in the road ones. And these accidents could be avoided.

Women look more in the future, they predict potential threats and they avoid them. I guess I don't need to mention the fact that the majority of criminals are male. Also in terms of addictions to nicotine, alcohol and hazard — almost three times they beat the feminine principle. Despite all the diseases, they go to the doctor much less often, which contributes to the worsening of the health problems."

"Quite a lot of this, " Kal howled.

" I haven't finished yet," said Semjase and continued her speech that Kal requested. "Men due to their genetic conditions perform considerably worse in unfavorable situations. Women perform much better and they don't break up straightaway, they try to find a way out of the situation. However, when men's life is abundant, all too easily and fast they get into the traps of luxury and they don't do best off it. What's more, perhaps this may be surprising but males suffer much more greatly due to broken hearts and they worry about work issues more. Most often they are hypocrites that are afraid to take risks. They get depressed and constitute seventy percent of the suicides across all ages."

"Is chromosome Y responsible for all those inconveniences?" I asked, "So little yet it triggers so many problems?"

"Unfortunately, yes. The hormone that it's owners boast about so much is also their downfall. It weakens the immunity of the organism. The cells of the immunity system die when they get in contact with testosterone and the male body has a lot of this substance therefore it has less ability to produce antibodies. As a result of this, it's more difficult for men to fight certain diseases, including cancer. The disadvantage of this chromosome is not unique to mankind. In the majority of animals, the males die quicker than the females. It will be worse with time. In a dozen or even several years or so, when the generation of children raised in plastic nappies grows up, people will find out about it with their own eyes. Why am I talking about it? Well, male babies wearing such diapers have a higher body temperature below the waist than babies wearing cotton diapers. These diapers are also worn longer than normal diapers for the convenience of parents, which adversely affects the health and the reproductive system as overheating of the testicles is a frequent cause of infertility. Well, I think I'm finished when it comes to chromosomal dependencies, but maybe I will remember something else, "Semjase summed up.

"I feel that there's much more to say about," I said and looked questioningly at Semjase. I liked this topic and I was hoping that Semjase would speak more about the differences and dependencies between those two opposite sex poles."

"That's true, Smaisi. I can literally flood you with statistics, research results, and the variety of contradictions that are between men and women. I even believe that this knowledge is very important, as it can positively influence the introduction of changes in many aspects of life in the future. The understanding of biology and its dependencies is equally important to the understanding of energetic dependencies."

"We want to be flooded," said Kal. He didn't have enough. Neither did I. Finally, we could somehow refer to the information contained in the channel directly to ourselves.

"As you wish," Semjase started and made a face that suggested clearly that we were not fully aware of what we had asked for. It didn't disturb her in flooding us with consequent facts. And, as it turned out later on, there were really many of them. — "You could say that men evolved into a relationship with a woman. While a woman is able to cope well on her own, men beside a woman can gain a lot, which may be surprising — a relationship with her extends his life even by several years. This is, of course, related to their mutual energy relationship. Single men of who — unfortunately — there are more and more out there, die faster and earlier. Women are mistakenly called the weak sex. It has nothing to do with reality and the real power that lies in them. Women are characterized by greater life force, they are more reasonable and much more resourceful than men. They have a richer inner life. For a long time, men have tried to explore the female psyche, but they only wander around and come to no conclusions that could lead them to the path of reasoning appropriate to the female gender.

Women are devoid of aggression. As an element of life — they protect, not destroy. Therefore, it is often said that if women ruled the world, there would be no wars and many other events that are the creation and influence of the male element on the surrounding reality."

"So, apart from the obvious fact that the male element is needed for the protection of the female — is it biologically only a gene carrier?" asked Kal, "But, however you look at it, thanks to it the species is able to survive. I'm talking about procreation."

"Yes, you've put it quite nicely. But it can't be simplified to such an extent. There is love as well — the vibration of love that joins those two elements. If it was only about the survival of the species, the acts of procreation wouldn't happen so often between males and females. In fact, from the economical point of view, it's a huge waste of genetic material."

"What do you mean by that?"

I could sense Kal's interest rising. We got the subject which every healthy teenager is interested in. It was natural then that Kal would get inquisitive. I was wondering though if that was what Semjase was counting on.

"In the majority of cases millions of spermatozoids are wasted before they reach the point where the fusion of cells takes place."

"It's logical I guess, that the strongest wins and that the ovum isn't always ready to be inseminated," Kal riposted to protect the honor of unnecessary sperm.

"Let me introduce you to a few facts and you'll decide on these grounds if it's not exaggerated. Will you let that happen?"

"Of course!" he replied. I could feel he was very very curious of what Semjase was about to say.

"According to estimates, all men procreate approximately fifty billion times a year. This gives us a million liters of male semen each day. Every second, two hundred thousand billion sperm are produced worldwide, which translates into five births. For comparison — women wanting to achieve a result of five births, they only provide four hundred eggs. And so, two hundred thousand billion meets four hundred. It is hard not to notice the injustice from a strictly productive point of view. So why such a difference and overproduction of genetic material in men? Unfortunately, this is mainly due to what I have already told you. Mutations from generation to generation have weakened the male genotype, which translates into sperm quality. A significant part of the sperm dies almost immediately because the body recognizes the damaged genetic material. So there is only a few percent left that are capable of fertilizing the egg. The more semen at the beginning, the more healthy and strong are left later, after filtering those damaged cells. Hence the overproduction. It's quite different with the male animals since they produce large amounts of semen to win over their rivals in transmitting their genetic material. In the world of animals, males are brought into existence solely for the purpose of transmitting genes and maintaining the species. They are not needed for anything else. How many animals together, like humans, care for their offspring? Really, not many. And there are millions of reverse examples in nature. One of the better animals — proving that males are single-tasked — is the mantis that eats right after fertilization a lover who was generous enough to give her his genes. For his generosity, the female will not repay him with gratitude. Or at least, that's not how it looks. There are also species where the male dies right after fertilization, having fulfilled its role. A perfect example of this is salmon. In turn, the male of the fish known as the sea devil is the size of the female's genitalia. It attaches to her body and lives like a parasite, and the female allows him to do so only to obtain the genetic material she needs to maintain the species. Another curiosity is the monkfish, which carries half a dozen genitals of its dead partners and decides for itself which phallus and genetic material she will use. Considering what nature is showing us, the human species doesn't lose its head" — she chuckled. It was, of course, a reference to the praying mantis — "And that's good for him," she added on the edge. I had to admit that she explained to us very well the role of the male in the transmission of genes.

"Fortunately, none died of the excess of expressing love,"

Kal laughed out and winked at me.

"You could be surprised," Semjase riposted, "not only many did lose their life, but also let be remind you that even Lemurians went too far with improving their genitals and increasing the sensations during procreation and this didn't work out the best for them. Sexual intercourse and conception is the synergy of two energies — it's magic yet humans are not conscious of that and are not able to use this magic appropriately. But I'll say more about it in a bit. Now, I would like to describe to you the difference between the sexes, but in order to do that I need to start from the beginning."

"That is?" I asked, not knowing what it meant.

"That is from the conception." she replied.

"Ah…" I sighed.

"That should actually interest you. Do you remember the article that you mentioned to us?" I couldn't believe that Kal just said that. I was about to retort when Semjase interrupted me.

"I remind you, private matters not during my guard, Smaisi" her words made my growing emotions fall and I again focused on the knowledge which I was so interested in.

I intentionally tried to express my thoughts so loud that Kal could hear it too.

"Smaisi!" Semjase, unfortunately, felt that too.

I blushed and apologized silently.

"Let's go back to the time of your first birth," she continued. I sensed there was more to this statement, but before I could ask, Semjase continued, "When the cells are connected, we are talking about fertilization. However, until the seventh week of pregnancy, the gender of the baby cannot be determined. It is the sperm that determines it. If it has two X chromosomes, it will be a girl, and if it has a Y chromosome it will be a boy. In the seventh week of pregnancy, the Y chromosome is activated, and with it the SRY gene that produces the sex, which produces a protein that activates the other genes. This is when the process of shaping the reproductive organs begins, and in the case of a male offspring, the testicles begin to produce testosterone. Already around the fourteenth week, the entire process of shaping the sexual organs is at such an advanced stage that it is possible to know the sex of the child. About the fortieth week comes the turn of a kind of a second birth — when the baby is born. As you already know, the child's sex is determined by the chromosomes, which are twisted strands of DNA. The X chromosome is inherited from the mother, and the Y chromosome is inherited from the father. Even though the female cell contains two X chromosomes, nature applies equality and only one of them is active. The difference between the sexes is determined only by the differences in several dozen genes encoded in the Y chromosome and they are responsible for the production of male reproductive organs and sperm needed later to extend the species. Not many people know that both sex chromosomes work properly in women, but one of them stays dormant. The dormant one can contain as many as twenty-five percent of the active genes. One percent of the human body's genomes work differently in women than in men. So, as you can see, it's not a lot, but it significantly affects the differences between the female and male elements. It is important for you to understand that genetic differences exist not only between sexes but between each individual person. These differences are more noticeable especially among women. In men, the X genotype works almost always the same, while the female genotype does not necessarily, and there are many modifications at the DNA level. This is why women are considered to be more complex than men."

"That's actually what everyone knows," Kal laughed out and looked at me emphatically, "I must admit though that I expected that there would be much less differences. My knowledge of this has definitely broadened."

"Let's see what you'll say when I finish," Semjase gently let him know that he interrupted her and then, not taking any further notice of him, she continued — "Women have one of the chromosomes X containing the gene which is responsible for the different structure of the area of the frontal cortex of the brain. This part of the cortex of the brain is responsible for the network thinking and the ability to process information that is hugely

178

diverse. The network thinking is definitely more developed in women, although much weaker in women who suffer from the Turner disease. With this disease, it causes worsened speaking and remembering mainly verbal information. When a woman has a chromosome XY, she still looks like a woman but there may be characteristics that are considered to be typically male. One of such disorders is testicular feminization syndrome, which manifests itself mainly in the fact that the body of such a woman does not respond to male hormones. There were even a few famous people suffering from this hormonal disorder. Genes located on the X chromosome have a great impact on a person's talents, especially social ones, and they translate into emotions — mainly empathy — and the ability to read them, for example, from facial expression of the other person. Although a person is used to the fact that he or she speaks, up to ninety percent of emotional signals are transmitted in a non-verbal manner. People have learned to speak and see, they have forgotten the gut feeling and the intuition that comes from their own heart. They had put some of their skills to sleep themselves. Thanks to these genes, nature has given women the ability to read other people's minds. Much faster than men, they are able to sense the mood of the interlocutor and the mood of their own children with whom in their early years, despite the lack of verbal communication, they communicate very well. It is then that they unlock access to their intuition, which is called maternal, but it is only because the blockade is removed as if on a task-related basis — for a specific purpose, which in this case is an attempt to understand their offspring and their needs. Men, on the other hand, feel dissatisfaction much more clearly and read low-vibrational emotions from the faces of their interlocutors. Here we see the relationship of shield and protection. The bad emotion is immediately caught as a potential threat to the female energy. You can actually see these differences in an infant within the first few days. Even one day old female babies can stare at the faces of their loved ones for a long time, while boys are more interested in the objects in their immediate vicinity. This baby habit persists and women maintain longer eye contact with their interlocutors than men."

"Y genes influence the looks and typically strengths conditions as well, right? Males have bigger muscles and they are generally bigger. Is this a matter of evolution or did mother nature decide on that?" I asked, "although in the case of many species, males are smaller than females. Hmm... interesting..." I paused, sending my considerations into space so that they could reach Semjase and come back to me with another message.

"The human body's characteristic is to adapt to the conditions in the environment in which it lives. On this principle, there was once a division of people into those living on land and those who over time created the races of underwater creatures. Evolution allows for adaptation. If you look at the topic from a closer perspective, women and men at the turn of the last millennia have specialized in fulfilling specific social roles and it is difficult to overcome these conditions in any way, although it is already happening slowly. A perfect example is raising a child. A man can successfully take care of the house and bring up children, but evolution has shaped him differently and he sees himself rather in competition that he experiences more at the workplace. He has an inbuilt program that tells him to earn as much money as possible. That's his field of battles and rivalry that he feels best in. Thousands of years ago women were forced to carefully choose their life partners that they could rely on when they were pregnant and later on — when bringing up, after all, common offspring. They were also taking notice of mothers of men that they were choosing because they knew that during their husbands absence they would need to support each other. It was, therefore, important that they could get along. These days, when a woman out of passion works as a builder or an excavator driver, everyone looks weird at her. Fortunately, over the course of several dozen years, a certain change has already been observed — women and men are again becoming closer and closer to each other and there is no longer so much pressure to perform jobs artificially assigned to women or men. This change will be going in a better and better direction and the time will come when nothing will be surprising because everyone will do what they love. Women hold not only a great energetic potential, but also they've been the guardians of the hearth. Women infuse with life the next generations which mainly take patterns from them. These days, more and more women consciously use their true potential, wisdom, resourcefulness and intelligence. In this century, women will become stronger and it will happen because the world needs this change. Women and men complement each other perfectly, but once again I will repeat that the energy balance must be kept, which at the moment is still upset. This is why now mostly female energy descends from space to the Earth's field, which is happening to harmonize the energy prevailing on the planet and restore order and harmony."

"Men are from Mars and women are from Venus" I said, "We have a saying like this here on Earth, it was created on the basis of a book, I guess. I didn't read it but since the whole book describes the difference between men and women, there needs to be quite a lot of them."

"It's true. There are plenty of differences, really — starting from the anatomical ones, through physical, ending with the differences in perception and brain workings—therefore, there are more conflicts between these two sexes. All of this contributes to the fact that even though those two energies can complement each other, sometimes it's difficult for them to get along."

"Could you…?" I requested, "at least for a moment. I don't want to go home yet," I looked at Kal to ask for his support but he was already supporting without even asking. Similarly to me, he was deep into this subject.

"I'm not surprised by that at all," Semjase summed up and she wondered for a moment — "Very well. Let's start with the anatomy. From the brain. The male brain is larger than the female brain and weighs an average of one thousand three hundred and twenty-five grams. Each cerebral hemisphere of a man is responsible for different tasks. The right one is responsible for the perception of form and space, while the left one took over the functions of thinking and verbalizing thoughts, i.e. speech. Thanks

181

to this, the man has a great ability to focus, but the problem for him is to concentrate on several things at the same time. When, for example, they are focused on some activity, they repeatedly do not hear someone talking to them, and it is not a matter of being tactless. They just focus so much on a given activity that they shut down, in a way, access to other information coming to them from space, especially if the focus on a given task is really big. It's completely different with women. The brain is smaller and weighs on average one hundred and forty-nine grams, but that doesn't mean it's worse. Women in most activities, in comparison, such as talking or observing, use both hemispheres of the brain at the same time, which is why they have an incredible ability to divide attention. They are multi-purpose. I know women who can read a book with the TV turned on and at the same time watch children playing out of the corner of their eyes. Not only that, in the event of a threat, the woman's reaction would be immediate, but she also knows what she is reading and hears what they say on TV. She can receive stimuli and signals coming from different places simultaneously. There are also other differences related to the abilities of both sexes, and they are dependent on differences in the proportions of gray matter and white matter in relation to the total volume of the brain. Gray matter is responsible for logical-mathematical intelligence, and white matter enables communication between cells located in different areas of the brain. Women have more gray matter, so for many activities they use two hemispheres at the same time because communication between cells is better. This is, in a way, a compensation for the lower capacity of the female skull — although her brain is smaller, it is more efficient than the male one. The female gender also has a better linguistic intelligence, which can be noticed even at the youngest age. Girls use both hemispheres to learn speech and just for speaking, while boys use only the left one, and thus girls learn to speak faster and have a better memory of vocabulary. They also talk more, and it is not just because of their chatter. They also read more and are able to master foreign languages faster. On the other hand, men have a much better spatial and topographic orientation, better imagination and hand-eye coordination."

"Exactly that is why when I tell you to trust me when we go for a walk, trust me instead of being fearful that we will get lost. When I say that I know where I am it means that I know." — Kal's interruptions were bizarre at times but this time they contributed to the fact that Semjase approached the subject more broadly. As always, he got his own, he was digging and squeezing as much as he could.

"I confirm that. You can trust him. It's true that even a man can get lost but it happens to him much less than a woman. In this matter, men use the right part of their brain much more effectively. Even a complicated web of roads on a map doesn't pose a huge problem for them and they're capable of knowing the terrain very quickly. The same goes for mathematical concepts. When planning a trip, a woman chooses landmarks she knows to know where and what stage she is at. While it is easier for her when she knows the way and the place, new routes are a real challenge for her."

"Good. So I will not tremble like aspen poplar anymore when you lead me into the big dark forest," I replied and Kal laughed because it sounded quite ominous.

"The organs are another thing that differs between the sexes. The structure of the genitals and the differences between them are obvious. Other organs, although they work the same, differ in size. For example, the heart of an adult man weighs thirty grams more than of an adult woman which means that when his heart muscle cramps, he throws ten milliliters more blood into the aorta than a woman does. Men also have a larger alveolar surface area, so that he can breathe in more air at a time. Due to this, they have better lung capacity, which is important during physical exertion. Because statistically men are bigger than women, more blood flows in their veins to power the body. Thus, the man has five and three tenths of a liter of blood, and the woman has only four liters. In addition, men's blood is richer in red blood cells, which are responsible for the transportation of oxygen and the oxygenation of the entire body, which also results in better efficiency of the body during physical exertion. The skeletal system is similar, although women's bones are, due to their structure, smaller and more prone to osteoporosis in later age. However, the most visible differences in bone structure concern the pelvis, which is adapted to childbearing in women, and the laryngeal cartilage, which is larger in men. Now, let's move to the muscles that make up forty percent of men's body weight. While women have only twenty-three percent of their muscle mass. Also, the muscle growth in men is faster. They achieve results in the gym more efficiently than women. This is due to adaptive conditions already initiated in distant ancestors. The body adapts to the work performed by the development of the muscles that are most needed and as it is usually men who do physical work, evolution has offered them such a gift. I was joking ... " Semjase giggled," I mean, this probably also has an influence on that, but it's mainly testosterone which increases the formation of proteins that are components of the muscles."

"It's good that I didn't take notes because if I had I would need to cross it out and I don't like any mess in my notes." Kal threw a joke in response to a small disinformation from Semjase.

"Touch Smaisi's skin" Semjase said to Kal and he reached out his hand and touched mine, "and now touch yours in the same place," she suggested and Kal did what she asked for, "can you notice any difference?"

"Yes, her skin is more soft and kind of warmer," he replied without hesitation.

"Excellent. That's the difference between you two. A woman's skin is thinner, which makes it more prone to all types of injuries and is more easily irritated. It is also smoother. In men, it is the leading hormone testosterone that makes the skin thicker and rougher and produces more sweat. The smell of sweat is also more intense in men. Skin sweating also affects the hair, so men have to wash them more often because they get greasy faster. The amount of hair in both sexes on the head is the same, but hormones mean that men have more hair on other parts of the body too. Men also have an issue with baldness that women don't. It's true that thinning hair is a natural process in women, but they will never completely lose their hair, which is very popular in men after they reach the age of 50. Another difference is the already mentioned susceptibility to various diseases. Women, statistically, live longer than men, but are more likely to suffer from varicose veins or diabetes. Their ailments are also anorexia and bulimia, practically unheard of in men's case. Women feel pain more acutely but have a greater tolerance to it. They can take more than men — it's an adaptation that allows them to survive childbirth. It's been proven many times that men wouldn't withstand the pain of childbirth. Men suffer more from heart diseases, but that's something I've already mentioned, so I won't repeat myself. Also, cancer reaches the two sexes with different intensity. Women most frequently suffer from breast, cervical and lung cancer, while in the male population, the most common are both lung and colon cancer. Most of the differences are found in the hormones which basically contribute to the differences mentioned above. Majority of the hormones in the bodies of both sexes are found in similar amounts, but not all of them. And it's they that influence most of the biological differences. In women, we identify hormones such as progesterone and estrogen, while men fight with their world-famous testosterone. Testosterone is the hormone of a warrior. It gives strength and vigor, but also influences violent behavior. Men have twenty times more of it than women. Now we know where the wars and eternal quarrels come from, when mostly gentlemen sit in governmental positions. Female hormones, on the other hand, are responsible for breast growth and regulate the fertility cycle of a woman. Also, they protect against any heart attacks. There is also oxytocin in the body of a woman, which can be easily called the hormone of gentleness because it plays a great role in the maternal instinct, it also influences sensitivity and adopting a conciliatory attitude in situations of conflict. These differences can be confirmed scientifically. However, it's different when we approach the topic from a completely different angle, namely from the emotional side. We already have a hill here. Because it cannot be easily tested and standardized."

"Oh yes! This aspect more than once meant that our

incarnations were not what they should have been. In addition, you were telling us how extensive a human's emotions are," I said, remembering the amount of suffering, only the one that was related to feelings I had for Kal in previous incarnations. There was no point in discussing other feelings and emotions. Emotions were like a bomb. Literally. Not kept in figures, they were able to give an extremely spectacular pyrotechnic show."

"You put it perfectly, Smaisi. It's important to understand here that each sex feels and understands emotions differently. The same event can cause a completely different reaction on each side. These are differences that cannot be avoided. And although everyone has individually set levels of their emotions and their intensity, which depends on their personal experiences, some emotional dependencies are common to the entire population of men or women, and I would like to tell you about it too. Men have difficulties in expressing their feelings and emotions; they like intimacy but at the same time they feel terrified of it. They like to reveal their emotions in front of others, but only when they can demonstrate their superiority and power. Women, on the contrary, love to talk about what they feel, words bring them relief and soothe them energetically. When a woman talks about her feelings, delves into them and works with them, she allows her to embrace them with love and understanding. The female part of society sees nothing wrong with talking about themselves, even constantly. For her, it means love for herself and for another human being. It's also a great sign of trust in the person who is listening to it. The woman, thus, also confirms to herself how much she loves and respects herself. For a man, love is felt when he is supported and admired by his woman. She, on the other hand, needs confessions of love, romantic gestures, understanding — for her these are proofs of love. Each of these energies also takes on a different responsibility. The woman is the goddess of the hearth that she has promised to protect, and she fulfills this role as wife and mother, looking after both her children and her partner. A man, on the other hand, tries to reign in his social life and focuses his greatest attention on it. Nowadays, social status and work are an indicator of how a man cares for his family, if he has one. The senses also work completely differently in men and women. Women have a better sense of hearing and smell, they can also see in the dark, while men see better at day but they are worse at distinguishing colors and they often are daltonists. Women have good memory and they remember a lot of information but they code it in their short span memory. Men, on the other hand, direct the majority of filtered data to their long span memory. They remember what, according to them, is most important. As you can see, dear ones, woman and man are the two greatest opposite energies walking on this planet. It doesn't change the fact though, that one cannot live without the other. It's the power of love — the highest and greatest vibration that flows directly from the heart space. This love is the beginning of an incredibly beautiful connection that initiates new life."

"Sexual energy!" Kal almost shouted out and we gave him a weird look,"What? You mentioned that you're going to tell us about it and I've been waiting patiently all that time." he explained and he didn't feel stupid at all. — "Even the Orions know its worth and they successfully sell it," he added a moment later, proud of the fact that he remembered what Semjase mentioned earlier about this energy.

"Indeed. I promised, I'm going to tell you about it because it's crucial from an energetic point of view. And you're busting with hormones," Semjase looked at me in a puzzling way and I turned red, "The remembrance of your past lives isn't helpful either in this matter," she only added and moved to the subject matter. "When two people are connected with a close relationship or when a sexual intercourse occurs between them, they generate a field of energy. The partners are the energy, they're electricity, polarities. When these polarities are activated, they create something in the shape of an electric circuit, thanks to which light is generated. This light can be perceived, some people will not see it at all, others only a little, and others still will see it very, very clearly. Whether you see it or not, the electrical circuit is always connected, but it is usually extremely short and is quickly interrupted as soon as it occurs. The key here is the duration of the sexual act. The longer the act is, the stronger the light will be and it will last longer. Thirty minutes is the minimum for this circuit to form. In today's world, however, it is a very rare phenomenon. People's minds are too tense and need a discharge which makes people make love intensely and quickly without letting this light to turn on. In many countries, sex is only seen as a reduction in tension and can be placed on a shelf next to a restorative afternoon nap. Unfortunately, it's not given the importance it deserves. When the energy that is produced during this act is suddenly and quickly expelled, it dissipates. Although a person expects full relaxation, in return after such an act he or she receives weakness and fatigue. So sex is counterproductive then. The same thing happens with a relationship that is only sexual in nature, instead of igniting love between both people, burns out very quickly when the desire is satisfied. What people should be striving for is reawakening sexual magic."

"What is it? Can you tell us a little more about it?" I requested. The word magic always attracted my attention.

"Sexual magic is the innate ability of female beings to use magnetic energy. This energy opens paths that allow you to access deeper levels of consciousness. When a woman is loved and appreciated enough by her partner, she feels stable with him and thus allows herself to enter the deepest levels of her being. When she feels an uncontrolled trembling over her body at the moment of orgasm and she feels safe enough to surrender to it and allows that trembling to take over her entire body — a wonderful magnetic vortex opens up for her. Its center is in her womb. This complete entry into the sexual act strengthens and rapidly expands the awareness of the magnetic field which is extremely important and necessary for the soul symbiote to nestle in her womb. A man whom a woman has trusted so much is in a state of elation and sets in motion an act of symbiosis and connection. It's called the power of lifting the released energy. Achieving such states is very nourishing and strengthening for the body. Contrary to quick sexual acts which have the opposite effect of what I was talking about a while ago. There is an alchemical key encoded in the female sexual nature. This key is revealed during the act of love. As two people continue to make love, and the connection and passion between them is growing, a tremendous amount of substances is released in each of them in their body and brain. It's thanks to this that a tunnel for symbiotes is created, and at the moment of conception, a magnetic field opens, generating an increase in magnetism and the ether of existence. This is the first birth. The birth of the symbiote of the soul. I will describe it to you exactly another time. A man at the moment of orgasm has two options. He can allow him to ejaculate or keep his semen. There is an immediate reaction in the woman's sanctuary if the ejaculation is done and the prior energetic conditions are met. The energy essence floods the walls of her inner sanctuary and the magnetic energy explodes — this is the opening of the spinning worlds within the inner worlds of the woman. If both sides are conscious, the magnetism released from such contact between the fluids — is immense. Knowing how the magic of the sexual act works is very important, as it allows you to draw these magnetic fields into the bodies of a woman and a man and consciously use the energy they have created. The second phenomenon occurs when the initiated and conscious woman begins to shake uncontrollably. The center of this body quake is in the uterus which begins to sway. This movement also creates very complex magnetic fields that both men and women can draw into their bodies again. You could say that a man is by nature "electric" and a woman is "magnetic". The nature of electricity is movement and action, while magnetism winds its nest and embraces it. Immediately after orgasm, the magnetic fields generated by the woman continue to spiral out and circulate. It is a time of rest and staying in the field of this magnetism. Without realizing it, men usually get up or go to sleep, thus giving up being in these magical energies.Well, it was supposed to be a long lecture, but at his own request he will extend it twice. It's time to go home. You have enough information for today. Kal is about to burst from excess testosterone here, "Semjase starts to loosen up a bit after a really difficult topic.

For the last several minutes I had to be careful not to blush because I received many intimate and very personal signals from Kal. Semjase only confirmed to me that she was also aware of what was going on in our heads during her monologue.

After a while, her laughter seemed to fade away, followed by the entire space around us. It was late morning when I opened my eyes. I couldn't help but think how I would use some of the knowledge I had just gained in my shared magical future with Kal.

Chapter 9

I may bring the keys, I can even open the door, however, you have to go through the threshold yourself."

Damian Buczniewicz

The future in the keyhole

When I went downstairs, my parents were not in the house, which surprised me a bit. I found a piece of paper on the kitchen table with a note: "We went for a trip, dinner is in the fridge ".

I wandered around the empty house for a while. I had to admit that I didn't like being alone. Especially recently. I'd gotten so used to Kal's presence that when he wasn't around, I felt incomplete. I realized that despite all my love for him, I couldn't allow myself to feel like that. The most important thing for both of us was that I fully love and respect myself, and Kal will reflect these feelings for me like the mirror that he really was for me. For a moment, I was wondering what to do with myself and how to plan my day. I knew that sooner or later, Kal would appear and we would spend part of the day together. I ate my breakfast and decided to meditate for a while. I entered the garden and lit myself up properly on the hill. For a moment, I was talking to my guide. He was aware of the level of my knowledge, anyway, why wouldn't he. He knew much more than I. In fact — he knew everything. I could have asked him about many things and, I didn't know why, I never did it. I preferred Semjase and other wonderful beings to pass on the knowledge to me that was needed to awaken humanity.

Kal appeared at noon. Surprised, like me, that the house

191

was empty, he started to wonder how to use this free day and space that was offered to us by my parents. I quickly got those dirty yet magical thoughts out of his head and we focused on the job. I was writing for a while and Kal was searching on the Internet for information he could use for his book about extraterrestrials. I needed to admit that his notebook was getting thicker with each week.

"You feed him well," I laughed, pointing at the file of pieces of paper that were already falling out, "You need to clip them properly before the mess creeps in".

"Relax, until this mess is mine it means that it's an order. I know where things are. When the time is right, I'll put everything together but it's still far from that".

"It looks quite vast" I suggested.

"It's only a drop in the ocean, Smaisi. We're not aware of how many millions of beings are located in our galaxy only, not to mention other galaxies. And the other universes — forget about it at all. My life wouldn't be enough to describe all of them."

"That's true. You need to focus on those that will be most important for humans — those that they can really get in contact with in future."

"I'm trying, but I don't know the future and it's not that easy."

"Semjase isn't in a hurry to reveal anything about it, and I can't see clearly my future incarnations. Perhaps it's not the time for that and Semjase is right by saying that if we knew too much we would badly influence the timeline and alter the events."

"I suppose that she knows what she's saying and we will learn about everything in the right time. We need to, similarly to other humans, learn to be patient. Although we know ourselves and the fact it's not easy."

"Yeah, we are terribly stubborn and inquisitive on top of that."

"I'm glad that Yriah liked us so much. I wonder if she'll ever take us anywhere else and what she would tell us about."

"I have a feeling we will meet her more than once."

Perhaps faster than you think. I heard Yriah's voice in my head. I looked at Kal and his radiant smile confirmed to me that he heard that too.

"We're looking forward to that," I replied but Yriah didn't respond.

We needed to be patient, although her message meant that we wouldn't wait for the meeting so long.

The afternoon passed on chatting. My parents were still gone, but it didn't bother us. Finally, after all those years of taking care of me, they had time for themselves. A second youth. As I was thinking of it, I suddenly felt a word in me: "Regression". It echoed in my head. I had no idea where it came from. After a while, I realized that Mommy had used this word before. She said that Daddy went through a regression and that it's a quite painful process of retrieving the memory. I decided to ask Daddy about it. I was certain then when I asked him he would tell me all about it. I was only wondering if it wasn't one of the ways for people to remember who they are and where they come from. I had a weird feeling though, that it wasn't about that kind of memory… I

I felt this though in space and I again focused my attention on Kal. I noticed that he was sitting and staring at the wall. He was neither blinking nor moving. I got scared slightly, but before I reacted, he came back to full awareness of this reality.

"What is it?" I asked.

"I saw a sun flare. It was a vision of what is going to happen," he excitedly replied.

"And?" I asked and couldn't wait and entered his memory.

The light of the flare was approaching the Earth with a great speed. Sky suddenly illuminated, as if the Sun switched on additional halogen lights. I felt that despite the beauty of this phenomenon, I shouldn't look at it, I also automatically covered my body with my blouse. I saw a beautiful and enormous aurora encompassing the entire sky that was visible to the whole world. I could feel the heat and on the trees there were seeds of fruit beginning to appear.

"Smaisi!" Kal called me back, "This is my vision. It's not

nice what you're doing. Maybe I wanted to tell you myself about it!" He was indignant at me.

"Don't exaggerate, please" I found the behavior slightly exaggerated.

Kal was very weird. He stood up and left the room. I was sure that he would be back but then I heard the front door slamming — it seemed that he wouldn't. I didn't understand his behaviour and I had no idea what I did wrong. I tried to connect with him telepathically but he completely blocked me. I became very sad and I had a terrible sense of guilt that I might have trespassed a boundary. Perhaps because only he received that vision he wanted it to belong only to him for a moment.

After several minutes I heard the slamming of the door again. Being confident that it was Kal, I ran downstairs quickly to apologize to him. On the threshold, however, I saw my parents. Disappointed, I put a fake smile on my face, not wanting to bother them with my problems, and I greeted them.

"How was your day?" I questioned.

"Fantastic," Mommy responded, "and how was yours?"

I already knew that my mask melted.

"What happened, Smaisi?"

I told my parents about the events that happened a while earlier. They both found my behaviour not quite alright and that the vision belonged to the person that received it and he or she decides what to do with the knowledge received.

"I watched only a little, " I defended myself.

"It doesn't matter, Smaisi. You trespassed on his free will. Would you like him to trespass yours?"

"No" I replied with full power and my behaviour became clear to me. I couldn't even apologize to him. He totally blocked me out. When I tried to connect with him I could hear only humming.

"He doesn't want to speak to me." I confessed with sadness, "I don't even have any way to apologize to him".

"Humanly" Daddy responded.

"But he blocked me out. I can't connect with him."

194

"Honey…" Daddy made a weird, sour face, "Do you have legs?"

"Yes, I do." I replied earnestly because at first I didn't get what he was about.

"Then, use them. And after that, apologize to him straight away and let it flow directly from your beautiful, illuminated heart", he threw my jacket in my direction and suggestively pointed at the door.

I got dressed quickly and having informed my parents that I wasn't sure what time I would be back, I left. I was walking quite fast and the freezing wind was lashing my face. I needed that. All that time I was wondering what to tell him so as not to make the situation worse that I created myself. When I knocked at the door, I was trembling like aspen in the wind. Kal opened the door. I looked at him in an apologizing way and I didn't need to say anything more. Kal spread his arms for me, and I threw myself in them and held him tightly.

"I'm sorry, I didn't want that. I don't know what tempted me." I confessed heartily.

"Curiosity. It was simply curiosity and I overreacted too. I would have probably behaved the same as you did. Will you come in?" he asked and the whole anger was gone.

"Yes, of course. Is your mom in?" I questioned.

I enjoyed meeting with her. She was a very kind and warm person. She sacrificed a lot to bring Kal up and understand his uniqueness. This task was more difficult because she was alone.

"She's upstairs. She is at an online conference. Work" he explained. "She should be done soon," he added, "You look cold. I'll brew you some tea."

I loved his amazing care about me and that he could feel everything perfectly. I needed to admit that it was very helpful in everyday life.

"Make yourself comfortable on the coach, I'll be joining you."

"Thank you, Kal" I whispered and he disappeared into the kitchen. I heard boiling water and Kal bustling in the kitchen. I mused off for a while and totally lost all my strength.

"You fell asleep." he woke me up with a slight tug.

I came round and the aroma of a brewed fruit tea hit me. I reached out to get the hot mug and to warm up.

"It's late, I'm not surprised you fell asleep. I'm tired too. Lately I noticed that my body needs more sleep."

"It's surely the energetic changes and DNA transformations. It concerns everyone. We're not exceptional."

"Do you want to go home?" he asked.

"I don't know. Perhaps maybe your mother doesn't mind, I'll stay here. I can feel that we will anyway be taken somewhere at night."

"As you wish. I don't think your parents would mind, my mom won't oppose that either."

Kal planned an evening with a movie and he even played it on. Eventually though we fell asleep after a few minutes, cuddled, even though the movie seemed promisingly interesting.

I woke up at the top of some kind of a mountain and at the foot of which there was a large lake. The sunset was reflected in it and the whole sky was in the shades of red. Huge forests stretched all around. I looked around. Kal was sitting right next to me.

"It's beautiful here," I said, moved.

"A romantic scenery. Perhaps someone has sent us for a date," Kal suggested and laughed at the irrationality of this idea.

"Unfortunately, it's not a date. Although it may seem so," Yriah spoke, standing behind us. She was floating in the air, slowly flapping her huge wings. She landed right next to us and sat on the rock. "I told you that we will see each other sooner than you expected."

"I could sense that," I uttered, "And I'm really glad that my intuition was right."

"It hardly ever does, you're not fully conscious though, and you're not using it to the fullest."

"Where will you take us?" I asked curiously.

"Where you always wanted to go. I'll show you a bit of the future which, if humanity wakes up, will become their everyday life."

"Finally!" Kal exclaimed, content with the fact he achieved his goal.

"You can travel to the future on your own. You're about to learn that soon. Everything comes in the divine timing. You need to be…"

"… patient" we interrupted Yriah's utterance.

"Yes, exactly. So? Are you ready for a trip?

"Of course. As always. And for such a trip, most definitely," responded Kal who was ready to absorb new knowledge at any given time of day and night.

"None is surprised by that," she laughed out, "Everything I'm about to tell you happened on your timeline and the time is only fulfilling. I'll tell you only what I can in this moment of time."

"Of course, we understand," I replied.

"Many beings of light that have descended on Earth, many times have requested not to spread among humans the message about the imminent destruction of the world and humanity. Nothing like that will happen and this is triggering in humans only fear and anticipation of the worst. It's contrary to what people should do now, which is creating positive realities. Moving away from materialism, they should focus on themselves and their own inner self. It's important because the technology of the future will be based on the connection between the inner developmental core with the state of consciousness of the environment. This means that the higher the collective consciousness of humanity is, the more changes will come for them in a faster time. It is impossible to accurately determine the date of an event and you can only be sure that it will happen sooner or later. For every event depends on the creation of the collective and many millions of factors can influence it on the Line of Time. These are really many variables and each of them affects the reality or creates a time shift of the event. While events may change in timelines and some may simply not happen, and others may appear in their place, they remain the same in the timeline. It's like a top-down plan that has to be fulfilled. Here I will refer for a moment to what Kal saw today. You saw the flare and space gave you a hint of what it would look like, what to watch out for, and when it might happen. This is the future at the moment, but in two weeks maybe even tomorrow under the influence of many factors and external factors, the time of this event may change. It may or may not. The solar flare depends on the state of consciousness of humanity, but you can be sure otherwise that it will occur in the two thousand twenty-first year. However, it is never 100% certain. Many people thought that the event of December 21, 2000, was a flare, and, in fact, it was the merging of the Earth's morphic grid and the entrance of Mother Earth into a completely different space. It was the complete closure of the third dimension. From that day on, for three consecutive days, high frequency bands of awakening descended upon Earth. The energy waves coming straight from the galaxy's central sun were directed towards the Earth. And although many people missed or completely ignored the signs visible at that time, expecting an explosive event, these few days changed a lot in people's minds, contributing to numerous changes in the near future. In recent years, there have been many visionaries and clairvoyants creating dark scenarios for all humankind — from wars to catastrophes to the complete annihilation of humanity. It will never happen, and these events are not in the timeline of humanity right now. Earth's polarity will affect climate change, but it will not be so catastrophic that humanity will have to fear it. Such intimidation of people or else to call it, unfortunately, can not only generate energy for the dark side. Many visionaries misinterpret their visions or are sent illusions aimed at generating energy for entities and beings who send these illusions. Many take such a vision and messages for granted and believe in them uncritically, although intuition tells them otherwise, because still what they see with their eyes is more real than what they feel with their heart and soul. Those who have a vision become a part of it and pass on their energy of fear so as not to keep it only on their shoulders. It really doesn't take much to change the reality in which people find themselves. The very change of consciousness as well as respect and care for your body and for Mother Earth are things that you know and feel inside you. However, people do not listen to themselves. Humanity has already been brought into a certain logical circle of events that will now have a place in their timeline. Slowly, there will be some kind of psychological transformation where the people freed from the programs will eventually be free in their creation. The time of the great meeting of many races and civilizations is slowly approaching. It will be a meeting of the terrestrial civilization with the earthly civilization of the future and many cosmic nations from outside the Earth. There will also be meetings of races inhabiting Earth, the existence of which humans do not know yet. The extraterrestrials are ready for this meeting, but humanity is not yet. Therefore, it cannot be a premature meeting for it to happen, the level of human consciousness collectively should be on a higher level than it is now. Otherwise, it will only have bad consequences. Such a mass disclosure of everything that is concealed at one moment would lead to the collapse of the economic and monetary system all over the world. Everything that has been told to you so far would suddenly fall apart like a house of cards, but life is not a game in which it can be straightaway built again. It takes time. I can say that the timeline is filling up and humanity is continuing towards its destiny, but despite the Internet and free access to information, of which we have more and more, few people know the truth and even more of them, even when they know, they simply will not believe in it later. The Internet has recently been filled with too many conflicting moments about future events. You have to filter them carefully with your heart otherwise you can really go crazy. The best suggestion is to listen to yourself. Do not think, however, that now is very bad; in the past, it was even worse. Only a few could write and read, and even if they could, they read only what they were told. The information was even more filtered and handwritten works were created in only one copy. Flavius and Długosz wrote for the proverbial slice of bread exactly what they were told to write. If they objected, they would lose food and often their own lives. So the past is as deceitful as the present, only the media have changed. The Internet, however, due to the abundance of information, allows leaks — small streams of truth, although lost in the oceans of lies, they are finally caught by the few. And this is how the truth finds an outlet. After all, the truth will always defend itself and find even the smallest gap to be noticed and heard. Much has already been discovered, but quickly swept under the rug, masked and sealed, giving access to only a few. If any truth was written down, it was immediately sent to potential dungeons located in the Vatican. You have no idea what a treasure trove of truth it is. They burn down the Vatican sooner than they let its documents see the light of day. The same thing happens with any archaeological findings. As soon as something is found that could reveal the truth about the past or provide evidence of manipulation of the human race, it is immediately covered up, and those who — as they say — let go of their mouths, are often murdered or die in strange circumstances, often in a pseudo-suicidal death. I will not even mention strange phenomena and objects observed in the sky, and not infrequently — it is also covered up and people do not even realize what they see and how many spacecraft of different races are in their close space. The main carrier of all kinds of lying propaganda on a huge scale at the moment — are the mainstream media. When worldwide hysteria suddenly appears in the media, it always means that there has been some kind of fraud and manipulation once again to bring humanity under control. The goal is known only to the elite and is always in line with their plans."

"Can you tell us, what was a media lie, for example? Any examples that we have skipped?" Kal asked.

"Of course I can. I have no secrets from you. I protect the truth. This is my role and I want to fully convey it to you. So let me give you a few examples according to your request. In the year 2000, there was media information predicting an attack by a computer worm, a virus that was supposed to destroy computer systems and the data stored in them. It caused chaos. The media is constantly talking about global warming which is a true lie resulting from the lack of knowledge of the natural processes of the Earth. People influence the atmosphere and the ozone layer, but they poison themselves by their behavior. Climate change will come

200

anyway because this is the order of things and this is the Earth's cycle. Despite this, people have been scared of it for many years, and the topic almost never fades away. However, a lot of good came out of this lie. Great associations stood up for the planet and more and more environmentally friendly power plants were built — water or wind. The fate of some animal species has improved as a result. So some controlled events can have a huge resonance with people. Nothing is ever just white or just black. There is a war against global terrorism all the time. Now let's ask ourselves who's in charge of all this? The elite s — they deal the cards.

They attack themselves and poison people's minds with fear. Lots of people have died in their terrorist games and games for power and control. What do you think was the attack on the World Trade Center? It was a carefully planned action, the effects of which are still widely echoed to this today and cause pain in the hearts of many people. As you already know, the next big deception and manipulation is NASA's voyages to the moon. So I don't need to elaborate on it any more. Another distortion is heliocentrism and what shape the Earth really has, but that's what you have planned for someone else to discuss and with, not yet," — she said mysteriously smiling, "Except for the alleged covid-19 pandemic that was so blown that half of the world was shaking for a long time and still continues, everyone remembers well the threat of pandemics of avian and swine flu that were supposed to decimate nations. All epidemics today have one goal — to scare people and force specific behavior on them. It was so in the past and it is the same this time. The elite wants to implement a new human identification system by introducing nanochips into their body. They know very well that the population will not agree to it voluntarily, but by threatening with the loss of life, they allow the commencement of compulsory vaccinations against the supposedly lethal virus and thus silently execute the plan to chip all people. We could continue to enumerate, and we probably wouldn't be finished anytime soon. The world in which people live is unfortunately controlled to such an extent that lies and manipulations are read as facts. It is actually very difficult for the average person to get to the truth. Even today, with all the knowledge leaking onto the Internet, shelling out what is real seems like an Oscar-worthy feat. One of the biggest lies is religion as well. You already know this perfectly well, and this lie has been dragging on for thousands of years. Many seekers of truth do not find its source. Later, disinformation spreads because they filter what they have discovered through their own imaginations, and fill the gaps in facts with guesses. This is how the half-truth is born. Lots of these seekers fell into their traps. They were absorbed by the new age movement, which is nothing but a secret elite agenda.

As a result, all those who act to the disadvantage of the elite and allegedly revealing the truth are on their side. Consciously or not. In a great deal of disinformation, finding the truth is incredibly difficult. That is why it is so important for humanity to wake up. The truth will then be at your fingertips. When people regain their soul memory, no one will ever be able to trick or manipulate them again. The elites who still rule this world, although they already use the remains of their power, they finance all the media. Including the Internet. So how is a person to find out the truth when every forbidden word entered in a search engine is immediately picked up by huge computer systems and then all materials that can convey the truth are removed from the web? How many will see an article or video? How many will believe in it and how many will pass this knowledge on? Even if there are a lot of these people, others will not take their word for it. Because that's how people are. They don't trust. No wonder. Nobody has taught them this, there is no question of trust when all life from conception to death is stuck after learning lies and manipulations. Humans see nothing, hear nothing, and even the feeling and intuition function has been taken away from them. Everything that the elite who rule this world do has one goal — full control over the lives of the human population. People are supposed to be like puppets carrying out the orders of the authorities without objection. This is not life, it is not the freedom that every being is entitled to have. It is a theater thanks to which those who hold the strings have the best fun. Even the stage of this theater was carefully planned. Humanity does not know that there are many more lands and continents on the Earth's globe than is commonly known. And here I will add that humanity does not know but governments and elites know it perfectly. Not to mention the knowledge of a huge underground inner world called Agartha."

"I understand though that what you've just told us will soon be revealed?" I questioned.

"Yes, the truth will come to light, but it will be happening slowly. Nobody would dare to throw at people all the knowledge at the same time, because it would not be well received then. People don't like changes, and such knowledge triggers them, and they are huge. Over the next decade there will be so many changes and such a great technological development in all possible fields that children who are now a few years old will live in a completely different world. Much more interesting and kind to the human species. That is why so many star children are being born now. Their inner nature is to bring harmony and love to all existence into this new world. These children do not have aggression in them, they have a connection to their soul and it allows them to see beyond dimensions. They feel with their intuition and hearts what is wrong and what is good. It is difficult to impose any programs on them because they are aware of their free will and the laws of the universe. Their parents do not even realize how much they know and how many things they do not say, although they understand perfectly better than many adults. They wait and accurately sense the moment when they can safely come out of the shadows and do what they were sent here to Earth for."

"And what about the travels in time? " Kal asked, "will they become accessible to humans?"

"Yes. The discovery of the possibility of time travel will enable a person to travel to the future and the past without any problems. Humans will also be able to travel across the vastness of the universe. It will be open to them. All this was not possible before. Time travel will result in the discovery of new forms of human life. Earthlings will eventually learn from extraterrestrials about new quantum technology and molecular nutrition technologies. Development will start to proceed very quickly in every field, which will result in the creation of artificial biological intelligence that will be brought into public life. This artificial technology will be used to operate all mechanical and electrical devices so that people will be able to stop working and do what they love. They will become free again. However, people must be careful, because the artificial intelligence which they construct and bring to life will become independent after some time, which could pose a threat to people. This will mainly apply to andro-robotic humanoid humans. People, having the possibility to travel in time, will also not be limited in traveling huge distances, because the travel in time will take place without the loss of real time. It will also be a time when the human population will be freed from the curses of premature aging. Medical beds using the latest technology and retrograde regression are enabling the human species to live longer than what will be possible thanks to the results of the latest genetics research, which will also be introduced. New technologies mean that the time of human life will extend up to four hundred years. Ultimately, the development of these technologies will reach such a level that human life will start to be counted not in hundreds but in thousands of years, just like it was in Lemuria."

When Yriah got silent for a moment, in my head again the word "regression" showed up. Because of the fact that I knew that in future this would have a huge effect on human longevity, it was certain to me that Dad would need to tell me all about it in detail. I suspected that it wouldn't be a punishment for him.

"It seems to me that it's a little more distant future."

"Yes. It's another century. The first decade though will introduce many changes that will be perceptible to people. There will be medical beds and they will change the face of medicine. Organic food will be introduced as well, free from any substances that are harmful to humans, the monetary system will collapse and a new one will appear in which there won't be any division into the poor and the rich and everybody will have as much as they need to live as they wish. Worldwide traveling will become easier and faster. In the next decade our friends — the intelligent race inhabiting the waters of oceans — will start getting in contact with human beings. It will be commonly recognized that they're a new race dwelling the Earth, that you had a pleasure to meet with, Smaisi. They will be called by humans Aqua Acticus. Soon after these events, the expeditions will start to the regions of Sirius and they will discover evidence of existence and heritage of the ancient ancestors. It will be revealed that for thousands of years the ancestors of Earthlings were escaping through pathways and they found themselves in the SOL system that they started to inhabit. Humanity will finally find information concerning their origins and merge with them."

"Semjase told us about it" uttered Kal.

"It's highly probable," Yriah confirmed, "These events will lead to contacts with very distant ancestors, the Ancients and with the beings of Sirius. There will begin a cooperation between humans and newly acquainted civilizations which will assist in rebuilding the human genotype and retrieve its natural form from the times before it was polluted with many genetic manipulations. Thanks to that, new races of humans will be born and their descendants. The course of events will be fulfilled and the whole cycle will come to an end. The human will again become the long lost real human being and will exist in balance with what is negative and positive. These are the events that are calculated to occur in the next hundreds of years and the sequence of their occurrence can interchange, which doesn't change the fact that they will happen."

"What else does the future hold? What's in store for us? This is all good news, after all. Humans should want to create such a future and become part of it." I said. I wanted to know as much as possible and I was aware of the fact that the desire to know the future wasn't only in me but in the majority of humankind.

"Again, you squeeze me out like a lemon" Yriah laughed out, "Oh, how I like this sour juice. The essence of knowledge in a few drops, while harmony and peace seeded into human souls. At the moment when the access to free energy becomes unblocked, the production of molecule food will be increased. They will deliver it to special points from which it will be collected free of charge."

"It will be free of charge?" Kal was astonished.

"Yes. Absolutely free of charge. Thanks to the technology of free energy there will be more produced than a human is capable of using up. The life expenses will drop to zero, almost. There will be no more slave labor and exploitation. The pension that people know so far will disappear because it will not be needed due to the fact that every person will get a kind of basic salary each month. Money itself will not be so important anymore, it will certainly not be a factor of fear for your survival. Due to the fact that most of the things needed for survival will be free, money will only be used to fulfill personal dreams and hobbies, such as travel or recreation. But they will not completely disappea r— people are too used to them. They will still be used to pay for services and products, but not on such a large scale, and special electronic wallets will be created for this purpose for each inhabitant of the Earth. Although there will be two attempts to completely eliminate money, they will fail, and it will continue to play a role in human life, but it will no longer be synonymous with living or not living. There will also be no monetary units, a single world currency will be created. Many will probably be pleased that animal breeding, the purpose of which is to slaughter meat for sale, will be completely abolished. The engineered technology will meet the needs of the human body for protein and animal proteins by creating plants that provide them. In addition, humanity will achieve the technological conditions for cloning meat, as not everyone will like the vegetable counterparts. However, I do not mean cloning animals for the purpose of killing them, but the cloning of a ready-to-eat meat piece after being cooked as it is done today. In order to obtain the meat for further cloning, the animal will be killed in a sanctified manner, in agreement with the creator, and only after the soul has departed from its body. This will keep the animal's body clean and will not be contaminated at death as has been the case so far. When this happens, no animal on this planet will be killed for consumption and billions of lives will breathe a sigh of relief.

Geneticists will discover this soon, but new solutions will not yet be introduced due to a lack of confidence in genetic manipulation. On the one hand, it is hardly surprising, but on the other hand, genetics, like the rest of the world, is neither black nor white, and when used in the right way, it will contribute to the colossal and rapid development of civilization. Were it not for the numerous blockades set by the elite, most of what is yet to exist today would exist."

"If only I could move there..." I dreamed up.

"Anytime soon. Oh... I would almost forget. Humans are about to become aware of what the elite knows — the elite that knows everything but doesn't say that to anyone. It's about the Earth's atmosphere that is not conducive to extension of human life. The attempts to introduce activities such as spraying, whitening and many others, have the opposite effect and cause people to die even faster. This will not change though either. Thanks to the fusion of free energy there will be a technology introduced that will produce the air. I know it sounds a bit weird and unbelievable but this is what's going to happen. Thanks to this technology, the air will become cleaner and much more healthy, it will have different yet much more suitable ingredients for the human body. It will form along with the terraforming of the planet — similarly to other innovative technologies — it will contribute to the extension of human life."

"Does it mean that there's something wrong with the air's ingredients now? As I understand, it's not only about the pollution."

"Yes. It's not the best for the human body presently. At the moment, the proportion of oxygen and nitrogen in the Earth's air is simply inappropriate for humans. The oxygen content is too low, not to mention many of the substances in it that adversely affect health when inhaled, but humanity is on the right track. Everything will happen as it is supposed to happen and time is only filling up and pushing people forward on the timeline of their destiny."

"Oh no! I just felt sad. Does it mean we're done for today?"

"That's what I've planned. And is there anything else you

would like to know?"

"I would like to know everything about such star children like we are. About Indigo and Crystal children" I revealed.

"Very well, but let me take you again in a few days. This is a vast subject. I don't want to explain to you anything in short. And now, go home" she snapped her fingers and everything around her, including her, vanished.

I woke up in Kal's arms. He was still sound asleep. I placed my hand on his chest and almost for an hour I was staring at how my palm was rising and falling to the rhythm of his slow and steady breathing. It was still dark outside. Still feeling a little tired, I closed my eyes and fell back asleep.

Chapter 10

"Healing
Humanity has learned to treat the symptoms of their problems,
expecting them to be fixed.
Healing requires finding the cause, digging out the foundations and creating
new ones... however, it requires tearing down all the walls first..."

Damian Buczniewicz

Regression

We ate breakfast at Kal's. After that, Kal walked me home. Of course, I revealed to him that I was going to ask Daddy about the regression. I wanted to know as much as possible about it, because the hitherto references to this subject suggested that the subject is very important. Kal didn't intend to skip the lecture and asked immediately when I was planning to ask for it. We made an appointment for the afternoon. Dad had no idea that he would be attacked, and after crossing the threshold of the house I watched my thoughts so that he could not read anything from them.

The day was passing as usual. For the majority of time I was writing and focusing on my task. More and more often I caught myself on the fact that I could write and write. It engrossed me up to the point that I started to wonder what's next after I finish.

None said this book will be the only one — I heard Semjase's voice in my head.

Ooo! Hello there. Will we be seeing each other today? — I asked, taking advantage of the situation.

I'm afraid that no. Not today yet.—she only replied and

disappeared.

I could feel exactly when the resonance with her frequency was finished. I could feel shivers running from top to bottom.

Immediately after lunch, Kal rolled into the house. He was climbing the stairs as if he weighed a ton.

"What's up?" I asked and couldn't help laughing.

"I ate so much that I barely walked up here and since I didn't want to be late for the lecture…"

"I would wait for you" I interrupted him.

"What lecture?" Daddy called from the corridor. His hearing was so reliable.

"Eee…" Kal stuttered out, not knowing what to say, "Well, a lecture about…" he interrupted and looked at me questioningly and I nodded — "About regression that you're going to tell us about" he finished off.

"Me?" Dad asked in slight disbelief.

"Yes, that's how it turned out," Kal responded to him and I only smiled radiantly.

"And what exactly took you on this subject?" Daddy kept asking. And something weird happened. He wasn't pleased at all that we asked him about it.

"If this is a problem, then we understand that," I said, feeling that something wasn't right.

"It's not a problem, Smaisi. It's just that I'm not particularly fond of these subjects. They're neither simple nor pleasant in experience. And you can believe me I know what I say."

"Mommy mentioned to me one time that you went through this process therefore we established that it would be best to ask you about it," I explained, "but if you don't want to, perhaps Mommy will be able to tell us something."

"No, there's no need. I'll grab something to eat and be back. Do you fancy anything?"

"I'm full, thank you" Kal pointed at his stomach, it was really noticeable that it was full.

"I'm fine too, thank you" I replied and both Kal and I went into the room.

"Do you think that we got his print?" Kal questioned.

"I wouldn't call it like that. Daddy loves telling stories and lecturing but, as you can see, not all the things that bring positive results is a pleasant process. When Mommy was telling me about it she said it was a painful experience for him. We know very well that the physical body has its limits and I have a weird impression that regression can be related mainly to the changes in the body and the changes in perception are the result of the former."

"You're right. I'm curious how he's going to approach this."

"You're about to find out" Daddy stood in the doorway and I started to wonder how much he managed to hear from our short conversation. Daddy sat down comfortably in the armchair and inhaled deeply — "These are not easy subjects and I hope that you are aware of that."

"Yes, that's what we suspect." I confessed.

"Regression is, to the greatest extent, the regenerative process of the human body, that is, the biological organism. This process later influences the feeling and perception of higher dimensions which is linked to changes in the biological body. This can be compared to turning the body into a light body. You already know what such a transformation causes. Well, but we have to start from the very beginning so that you understand everything well. So let's start", Daddy took a deep breath again and began his lecture — "DNA is a segment that carries genetic information. Currently, humans use a very small part of their DNA segment. For humans, the human body should be the most valuable thing, because it is the carrier of their soul and existence in a given incarnation. Therefore, people should not destroy it by themselves and under no circumstances should they allow it. But that's what happens. Destruction comes from all sides. The body stores for you a lot of valuable information that allows you to achieve more and more. It supports people in opening to their inner awareness and exploring not only themselves but also all other information about the world and life. As you know from previous lectures, human cells are divisible.

In this frequency to which the human is currently, assigned, unfortunately, he or she is prone to aging of cells and, thus, of the entire human body. Cells have a specific counter that calculates all molecular overwrites and divisions. There is a limit to these divisions, and it applies to all human cells as well as to other multicellular organisms. You already know that the cell, depending on the conditions — favorable or not — chooses immortality and self-sufficiency or reproduction and the transmission of genes and information. It is subcellular and cellular memory. The aging of the biological body is the result of incomplete duplication of DNA sequences at the ends of the chromosomes, which with each successive cell division lead to the fact that the telomeres at the ends of the chromosomes shorten. The shorter the DNA telomere tail, the more divisions have occurred. Thanks to this, we learn how old the cell is. When a certain number of divisions occurs and the counter cannot go any further, the cell, unable to divide, will self-destruct. This process is called apoptosis, but it can be stopped and even reversed. Cells' telomeres can begin to elongate, which is influenced by an enzyme called telomerase, which is active mainly in stem cells, making them practically immortal. Despite the fact that DNA and light molecules have been disconnected by humans and mutations, they are still connected but inactive. There is a form of energy between living tissues. This makes it possible to activate telomerase in cells. Even modern medicine can do it. In this process, chromosomes are protected and controlled by telomeres and telomerase, which as an enzyme is responsible for the restoration of telomeres. As a result, after using the modified RNA, telomeres are extended by up to a thousand nucleotides. But that's not all. Such cells have a 40 times longer lifespan due to the increase in the scale of the division counter. There is also no possibility for a cell to turn into a cancer cell."

"And it's possible to do that? Why, then, contemporary medicine doesn't use this method?" I questioned.

"Guess, Smaisi. As everything — this is being blocked as well. Because humans need to be afraid of death and should suffer, spending their last money on treatment of a variety of diseases that shouldn't concern them at all."

"So then how to activate that? This telomerase?" Kal continued asking. As always, he approached the subject very technically.
"

The activation of this process requires the use of telomere biology. Telomerase can be injected into the body. Therefore, it is possible to control the aging process with a mixing that contains telomerase. As a result, the cells of the biological body are able to rejuvenate thirty years in just three years. However, I must point out that the telomere is not a panacea, it must not be treated this way. Aging is not only a process that involves shortening the telomeres in the human body. Other processes take place parallelly. And here we move to redumeres, small molecules found in the structures of DNA. There is a certain dependence between telomeres and redumeres. Redumeres are shortened in the same manner as telomeres that I mentioned before, and are actually responsible for the simultaneous aging process, while the length of the telomere is, in a way, an indicator of the changes that are taking place in the cell. They control this process. Thus, the aging process of cells is also conditioned by the shortening of redumeres, although they are of secondary importance in the aging process of the whole body. They largely affect the aging of certain parts of the human brain, which is the main organ. In the human brain, most cells do not divide because there are redumeres that are shortened by a completely new process. Everything takes place in the hypothalamus, in the special structure of the brain that controls the pituitary gland. It's this part of the human brain that is responsible for the regulation of the endocrine system of the whole organism. In the brain, the shortening of redumeres occurs as a result of DNA strand breaking up during the synthesis of RNA and DNA molecules. These ruptures only occur when the cell is overstimulated by certain chromosomes."

"Holy Moly!" exclaimed Kal. Even he wasn't ready for such a deep dive into the concept and that was just the beginning.

"I said that it's a tough subject. It's not possible to digest after the introduction of only a few sentences. Without the recognition of processes that occur in the body you won't be able to comprehend the whole mechanism of regression. And that was what you wanted, right?" Daddy asked to be certain.

"Yes, indeed…" I said this time, although I wasn't so sure about that.

Kal was still sitting amazed, trying to understand the first part of the lecture. But since we had already entered it, I had to admit — slightly blindfolded, we had no other choice but to continue studying and take from it as much as we could.

"Do you want a little break?" asked Daddy.

"I guess it's too early to take a break. It's been about fifteen minutes" Kal noticed, anyway, rightly so.

"Well, let's go on with the topic then. We should now move on to the fact that the human brain has a physiological system that is interdependent with many external influences. It reacts to changes in space and changes in the strength of the primary field, including the gravitational field. These are the interactions of the energy wave of light photons. This results in calcium grains in the pineal gland. Its excessive calcification blocks human skills in conjunction with soul awareness. It is the pineal gland that is responsible for the integration of changes in the intensity of the photons of light and cosmic rays depending on the vibrations and frequencies that come from space, therefore, it must be decalcified and clean. The flows between light energy and material light and other universes take place in a torso-vibrational field.

This can be compared to a stream of water that can flow freely through various spaces. Similarly, energy flows from one world to another. However, it does not take place without numerous swirls along the way that affect the changes in the flow of these energies. The speed of the flow of these energies is invisible, then one can talk about the omnipresence that exists everywhere simultaneously, which occurs only when the speed of light is exceeded."

"How does this influence the process of regression?" Kal suddenly asked who, like me, had an impression that we were moving away from the subject matter.

"Well, the spectrum and waves of this light and energy cause that there is compression and pressure on the neighboring pineal cells, thanks to which it releases active chromosomes. This process takes place most often and intensively during the New Moon. The energy flows are at their greatest then. The pineal chromosomes, as a result of emission of waves of light, reach the hypothalamus and rapidly activate RNA synthesis, and telomeres and redomeres begin to break. This whole process can be called the regulation of the human monthly biological rhythm. This process is very necessary for the proper development of the body. It is like a biological clock whose task is to measure the rhythm of life of the human body."

"So in short, and simplifying it a lot, is the shortening of the telomere and redumeres responsible for the aging of the human body?" I asked to be sure if I understood at least the merits of what Daddy said.

"Exactly. It is a process that has been programmed into the human body. The cells of the body and telomere lengths allow in a fairly simple way to check what stage of aging a person is at. A healthy person will have longer telomeres than a sick person. Diseases accelerate the aging of the body. However, as I have already mentioned to you, it is possible to lengthen the strands of chromosomes even without biochemical interference in the human body. Molecular medicine and molecular nutrition will contribute to this in the near future. At these times, the telomeres elongate thanks to herbs such as baicin and astragalus. The body itself requires healing through connection with nature and a proper diet. Just leading a proper lifestyle combined with physical activity and reducing stress, reduces the degeneration of the telomere thread and prolongs life."

" Any suggestions concerning the style of life?" Kal asked,"More specific ones?" he added after a moment, having noticed Daddy's questioning look.

"First of all, a high-energy diet, consumption of living water, gluten-free and meat-free food that is free of lactose and complex sugars. The alcohol should be completely gone. And most importantly — preparing dishes with affirmation and positive programming of a given meal. The day should consist of the right proportions of work, sleep and relaxation. Meditation and physical exercise are also important. It is important that our lives do not lack challenges stimulating our creativity. Contact with nature, forest, water, even work in your own garden, contribute to the fact that human life is filled with harmony. One cannot put everything that is bad on the shoulders of bad genes. Humans themselves can do a lot to slow down the process of shortening of chromosomes. A lot of fruit, vegetables and cereal products will adapt to the molecular nutrition of your body. However, what can influence the process of aging most is your consciousness and the perception of yourself and your body as an integral whole in which you have to take care of each of the elements."

"Which, let's face it, humans don't do" Kal summed up.

What occurred to me was that we reached the end of the lecture or at least that's what I thought.

"No, they don't but they're also being lied to when it comes to the possibilities that are available for them at this moment. Available in infinite amounts. Completely free of charge" Daddy talked in riddles and although I knew what questions he waited for, Kal was first.

"What are you referring to?" he asked and for the first time since the beginning of the lecture there appeared a wide smile on Daddy's face.

I still didn't understand why Daddy didn't like the topic of regression. Perhaps he skipped part of it in which the quick regenerative process was causing physical pain.

"Smaisi, the process of regression is not only about regeneration and prolonging of life, but also a process of remembering who you really are. Regression as a term defines the regeneration of a physical body — it's the remembrance of what it's been made for thanks to the Shiru matrix as well as the access to the memory of your previous incarnations. Maybe you were about this kind of regression?"

216

"I don't want to be so demanding, but…" Kal interrupted, slightly suggesting that Daddy was to tell us something.

"Yes, I'm returning to the previous subject. I meant water, to be specific, sea water, salty. Such water has amazing healing properties, prevents stomach ulcers and stops the development of cancerous cells. It happens so due to the minerals in it, such as calcium, potassium and magnesium, which damage the inner cell membrane of bacteria. Water obtained at a depth of two hundred meters completely inhibits the growth of tumors and cancer cells."

"Well, it's actually abundant on Earth", I confessed happily, looking into the future with optimism. From what I have learned so far, it appeared that many things were already available and could effectively save people's lives.

"It's not difficult to be surprised that this information is being blocked. Imagine molecular technology and cell self-healing. Additionally, organisms that get sick and do not age. All pharmaceutical companies would die in a few days. Not only that, all the poison-soaked drugs that have been produced so far would have to be disposed of safely by them, which would entail huge costs combined with a total loss of profits. The truth is that you already know perfectly well that drugs are one of the many manipulations of the elite, a way to profit and control the human population better. Artificial epidemics are ideal examples here. After each such epidemic, pharmaceutical companies' stocks skyrocket and billions of dollars fall into corporate accounts. Concerns are driving up the production of worthless vaccines, often not properly tested, causing numerous post-vaccination reactions that even doctors are not able to correctly qualify. Thanks to molecular regression, it would no longer be necessary, and the transplants would not be needed as the cell would regain its ability to self-regenerate.

I mentioned this because the organ transplant network is another gang making billions. The prices of organ transplants are staggering and not for the pocket of an average person. Again, only the richest of the elite have room for maneuver. But that's not all. Thanks to the improvement of regression processes, it is possible to cure many diseases such as Parkinson's or autism, which is so popular in children recently. Unfortunately, as was the case many times, laboratories trying to implement the regression process were closed up very quickly. We still live in a world in which concerns and elites control everything, but the dawn of a new era is near." With this optimistic opinion, Daddy ended his lecture. It was not what we expected, but it brought a lot of valuable information that could turn out to be very useful in understanding the processes taking place in both the body and consciousness of people.

We were up with Kal until late evening. We decided to relax as that day's topics were not easy. For the first time in a long time, we threw away all the past and the future, and played chess for several hours trying to stay in the here and now.

Chapter 11

"Expectations
Our expectations show us that we're still defending ourselves, escaping, we
have a conviction that material things or other people will make us feel
complete whereas by doing so we reject the fact that we are already perfect..."

Damian Buczniewicz

Star children—Indigo and Crystal

For a few days, completely nothing was happening. The energies that were descending from the space were stronger and stronger, which could be felt not only in the body but also in the emotions. Their built-up could lead to outbursts of anger or a sudden sadness and ended up completely euphoric. The emotional swing of the highest class.

For St. Nicholas Day I received from Kal a snow globe. I bought him a sweater and I was slightly afraid that he might not like it. He surprised me with his enthusiastic reaction to it, though. He put it on immediately and walked proudly all over the house. I, on the other hand, shook the crystal snowball every now and then, causing a small blizzard inside it.

Between the tormenting of my internal emotions and me overworking everything that was going to be overworked, I tried to sleep. But it was not going too well. In tides of the Schumann resonance, when the frequencies jumped high above the average, I got some revelations and mainly then I sat in front of the computer screen.

219

One day before noon we went with Kal for a walk. We were strolling in the park, naturally talking when a boy stood right in front of us. He was maybe six or seven years old. He stopped and stared at us silently at the beginning. We let him do that, however, we were slightly puzzled, we didn't understand what was going on.

"You're the same" he said, "Cool" he added after a while and he was just about to leave when Kal stopped him.

"What do you mean?" he asked the boy.

"From one soul. I see you. Old souls. Experienced. I'm here to help as well. It's not my time yet, but soon" he said and it sounded as if he had never said that to anyone before.

I felt strongly inside me the word "secret". Our secret. The secret of star children.

"And can you see me?" he asked after a moment, completely serious.

Perhaps for others this question would sound quite weird, but not for us. I closed my eyes and tried to call in the image of his being from a higher dimension. He stood there. Beautiful angel warrior. He had been growing up to his mission here, his wings were still tiny. He was waiting until he would be able to fully spread his wings and fly high in the sky, taking with him as many beautiful beings as possible to the fifth dimension.

"I see you…" I said quietly.

"Cool. Not many can see me. Mommy saw me once, only for a moment. Then, she was looking for the wings on my back."

"Did you tell her who you are?" I asked him.

"No. Mommy isn't ready. Not yet. I'm helping her now. It's a good time for awakening. I'll tell her then. She can feel that I'm a bit different but she doesn't know why. She will probably be amazed anyway. But with so many new things that will come, this will be for her the least shocking" he continued as if he was tens of earthly years old. Enormous wisdom and tenderness was radiating from him and one could feel in him a huge amount of love.

"I believe that everything will be how it should be," I said to him.

"It will be beautiful, I can see that" he replied and having said goodbye, he left. It's good he did that because Kal was almost ready to start questioning him about what, in his opinion, the future was bringing.

"That was…" I started.

"Unbelievable", Kal finished off for me, "I don't know why I have a feeling that this wasn't accidental."

"There are no accidents, Kal"

"I know that right"

"Yriah" we said at the same time and blurted out laughing. We already knew who would take us for a trip and what it would be about.

The day was passing for us in a cheerful anticipation for a night adventure and a promised meeting with Yriah. I counted that what we were to learn from her, would explain to us a lot also about our origin. The boy that we had met that day was a confirmation that star children are among us and they are waiting for the right time to fulfill their mission and start to change this world for the better.

In the evening, as never before, we said goodbye quickly so as to get to our best as fast as possible. We really did care to go on this trip. It had been a long time since our excitement was so high. I fell asleep almost immediately.

"Welcome" I was woken up by a voice. I was surprised that I was still in my room. Yriah sat comfortably in the armchair and Kal suddenly materialized next to me.

"We suspected that you would come today," I confessed.

"I've sent you a hint" she admitted, "That's my earthly pupil.

"A clever boy" Kal praised him.

"Oh, yes. You aren't even aware of how much. He's one of the star children who, thanks to his achievements, will make history on Earth. Similarly to you two. The tasks of star children are different, some of them smaller, some of them greater. Each of them though is equally important. Today I'm going to pass on to you broad knowledge. It's about the quantum leap in the evolution of human consciousness. The great era of changes is approaching which you already know very well. Not everything that will be

221

happening can be perceived as beautiful. There will also be such events that will leave an imprint on humanity. Children of a new era that have already appeared on Earth will have to go though the time of the so-called transition between eras, a time in which many intense changes will take place. These are Indygo and Crystal children. Some of them will see the beauty of a new era only at the end of their earthly life. But that was the choice of each of the souls who came down here at this amazing time. It's important to accept that you understand what is happening. This will minimize the chaos that will be part of human existence for a short time. Many of the upcoming changes and the awakening itself do not suit the elite and do not fit into the present new world order. The elite will try to do their best to subjugate the Star Children. However, they are not as easily manipulated as the rest of society. It is due to the memory of their soul and the awareness that is awakened in them more from the very beginning. But we'll get to that in a moment."

"They're already here right? Many of them?" I kept asking, although it was clear to me anyway. I was one of them.

"Yes. Look in the mirror. There are millions of them on Earth now. These are the beings that will be constantly developing. Their first step should be awakening to the awareness of their own existence and origin, discovering their skills and isolating the distinguishing features of the new generation. They are the children of the new age. Many of them are still asleep and waiting for their awakening. The youngest generation of star children pose a great threat to the elite at this stage of awakening. Those in power will want to force them to socialize, persuading their parents that they have numerous diseases and disabilities, from ADHD to autism. This is only to isolate them and stifle their creativity. However, these children are resistant to commonly known diseases and have features that distinguish them significantly from the current nation. The uniqueness of these children is noticed by their parents' soul, although they will not always be able to classify it correctly.

Most of them will accept their uniqueness even though they

will be told it is a problem. The time and generation in which they were brought up also have a great influence. The younger generation growing up in peace and prosperity have a completely different view of the world than the older generations on whom war, poverty and often hunger left their mark. There, having a pair of shoes was a joy beyond measure. Especially in villages where there was no wealth. Children brought up in the age of digitization and developing technology will be completely different. Changes in the global consciousness of people have been taking place for a long time. Indigo children started it. It is impossible to fix the world you see just like that in one moment. It's a process. Like everything else. The emergence of a new race of children is a sign of a new beginning; the global evolution of consciousness that is governed by the universe itself. Everything happens exactly as planned. Time is filling up. Children of the new era, the souls of luminous beings incarnating on Earth have access to dimensions of reality that are inaccessible to the present generation of people. It changes the world beyond recognition. Their way of perceiving and accessing information contained in space will allow them to take control in the future. They overthrow politics and the current monetary system because it will be outdated and unfair to them. These creatures have love for everything that exists and feel it deep within themselves. The entire economic infrastructure will be modernized by them, it will become better for people. Reality will change one hundred and eighty degrees. It is no longer possible to stop this change, although the inept attempts of the elites still cause problems. The alienation of the star children has been noticed for some time by parents, educators, doctors, even psychologists and many other people who have been in constant contact with children for years. They are also completely different than even thirty years ago. The first to notice are the differences in their behavior, but not only. They have a completely different mental and emotional, even spiritual mentality. They have completely different needs, feel differently and create goals for themselves.

They come into the world to show everyone a new direction.

Often, however, because of what they are like, they remain misunderstood. Even parents have a problem with adapting to their needs and accepting a completely different perception of the world because they cannot look at it with their eyes. They try hard to stuff them into the systems and programs that they themselves grew up in. This is a huge mistake."

"I know that from my own experience," said Kal.

"Your mom accepted your uniqueness so quickly. She wasn't blocking you. The blocking is the worst. These children, when they are small, see a lot and feel a lot, they also understand a lot. Much more than anyone could imagine. The problem appears only at the very beginning of their incarnation path, because then not everything is clear to them, they only sense who they are and that they are different than everyone else. They even feel uncomfortable as if they came from a completely different planet. Blockades from loved ones may cause them to close themselves off to their own strength and possibilities. This has happened to many Indigo children who are just now going through their awakening process again. That is why it is so important to show humanity the direction to a better future. They need love and acceptance of their innate gifts that many may find unacceptable. Knowledge about them is important so that they can develop their potential without blockages and with full support and perform the task with which they came to Earth."

"What kind of beings are usually star children?" I questioned.

"They are various beings. They come from different planets, dimensions, and spaces. The average humans usually come from lower solar dimensions, that is, from the third or fourth. Indigo children come from the fifth, whereas Crystal children come from the sixth and above. Both Indigo and Crystal children are incredibly sensitive, they possess numerous psychic abilities. They have important goals to fulfill on Earth — different for each of the group — that they achieve via completely different means and abilities."

"First, there were Indigo children, right?" I asked a

question.

"Yes, Smaisi. They incarnated first. The main wave of their birth fell in the seventies and eighties of the last century. Their difference was visible right at birth, because they had so-called adult eyes. They knew how to fix their eyes on one point very early on. It clearly felt when they were looking at someone. As they grew older, the Indigo children grew up more and more difficult. They caused problems, they rioted. Their difference was very palpable. After the year nineteen ninety-two, their birth number multiplied, and since then more and more have been born into the world. Indigo children are defined as having silver rays. These rays are responsible for amazing intuition and feeling, for removing blockages and standing out above programs. Thanks to them, children are open to deep wisdom and soak up the self from their surroundings as much as they can. They also have special abilities. Their special gift is the ability to heal nature and the Earth. The awareness of Indigo Children opens them to higher dimensions to the crystal level."

"What do you want to say?" I completely didn't understand, what might have Yriah meant. For the first time I heard a term describing the level of consciousness as a crystal.

"Let me explain. The crystal consciousness starts on the seventh level and its full opening takes place on the ninth level. Indigo children, when reaching that level, have access to the galactic consciousness and can connect to golden rays that offer them getting to the universal consciousness. The "time" of Indigo Children comes in three decades — from the seventies to two thousand when on Earth there slowly started to appear Crystal Children."

"Why were those children called this way? Indygo..." Kal asked further.

"The name comes from their light violet Aura color. For comparison — for the majority of people the color of their Aura is yellow or green. Indigo Children know more than their peers and their parents.

The color of their aura is also closely related to the third eye chakra which, as you know, is responsible for clairvoyance as well as the perception and feeling of energy. Children with a purple aura are distinguished by their unique temperament. Their goal is to destroy old systems to make room for new ones. They perfectly feel dishonesty and untruth. It's hard to lie to them because they intuitively sense the deception. The same is true of manipulation which they rarely succumb to. Even if they wanted to, they would not be able to submit to some things, which is not in line with their feelings and beliefs. They are much more demanding — both to themselves and to others — and therefore they often cause conflicts as they are staunchly defending their rights and reasons. Despite much better developed spirituality, they tend to get angry and even brutal, which results from their internal disagreement with a given situation. Indigo children can be recognized by their many characteristic behaviors and psychological characteristics. However, no one has yet been able to reliably document this. Failure to correctly identify Indigo Children may result in their environment ignoring their differences and cause blockages and frustration in their minds. And yet they came into this world to change it for the better. If the parents of the Indigo Children were aware of their origins and changed their approach, their mental balance would be maintained and possibly today as a humanity living in a slightly better world."

"What else distinguishes them?" Kal was digging, although I had no idea why.

"Hmm... Let me think. They have huge problems with adaptation. They're very impatient. They don't like waiting. They want to sort everything out now. Waiting in a queue is a real tragedy for them. They can have problems with concentration which translates into performance at school. Moreover, they do not accept top-down imposed patterns and authorities. It often happens that they are rejected due to their individual approach to everything. Nobody sees and understands the world the way they do. They also have a strong will. They are extremely curious about the world, especially if a young soul takes on the body. They are also said to possess royal dignity which is visible in their behavior. They subconsciously sense the purpose of their life and have a high self-esteem. They are distinguished by a special intuition, they are very empathetic. Their advantage is high emotional intelligence. Some of the Indigo Children have the ability to use extrasensory perception."

"This royal dignity definitely reminds me of something. " I looked at Kal and we both burst out laughing.

"Yes, it is the positive value of the Indigo children, but at times it is also an obstacle. They believe that they deserve to be on Earth. They are surprised when someone questions this fact and they don't hide that. They often tell their parents who they are and whether the parents believe it or not is a completely different matter. Indigo likes creativity and creations. They hate blindly following programs and imposed standards. They always find their own way of doing something, often better than the generally known. When there are no other Indigo children in the environment, they often feel different and then turn inward, which may result in the conclusion that their behavior is antisocial. School science is ignored by them, which you can perfectly notice in yourself, because they internally feel how many lies and manipulations are slipping through the children's minds and are coded in them. Indigo children do not want to submit to it, which repeatedly leads to problems, it is not easy to make them feel guilty until they feel that they are actually at fault. So this method of bringing up completely fails in their case. Unlike many others, these children always say what they want. They are not ashamed of their needs and dreams. It can be said that these wonderful children are a completely different species of man. Highly talented and empathetic. Their IQ most often oscillates around one hundred and thirty — this is the level of intelligence found in one in ten thousand people. At the age of three to four, they can already master computer skills if they are able to do so. They have a gift for rapidly processing strictly technical information in their minds, and therefore will make a significant contribution to technological advances in the decades to come. There is nothing impossible for them, especially since many of them already remember who they are and where they come from. Just like you. Thanks to them, the era will come in which they will show others how to work more efficiently with their mind than with their hands."

"Wow! They have really many interesting and unique characteristics!" Kal exclaimed.

"That's true. However, many of these traits haven't made it easier for them to live in society up till now. The great amounts of creative energy pushing the Indigo children to act constantly have been perceived from outside as something strange. Their mobility and hyperactivity, as well as very quick and skillful transfer of their focus into various fields contributed to the diagnosis of various disorders. Starting from ADD, that is. the syndrome of concentration disorders, to ADHD, which I don't need to explain. This only confirms how many Indigo Children are among us. Unfortunately, incorrect diagnoses led to the fact that these children were completely unnecessarily stuffed with many drugs which — apart from silence and peace for their parents — served as a bonus to lull all the gifts and opportunities that these children had at their disposal. They began to forget and the realization of the mission of their soul was relegated to the background. Many are waking up only now. As information about Indigo Children began to spread on the Internet, it makes it easier for these adults to re-identify. Many books have been written about them, even films have been made. The knowledge of their existence begins to spread, which has even contributed to the creation of special schools aimed at developing the abilities of these children instead of blocking them. So everything is going in the right direction here, and let's hope that the past and future generations of the Indigo Children will have a much easier time finding themselves in this space and at this time and their mission will be fulfilled as planned."

"Do these children have any assistance in the higher realms?" I asked. I remembered how Yriah had said that she supported her incarnations at this time and she helped them on their path.

"Of course. Everyone has spiritual guidance. However, not

228

everyone gets it at the same time. It depends on their mission and the awakening stage they are in. So they probably have more or completely different abilities."

"Will you tell us about them too?"

"That was my plan. And you're right, Smaisi, there's definitely less being spoken of Crystal Children. It's linked to the fact that they started incarnation on Earth much later. After 2000."

"There's a lot said about Indigo Children indeed, but when I was searching on time there was much less information about Crystal Children. And from what you've already told us, they're from higher dimensions."

"Yes. The generation of Crystal Children is born with golden rays. These children most often incarnate on Earth from the sixth dimension and very quickly manage to ascend to higher levels up to the ninth. For them, however, this is not the end of the journey. They move rapidly back to the thirteenth dimension where they connect with the consciousness of existence. Alternatively, they can be called universal consciousness. Most of these babies keep golden rays and magenta rays. If we were to develop the name of crystal children, we could say that they are a rainbow crystal because in their aura you can see all the colors of the rainbow. Right after birth, they seem to be attached to the thirteenth dimension. It is thanks to this that they very quickly open up to their abilities and possibilities and begin to fulfill their mission early."

"So you can say that they wake up with full awareness of their powers and the ability to use them much faster than the Indigo Children, right?" I asked to be sure, thinking these were the only differences.

"Yes, Smaisi. That's true. They're ascending quicker and are much more conscious and aware of who they are, practically from their birth."

"What does it mean their aura is rainbow?" Kal interjected, which surprised me because his question sounded as if he had never seen a rainbow before.

"Their beautiful subtle bodies look like crystals. This crystal will break the light into seven or eight rays, creating a rainbow. In their body, all the chakras are already properly balanced. They come to Earth ready for the upcoming changes — perfectly prepared for them. They are filled with full harmony of light. The golden rays come directly from their eighth chakra which is fully developed with them. In the aura you can see the colors gold, orange, yellow, ruby, magenta, blue ... You could keep enumerating them. Hence it is said that their aura is a rainbow. But gold is definitely predominant."

"They must be wonderful souls," Kal said thoughtfully but I felt that he was wondering if he was an Indigo or Crystal Child.

Up to then, we had known ourselves as star children. This meant to us that Indigo and Crystal Children were as if two types of the same name that we took on to determine souls that possess special tasks to accomplish here on Earth.

"You're right, Kal. They are wonderful just like any other soul that you need to remember as I remind you now. Their uniqueness is based on the fact that these souls have already surpassed all possible dimensions and are timeless. They have a very strong connection with energy and etheric light. The crystal, when exposed to light, shimmers with rainbow colors, just like the aura of these children. This is where their name comes from.

"Aura colors are of huge importance and they give character to a person, right?" I asked. I was aware that I was weaving in a completely different thread to the topic, but since the rainbow has been mentioned, why not find out more by the way...

"Of course, they are. However, you must know that the aura of a human, depending on the stage of the journey, can be shifting even during one incarnation on Earth. Then, it indicates the spiritual processes that take place in a given person. You can also have an aura in several colors. Everyone is unique. But there are certain values assigned to the different colors of the aura. And, certainly, in accordance with Smaisi's cunning plan" — she glanced at me, amused — "I can shortly describe them."

"I would appreciate it," I added, slightly apologizing.

"The red-gold color in a person's aura is a symbol of the

fact that they've achieved a spiritual union, a union with the soul. The golden color itself symbolizes many very desirable qualities, which are deep faith, incredible wisdom, achievement of the highest truths and filling with the highest cosmic love. It is also a symbol of glory. When we add ruby to gold, we will be able to read divine wisdom, rebirth and all-embracing peace in a given being. Such an aura and its rays raise to higher levels of consciousness. The next color is magenta. People with such aura have the ability to heal energy both by transmitting it as well as praying and affirming to the person in need. The orange color of the aura is responsible for wisdom and great ambition. People with such aura often make great careers. When someone has an aura of yellow color — we say about them that they're filled with joy and optimism towards everything that surrounds them — every day they discover life again, they give themselves a blank sheet at a time and look at the world a bit like through pink glasses. Optimism somehow forces positive thoughts and creations, which makes people with this aura usually happy as it returns to them with energy and manifests itself in matter. If we add green rays to the yellow color, we get a person with the powers of a healer. When the green that comes in it will be more of an olive tint, we can say that the person has inborn wisdom. The blue color of the aura also informs about the healing abilities, but its owner also has a lot of peace and often falls into a quiet state. In addition, they're characterized by communication and media skills. Blue also symbolizes the hope that this person always has within. When you see the turquoise color in the aura, it will signify awakening. Violet color adds to awakening the knowledge of the existence of the universe. When the aura is dark purple, it means great honor and truth from the soul level. The best aura, however, that defines a being that is really far on its way of awakening is the white aura. It signifies a great unwavering faith which no one can undermine because faith has its roots in the inner truth of the being. They just know. This aura also symbolizes the reality and the perfection that a given person has achieved on their journey — this is the level of total enlightenment. Such a person is usually happy and searches for the truth all the time because they know that knowledge is so vast that they will never be able to fully comprehend it. This is what drives them."

"It's incredible how much we can learn about a person based on their color of aura" I summed up.

Kal was sitting calmly, I felt that it didn't impress him that much.

"You are White, Smaisi," he said, "White and luminous like a snowflake in the sunlight. Beautiful," he added.

"He's right," Yriah replied.

"And what color is mine?" Kal asked. Clearly, he never managed to see it.

"Yours is white as well," Yriah replied which triggered in him enormous happiness that in a second appeared on his face,"Would you let me come back to the subject of Crystal Children? Of course, if you want to learn more about them."

"Yes!" I almost shouted out.

"I didn't dare to doubt," Yriah laughed out and returned to the story about children with rainbow rays, "Crystal Beings are characterised also by their peculiar looks. They have beautiful big eyes with a deep look. It can be even said it's hypnotizing. In their eyes, one can see huge wisdom that is significantly beyond physical age — especially in young children. Crystals have a completely different temperament than Indigo. Their inner being radiates with peace and harmony. They are happy and understanding towards others. They are filled with pure love for all that exists. You could say they are perfect in many ways. That is why they are to contribute to many changes and introduce humanity into a new era of rapid technological development and at the same time show how to live in happiness and harmony. They are the seeds of the change that the creator sent to Earth at this time. They are on fire for a completely new reality. The Crystal Children were sent to show humankind the path of their evolution in the only right and right direction. To a world based not on fear but on love and trust. However, what is important — we distinguish two groups of crystal creatures."

"What do you mean by that?" I questioned.

"Children that were born as Indigo, while transforming into the subtle body, they change into crystal. It happens so when their consciousness expands and the transformation of body into luminous body is ended."

"So Indigo Children have a possibility to get into a higher level" Kal pointed out.

"Yes. Every being can do that. But it's the easiest for Indigo Children. In the second example we have children who were born on Earth as crystal beings. They have inside themselves cosmic high vibrations and their bodies are ready for receiving high frequencies of light. These children wake up very suddenly in their due time. More than once, it's a drastic transformation. Then, it's almost immediate that they can recognize their identity. That's when their mission starts here. Crystal Children, from the moment they're born, have the ability to draw the attention of others and it's not only connected to their hypnotizing and wise look. They're like a magnet that attracts. These are their Hugh vibrations that work on others in this way. It's their innocence and love they're filled with. They have a gift of seeing auras and their own clear aura works as a shield that allows them to dwell just for a moment in another world. These children develop faster but they are shy by nature. And that's how they stay for the rest of their lives although they get in contact quite easily with others. They're highly sensitive to any manipulations and fraud. Even adults find it difficult to manipulate them. They detect all lies and insincerity with the speed of light. Dishonesty offends them, therefore they are always truthful themselves. A very characteristic feature of crystal creatures is their telepathic abilities. Their communication is very well developed at this level. They specify their thoughts very quickly and communicate them both verbally and nonverbally. They perceive sounds completely differently. This is one of the reasons why Crystal Children are often diagnosed with autism. They start speaking late, because they do not see the reasons for that if their thoughts are passed on in a different way and their needs are met. Their acute hearing makes them react differently to background noises. They also have a philosophical sense and many gifts which the universe has given them and which they can use to their fullest. They are in contact with nature and exchange energies with trees, shrubs and the earth. They see the future because they have access to information held in space. They can heal others. Star Children were born into the world at almost every era, but this happened very rarely. But now comes the time when almost all babies will be born as Indigo or Crystalline. Crystal children are unique and from the very beginning parents learn to communicate at the level of the mind, they subconsciously feel that delay in speech is not a bad thing. Very often, children also use sign language created only for their own purposes and use numerous sounds. Incomprehensible communication resulting from their uniqueness and is often diagnosed as autism. However, these children are not autistic. Since the Crystal Babies waited for the coming of the Crystal Children, the number of diagnoses for autism has increased dramatically, but most of them are simply wrong. We talk about autism when there is an error in chromosomal dysfusion. Otherwise, it is simply a lack of understanding of the differences between these beings and the needless classification of them as dysfunctional or even underdeveloped."

"How to distinguish that without proper knowledge about it? I think that in this matter the inaccurate doctor's diagnosis is not his or her fault but rather the result of lack of knowledge."

"You're right, Smaisi. In the majority of instances, this is the way. The difference between autistic children and Crystal is mainly about the fact that autistic children live in their own reality. They're indifferent to contacting other people and they don't feel the need to communicate. It's not necessary for them. With the Crystalline Children it's the contrary. Their communication is at the highest possible level, unfortunately, for the majority it's misunderstood and unsurpassed. They've got a high sensitivity and kindness which makes them hug sad or unhappy people, sharing their gift of healing. You can't call such behaviour indifference for another individual. If someone analyzes their emotions after meeting with such a child, they will immediately notice the difference. And this, for the external people, a small yet noticeable difference between autistic disorder and exceptional being who is on a completely different level of consciousness and communication."

"Taking into consideration the fact that Indigo Children as well as Crystal Children have come here for a mission, has it been divided into stages? Or was it carried out with the waves that they were descending into incarnations on Earth?" Kal asked.

"In a way, yes. Indigo, thanks to their rebellious nature, had the task of tearing down old structures and breaking false patterns. Crystal ones, on the other hand, indicate the way and direction which humanity should follow. So Indigo breaks apart what is old and Crystal are building what's new on completely new foundations. These Star Children came to Earth with weapons and gifts that enabled them to complete their tasks. As I have already told you, they are creatively gifted in many fields, nothing is impossible for them. They share their gifts with others and it is only up to people whether they decide to use these gifts and awaken their own consciousness, stand by their side and support these missions. To make you aware of how numerous these few Star Warriors came to Earth, I will say that today as many as seventy percent of babies born are Starseeds. Soon the proportion will increase to ninety percent and nothing will be able to stop these changes. The Earth will be filled with the love of the creatures living on it. Crystal Children have amazed scientists for a decade. There are many documented cases where they were not afraid to show their abilities. This phenomenon will become more frequent over time."

"People are unaware of how many starseeds are currently on the planet. What a variety of beautiful luminous beings there is," I concluded. I thought Yriah had finished her lecture, but she decided to answer me.

"All beings descended on the same conditions, passing through the curtain of oblivion. Few realize that almost everyone comes from a different planetary system, from a different star that can call its home and with a completely different level of consciousness. Each of these creatures has an individual mission on Earth. Due to the fact that the cosmic levels from which the Star Children come have different radiation and cosmic vibrations, we can speak of cleaner and undisturbed energies that allow these children to wake up faster. The astral plane will be closest to the earth level, just above it. It's called the fourth dimension. Every being that incarnate on Earth carries within itself exactly the vibrations from which it came, is almost a dimensional part of itself. This can be compared to the multitude of races and cultures around the world. So the Star Children carry within them the seed of the dimension from which they come and flourish to that level during incarnation."

"You said before there were coming to Earth such beings yet less frequently," Kal interrupted, wanting to get the continuation of this thread.

"You're right. They were a very highly advanced symbiote. Each time they came on a special mission. They are people who served the planet with great commitment. We are now living in an epoch in which cosmic rays have decreased. From the planet Alcione, located in the Pleiades system, the energy of a completely different magnetic field reaches Earth, the strongest one from space and cosmos. This will bring about many changes and open the door to a new golden age for humankind. It will be a flowering of beauty and love. However, you cannot just embed this event. Diamond and gold are beautiful, but they also need to be polished and prepared to become such. The same will happen on Earth. Cleansing to create something new often means burning out in the fire of what was bad. The uplift of humanity and the planet will require this purification. And that is why many higher dimensional beings will appear on Earth to safely guide humanity through this purification. Just knowing about the processes that exist and which will follow one another can limit the general chaos which results in the loss of millions of human lives. However, they know it themselves, but that's not all. These beings also carry a message and with their mere presence they increase the vibrations of space and those around them. The higher dimension a given creature comes from, the more devoted it is to its mission and work for humanity.

It is filled with unconditional love and willingness to help other people. Due to the fact that these beings will come together, more and more will now seek each other and unite the vibrations that are being directed. They only want to help others in the process of transition and transformation so essential for the entire universe."

"Are there as many women as men?" I asked automatically.

"It can be said that sixty five percent are women that symbolizes the inner energy and the rest thirty five percent are men, creating the shield with the outer energy."

"Can they be noticed in the crowd? Can they be distinguished somehow?

"Hmm… Very often they have cat eyes with a changeable color—it's difficult to state if they're grey, green or blue. These are people with huge hearts. As one said: "you will recognize them by their deeds". They

They are sensitive to changes in the electromagnetic field, to light, sounds and smell. What is interesting, their body temperature is slightly lower. They are more susceptible to chronic diseases because they are in vibrations that are far from their own, though that will change now. They are often born with birthmarks. They have a gift for healing themselves. They have a great sense of truth, know and feel that they do not come from this planet and can connect energetically with their native source. They often get depressed, which is associated with a hormonal imbalance in their bodies. Most have had mystical experiences since childhood — the ability to be telepathic and to be attracted to thoughts even from far distances. They are happy and full of humor. They like colors and are happy to wear colorful clothes. They love nature and animals that are drawn to them, sensing their love for all existence. They have many abilities that I have already described to you. Their ability to look to the future with prophetic dreams and visions is almost the order of the day. They also have healing skills, but do not necessarily realize they are using them. They love gemstones and often subconsciously read the meaning of certain symbols. These creatures, often coming from distant galaxies, came to Earth of their own free will. Very often their private life is not important for them as they have already lived through a whole lot of them and they focus on bringing light and love to the Earth that will help to raise the planet and humanity. They know their mission is to awaken the awareness of others, and they feel it. They are like teachers who erase what is old and bad, open the way to a better tomorrow, creating an ideology that is compatible and best for all existence. These beings are here to help people. People can also help them by opening themselves up to the light and energy of awakening and accompanying them on this journey."

"Am I a Crystal Child?" Kal couldn't help it. Throughout the lecture he was trying to fit the features of both Crystal and Indigo Children. It seems that it didn't go well so he decided to ask Yriah a direct question.

"Yes, Kal. You're a Crystal Child." Yriah looked at me and added, "and you are first," having said that she suddenly disappeared and left me with my mouth full open.

"Uhm, what was it all about this " first one? "Kal asked.

"I have no idea, I can hear it for the second time but every time someone cuts off and I'm not able to get anything more."

There's time for everything. I heard in my head Yriah's voice and everything faded away.

Chapter 12

By judging or name-calling anything you lose the possibility to see what it really is..."

Damian Buczniewicz

The evidence of existence of other races on planet Earth

I woke up exceptionally rested. I laid in bed for a bit longer, dwelling on various topics. Recently there were many of them swirling in my head. We had a few days off with Kal from messages so that we could integrate them all.

Recently we were receiving completely different messages. For the last few days, Schumann Resonance was going crazy. By saying: crazy, I wasn't exaggerating. Taking into consideration the regular frequency of eight hertz, the last few days broke the record, showing five hundred and eight hundred hertz respectively. These were huge energies and these waves had a direct influence on Gaia. Only in the last week there were forty volcano eruptions in the whole world, with earthquakes listed every now and then in many parts of the world, all of them had a strength of more than six on the Richter scale. They were not, therefore, harmless quakes. Many people have been evicted. As if that was not enough, the more and more frequent outbursts on the Sun have caused geomagnetic storms on Earth with the strength of G3, making it possible to see the auroras in many places in the world, not only at the poles.

The changes were visible to the naked eye, especially for those who knew what to look at and what to monitor. Most of society, however, lived in blissful ignorance. Of course, television did not make it easier. Despite so many natural disasters, from the metal poodle, it was possible to learn almost nothing about it. Silence. Swept under the carpet as always when something could cause people any interest in the ongoing processes. It is as if we suddenly live on another planet where there is peace and each day is similar to the previous one.

All climate change events were closely followed by Daddy. Not only that, he even drew a map of volcanic eruptions and places where the quake had occurred. It worried me a bit. He did it with such precision as if he was afraid of something. On the other hand, since the energies influenced people, it was not possible for the Earth not to feel them on itself. All the time I remembered that we are in the process of its polarity reversal. All the people who can be called awake have been following the information related to the great day of December 21st, although as we have already mentioned, it was not supposed to be something big that would be noticed by everyone. I was hoping that at least some of those still sleeping would start to perceive more thanks to the energies of awakening.

Last week was terrible. In the mornings, school and its manipulations, and in the afternoons, writing. Then Kal came. My book, like Kal's notes, swelled more and more. I was pleased with myself, but I was a little worried that there is still so much to describe.

I was glad to finally get some rest and hoped that this weekend would bring us some surprises. I was counting on Semjase to decide to visit us again. We hadn't seen her for a long time.

I went downstairs and I wasn't surprised that Kal was already sitting at the kitchen table, having a discussion with Mommy.

"Hello sleepyhead," he said.

"Who's sleepyhead?" I was surprised.

"And have you looked at the clock?" he asked and only then did I realize that I hadn't checked the time. My gaze drifted to the kitchen clock which showed a quarter past ten.

"Uuu… I actually did sleep a bit" I blushed.

241

"Apparently your body needed it" Mommy interjected.

"I slept very well I must say, I feel so brisk."

"What are you up to today?" Mommy asked.

We didn't plan anything special for this weekend. Recently we hadn't made plans for the next few days. We were living in the moment and that's what we were focusing on.

"How about a walk to the park or a shopping mall? It's time for Christmas shopping" Kal suggested.

It completely got out of my head that I need to have a present for someone other than my parents.

"OK, we can do that," I replied. I started to wonder if we went together I would manage to hide what I got for him.

"Anyway you won't be able to hide it from me" he replied loudly to my thoughts.

"That's true. Do you know what you want to receive?" I asked.

"I think that when you find it, you'll know," he only replied and started to eat his fruits.

We spent a few hours in the shopping mall, yet I didn't manage to find anything that would be a suitable present for Kal so I returned home with my hands empty. I decided that I still had a lot of time and I would definitely manage to buy something unique for Kal. Kal bought a few gifts, mainly for his mom. At least he made use of the trip to the mall.

We spent the afternoon at home. Freezy weather and minus temperatures were not favorable to have long walks. Each of us again closed up in the worlds of our earthly tasks. I was writing and Kal was still creating his album. The evening came so quickly that we didn't have time to figure it out. Kal returned home and I, following Mommy's recommendation, decided to take a longer bath with the addition of sea salt to support the body in the processes of intensive cleansing that was now taking place, I poured water into the bathtub and lay down comfortably, putting a towel under my head. The warmth of the water soothed me and made me feel sleepier. I also felt the influence of sea salt. The energy passed through my body to release everything that was in my body. After a good thirty minutes, I looked like an old grandma and decided that it would be enough to get wet. I sat down in front of the computer, trying to finish the thread that I started earlier, but my eyelids drooped, the fatigue was stronger than the willingness to work. I went to bed with renewed hope that that day we would meet Semjase and take us somewhere with her.

I woke up and looked around. I was standing in the desert and right behind me there were pyramids. Kal appeared next to me after a few seconds.

"We'll learn some history, right?" he asked, glad that there would be a trip.

"Very possible" I replied because I remembered how Semjase told us about the pyramids. Perhaps there was to be a continuation of this thread.

"Welcome, " he heard her voice and soon after she stood in front of us.

We were surprised that she was wearing very earthly clothes. She was wearing jeans and a t-shirt. This even suited her. Anyway, how they say it, a good-looking person looks good in everything.

"Thank you, Smaisi," she replied to my thoughts.

"You're welcome."

"Today I would like to take you on a journey in search of evidence of the existence of ancient beings on planet Earth. They left behind much, but little has been discovered by humans. So we're going to dig out some secrets today that will have a chance to open people's eyes a little more."

"Wonderful," I was happy.

Kal was happy as well. He loved historical facts, especially those that hadn't been discovered yet. I needed to admit that we recently had learnt a lot about the future, we were missing the insights into the past.

"Okay, then let's get started. Not everything that previous civilizations have left behind is visible to a human. Currently, as you know, the seventh generation of humanity lives on the surface. The previous generations have left a lot behind. Their traces are ubiquitous. One of the greatest remnants of the generations of that time are the great networks of underground tunnels stretching all over the world. They are also located near Europe. But that's not all. Even beneath the ocean floor there are huge bases and caves connected by tunnels to those below the land. Currently, they form a network of underground highways that expand and connect the whole world. The tunnels are guarded and few people know about them and only a few have access. The tunnels beneath America's surface are so vast that you could really say they are a subsurface highway. They can be driven on vehicles with electric motors, but only for limited distances. There are other ways to travel fast and far. Underground there is a network of transport tubes, known to a few as the Sub-Global System. From these tubes, transporters are launched, which, using magnetic levitation and the vacuum method, reach incredible speeds. They can be compared to trains on the surface, with the difference that underground trains run faster than the speed of sound."

"How can you get into these tunnels?" Kal asked a question.

I could see him planning a tour there in his mind.

"Basically, every state of the USA has an entrance there. Also, the military bases have their own entrances. In New Mexico and Arizona there is the greatest amount of places of access. Then, there's California, Montana, Idaho, and Colorado. Wyoming has a road that leads directly to the underground highway but it is not being used currently. This could be quite quickly changed though if such a decision was made. The road requires only some modernization that is necessary for safe traveling."

"Can you tell us exactly where this road is located?"

"Why? Are you going to travel there, Kal?" Semjase asked and laughed out, "I can take you there even now, I don't believe that it was necessary though. Underground tunnels are located everywhere. Of course, I'll tell you," she said to Kal and he immediately cheered up, "The road is located near Brooks Lake. The underground installations that lead to the tunnels are located in the Wasatch Range area, Great Salt Lake, and Lake Powell areas as well. The following ones are by Dark Canyon and Dugway Proving Ground. They're located in many places in fact, creating an

244

underground transportation system called Archuleta. This system connects with the roads that lead to Mount Shasta, located in North Carolina."

"Telos," I said.

"Exactly. They lead to Telos. The dwellers of Telos use this Web of tunnels for transportation as well."

"How is it possible that humans haven't found these entrances?"

"Some of them have been discovered. But as you know, everything is immediately swept under the carpet and the explorers get blackmailed. The entrances are well hidden, even camouflaged. You could say that they look like sand quarries. Often these are entrances to old mines where you are not allowed to enter for safety reasons. There is also a great tunnel between the Euphrates and the Tigris. It used to be the seat of a space colony that founded its civilization there. At the end of this tunnel is Kuwait. It is also a portal used to manipulate the human race. In many places on Earth there are numerous excavations and artifacts that clearly suggest that other civilizations lived on it, sometimes much more developed than the present human population. These numerous proofs are, as I have already mentioned, carefully guarded not only by other nations and beings, but also by the Earth itself and time. Global disasters have contributed to the fact that under the post-flood soil cover in some places there are still ancient remnants of civilization, up to seven kilometers underground. So you can see for yourself that finding and unearthing some of them is almost a miracle. And there is a lot of it — including the technology of stellar civilizations that could revolutionize the world of that time. Funnily enough, most of the finds that were obviously publicly informed are about creatures and animals treated as primitive. Dinosaurs and other related excavations have been documented largely because they concerned the past of reptilian civilization. Another reason was that the population of dinosaurs was so huge and so scattered around the world that numerous remains could not be effectively hidden. People would sooner or later dig into the next ones. All material remains are evidence of the existence of only races and species that inhabited the Earth on this particular level. But what about everything that is still not visible to people? Even the elite believe in false light and serve it, can do almost anything for it. It is also a manipulation directed at the elites, which often do not realize that they have fallen into their own trap. All the remaining knowledge about the multidimensional space is completely blocked even though even in the Bible there are references to the existence of higher dimensional etheric beings. Hiding ancient evidence at some stage was no longer enough for the elites as people's level of consciousness began to increase. Humanity succumbed to the energies of awakening. The elite knew it would happen. So they were forced to introduce other measures for human control. They have the capabilities and technologies to literally invade the human mind and hack it. They use bioelectronics for this, introducing viral mutations into them that alter DNA. A lot of interference on their part is also a programmable matter that humanity does not know even though it is surrounded by them. Many innovative things that they allow to introduce are aimed at further control of people at all levels of their existence. However, I will tell you about this exactly another time."

"When?" Kal asked a question.

"Sooner than later. Let's stick to the subject matter today."

"Okay, then" he replied and focused on the main thread of our meeting again.

"Before we move to the following evidence, I would like to point out to you that at this moment in time there are two different thought currents on Earth that are fighting with each other. These two collective thought forms have a huge power. It's a war — in which stand up people whose consciousness is waking up more and more and those who remain faithful to the system and its manipulations. Unfortunately, the fight isn't entirely even. The only weapon that they have at their disposal is their own consciousness and strength of spirit. The war is currently taking place all over the world, it's visible not only in private fields but also public and every human is its link. Now it depends on the humans who will win.

Although there are powerful light forces and our galactic brothers from many planets and stars on our side, humans need to end this. None will resolve the problems of humanity for them. A huge internal fight will be conducted by people who work in the field of medicine, law, education, and those who are closely connected with religion, ecology, and finances. They as the first will face the choice between the programmed, yet well known safety, and innovative ideals, which will be intuitively closer to them. Not easy experiences will teach everyone that it is worth distinguishing the voice of the heart and intuition from the engrossed in speculations and chaos mind. Thanks to this, humans will start to control fear. They will become masters at that. Everything that will be taking place simultaneously with those events, will contribute to their self-confidence and will dissolve their fear. Fear that is different every time — of health, life, money. Everything will be solved and humans will be free. The final and, at the same time, the last nail in the coffin of the elite will be the great transformation of human DNA that will open human chakras to the full spectrum of light and thus — mass awakening of consciousness around the globe. However, these changes will not be a pleasant process for everyone. If the new frequencies and vibrations meet the opposite polarity, the effect of the inflow of this energy may be similar to an attempt to transmit through a thin rusty wire a large amount of high voltage current. People with low vibration and a cold heart may feel this in their bodies as if they have blown fuses. These changes and high energy will have a debilitating effect on the body.

You will be able to observe the bursts of energy as well as its complete release. All ailments will be a signal that the body is resisting these energies. Then it is best to transform and enter the heart field focusing on positive visions of the future. It is not advisable to go into fear of your health, because these symptoms are nothing but symptoms of transformation. Creating warmth in love and happiness will be the best medicine for people. Well... Now we can come back to the topic."

I could feel that Semjase interjected that for a reason. More and more I could feel weird imbalances in my body. Perhaps it was a suggestion not only for humanity but also for myself.

"I've heard a term: forbidden archaeology. Something tells me that a lot of evidence is there," Kal suddenly threw in, wanting to direct Semjase into the right topic. As always he only confirmed how impatient both of us were.

"Yes. It's a huge void filled to the rim with secret discoveries. There are documents concerning the most shocking excavations and discovered constructions. Among them, Nephilim Skeletons. After close examination of a few remains, it's been stated that there are unknown fibers in the bones of these beings that give strength to the bones. I'm referring here to the discovery of Lloyd Pye, who named one of the skulls the Star Child. The skulls he studied, and this one in particular, had features that clearly indicated advanced genetic engineering. There are many such discoveries in the world of forbidden archaeology."

"Why have you taken us here? " I asked suddenly, looking around again.

"Giza is one of the extraordinary places. It's special."

"Why?" I questioned.

"It just so happens that this Egyptian city is the chakra of the Earth. It is here that terrestrial and cosmic energies accumulate. From this city, there come out beams of radiation which form the energy system of the entire Earth. These energies, however, go much further. They find their way to the identical shape of the star system above the pyramids. The Great Pyramid was built two and a half thousand years before our era. It was then that Orion was at its lowest point with respect to the Earth. The next points of cosmic connection arose during the construction of the remaining pyramids about eleven thousand seven hundred years before our era. During the southern climax of Sirius that was twelve thousand two hundred and eighty years before our era, there was the deployment of buildings in Giza. The creation of a horizontal corridor leading from the Queen's Chamber was dictated by the positioning of the Vega or the polar star at its northern culmination, which fell on twelve thousand and seventy years BC. At that time, underground corridors were created in Giza in the

Khufu pyramid, known as the Great Pyramid or the Cheops pyramid, and in the Broken Pyramid of Snorf located in Dahshur."

"So the pyramids are a reflection of the arrangement of the stars?" I asked.

"Yes, exactly. They were created in the most prominent moments. And that's not all. Imagine that the river Nile overlaps the Milky Way and the three pyramids of Giza are positioned towards one another in the same way as the Orion Belt stars. What's more, the angle and the inclination of the pyramids in relation to the river accurately reflect the constellation of Orion stars in relation to the Milky Way. Giza is therefore a terrestrial star map and the site of many portals."

"That's incredible," Kal summed up Semjase's confessions,"Is it the end of the terrestrial star map?"

"Of course, not. Not far from Giza, in the cities of Abu Rawash and Zawiyet-el-Aryan there are located two pyramids that were built at the times of the fourth dynasty. Their localization reflects the places of two Orion stars. The whole terrain with the River Nile creates a reconstruction map of the sky.

Part of this map also includes another two pyramids erected by Pharaoh Snofru, who was the father of Cheops, and they are located in the city of Dahshur. These pyramids reflect the constellation of Taurus. During the fifth dynasty, numerous smaller pyramids were built to complement the star map. It should come as no surprise that the Ancients had better technology than the present. The statue of the Sphinx itself is an expression of the fact that they were advanced. Despite the passage of time and the heavy rainfall that occurred in this area about five thousand years before our era, the Sphinx is still quite well held. It was carved in the rough bedrock. It also has a separate story."

"Will you tell us?" Kal asked further.

"Sure. Scientists say that their calculations show that the Sphinx was created around two and a half thousand years before our era. The truth, however, is somewhat different. The Sphinx now looks completely different than it originally did. In the past, his head was larger, but numerous modifications were made by many pharaohs, which finally led to a distortion of its proportions and current appearance. The Sphinx is considered a Leo, which is also associated with the constellation of stars. On the day of the vernal equinox, ten and a half thousand years BC, the Sphinx's gaze was perfectly focused on its counterpart in space, the constellation Leo. This, then, is the true date of the Sphinx. So as you can see, it is much older than you think. In antiquity, great buildings were erected according to the alignment of specific stars in the sky. Let us remember, however, that what we see is only a small fraction of the entire universe. The purpose of the ancients was not to map the sky, but to reflect the energy signature of a place. These structures are nothing more than a reflection of the position of the pyramids in relation to the stars. They are energetic vibrational reflections of their natural location. The knowledge of the ancients exceeds the wildest expectations and surpasses all technologies known to people at these times."

"That's very interesting. Even though it's not possible to hide the pyramids and they're the obvious evidence that the ancient civilizations had highly advanced technology, it's still stubbornly claimed that it was otherwise. Some people still believe that humans carried these stones one after another" Kal interjected.

"I must admit that it's really funny. Oh well. The manipulations of the mind go deep. To me, it's more unbelievable that humans build the pyramids with their own strength rather than using technology that would help them. Oh, but everyone needs to analyze this in their own minds and feel where the truth is. Another thing is that not many people actually know what is inside the pyramids, the precision with which they were built and the existence of substructures inside them. And this means that they can't rationally approach the thesis that suggests that the pyramids were built with naked hands and with the use of primitive tools."

"Humans have a lot to reveal," Kal summed up.

"It's true. Many things are not visible to them even though the evidence is in front of their eyes."

"You have something in particular on your mind, right?" I inquired, feeling the second bottom in this sentence.

"Surely, I do. It's Stonehenge and the magnetic field it creates all the time. These stones show radioactivity and this can be tested. They stand in specific places not by accident, more precisely in the center of key circles. They still emit radio waves. The information that the stones show radioactivity is quite important because it completely destroys the knowledge that geologists have about the origin of these megaliths. The fact is that the frequency of the radiation and the radioactivity of these two stone circles vary. Still, scientists will find it bullshit, and the evidence is right in front of them. The great circles in Stonehenge and Avebury are as much as one hundred meters in diameter if we count the surrounding shafts. They also reflect the constellations of Orion's belt. Higher geometry was used to correctly position the stones, which is another proof that primitive civilization could not do it. Most importantly, the Stonehenge stones are only a part of the entire mapping, the rest has been underground for thousands of years."

"So have humans never really checked that?" Kal considered loudly.

"No, and even so, we need to remember that the evidence has always been hidden. And the answer is hidden in Great Britain. Knowing where the Orion Belt is, it's enough to place it in the right scale onto the earthly plane. This will not do any harm to the scientists, instead, it will open their eyes to what Stonehenge stones actually are. The place in which Stonehenge is located, determines the direction of the astronomical Summer Solstice. The stones have been placed on a gold cosmic band, but not only this one as this is where the various star bands are aggregated. Stonehenge also indicates the astronomical time of the Solstice Equinox. The avenue that leads from Heel Stone to Stonehenge is not a road on which monoliths were painstakingly pushed or pulled. Their arrangement is pure mathematics combined with extensive knowledge of geometry, physics and astronomy. Stonehenge was built before the great cataclysms happened, due to which the counters were flooded and the great stone circles were covered with the ground. It was only thanks to erosion that boulders began to emerge from under the surface of time. Their tops point to the north-eastern direction, the same as the golden bands. It says a lot about the cataclysm that came from the Southwest. It happened ten thousand years ago in the Atlantic Ocean, and you know perfectly well what it was. The great trail of Atlantis, due to the cracking of tectonic plates, collapsed suddenly into the ocean. This triggered a powerful tsunami. The waves were one hundred and fifty meters high. They destroyed everything they encountered on their way. All life that existed in Europe at that time was extinct. As the tide passed Europe it did not stop but continued to spread in all directions. It was then that European civilization was completely destroyed. There are, however, stones showing the time of the cataclysm events. Stones located in Poland and many other corners of the world can convey real knowledge to humankind. However, not understanding the mystery of the great stone circles, humanity seeks this knowledge out of place and clings to many contradictory theories."

"I've read about..." Kal began but stopped as if he wasn't sure if he should mention it or not.

"Yes, Kal," Semjase had read his thoughts, "The stone circles are considered to be Earth chakras. Stonehenge as well as other stone circles all over the world are places of ancient wisdom. Many answers about them are hidden in Sanskrit, the oldest hindu writings. It's there that the word chakra is used to describe the stone circles. This word means a circle, a disk, a missile, it may suggest an astronomical circle, or mystical circles and diagrams. It also means, as you already know, energetic cavities in the human's astral-spiritual body. You already know the human chakras and their application, but it is worth knowing that in the case of stone circles this word has a slightly different meaning because they have a completely different function. Stone circles are not, as many suppose, the chakras of the Earth, but only a clue how to find these chakras. Chakra in Sanskrit means a circle and it symbolically refers here to destiny, the circle of life. In Buddhism this is called the wheel of life and death. The word has another meaning, however. Namely: "rolling of the royal wheel of the universal kingdom and justice". When the chakras are closed in the human body, they are small, inconspicuous, because there is no energy flow. When they open, they begin to radiate energy like living fire. This energy spreads out and flows through all the chakras. Each chakra then looks like a small beautiful sun. The energy vibrates in them and spreads to the surrounding area. The Earth chakra is a place of power that manifests itself in the shape of a circle. It is a disk containing codes and ancient knowledge. Chakras have existed since the dawn of time, from the very beginning of human civilization. They are the backbone of human existence, they show who you are."

"Do you want to say that Earth chakras can pass onto us information about ourselves?"

"Exactly, Smaisi. In Stonehenge, to be precise in its constructions and the energy, that is a peculiar frequency of waves—there is a wisdom encoded about the size and origin of each disc."

"What has to be done then to find these pieces of information?" I asked.

"Humans need to research the stones well, locate the disc and give a signal. Thanks to that, the message can be received and your origin and its data activated. The chakras of your body and Earth are always connected, not only with each other but also with everything that surrounds you. This connection, though, has been distorted. The civilizations of Orion created their own connections whose aim is to maintain humanity on a low frequency level. There has been a web created, a certain block, which is used until today. The elites are supported in that by the devices that emit frequencies such as HAARP or electromagnetic technologies. But we'll return to that another time."

"Is it possible to decode the information off the stone circles?" I inquired.

"Of course, but your current science is not capable of grasping that. It's not the result of low intelligence, it's rather because humans hold on tightly to certain theories and hypotheses. They don't look for answers more broadly. That's why they haven't discovered the secrets that Stonehenge and pyramids hold. Only if the backwards theories are rejected and scientists open to the new perspective, suddenly everything will appear so clear, simple and logical. They will be surprised they haven't discovered that earlier. They haven't because they rejected the idea that ancestors could be more technologically advanced than the temporary civilization. And it would be enough to ask a question how these primitive people, as they're considered, could build buildings that were so intelligent, concise and complicated technologically, fully based on science and its laws. How? Only by using technologies and abilities exceeding human imagination. What's more, the ancestors wrote down their knowledge for their descendants, leaving it in Stonehenge and in many other places, but their descendants still can't read them. Here's a nagging question: Are the temporary scientists capable of grasping their ancestors' intelligence and, in fact, confirming that they come from them?"

"But why have all the information and channelings been left on the stones or inside the pyramids? I asked.

"It's connected to the strength of the medium of a given message. Megaliths and stones can survive many of the harshest weather conditions, from flood to fire to glaciation. They can wait to be discovered under a thick layer of earth for thousands of years without being damaged. Clay tablets or books would not survive this. Your ancestors knew exactly what they were doing. These stones were placed in a very intelligent and over logical way that, upon closer reflection, will be understandable to everyone. They're the timeless transmission of astronomical knowledge, but not only. It is mathematics combined with physics and an admixture of mysticism and all that is contained in symbols. If scientists focus on the symbolism of the painting, they will quickly come to the correct conclusions. However, there are pitfalls here as well. They result from the fact that each symbol can be treated both literally and figuratively, it can mean something completely different than what it represents in the image. Therefore, to be able to understand them, a double interpretation of the written symbols is needed. You have to create a logical interpretation of the symbol itself and its relation to what it represents."

"Why is Stonehenge right in Europe?" Kal asked, "I have certain assumptions but..."

"They are right, my boy. The European continent was the cradle of higher civilization culture, which is why it was in Stonehenge that mathematical and geometric knowledge was recorded. And soon, what you can read will completely revolutionize all current scientific views and will confirm that you are the descendants of a lost civilization which has left behind not only numerous legends and myths but also legendary megaliths containing knowledge. Only then will the true history of Europe be discovered and understood. The discoveries of Stonehenge, developed by many scientists whose soul consciousness will be at a high level, will help in this."

"What other evidence has been left for us that we can't see although our vision is so sharp?" I asked and it was only after a moment that I realized that this sentence was very... Very poetical.

"Haha!" Semjase laughed out, "Well, someone here is writing a book. I'm not surprised that your sentences will be getting more and more beautiful, getting into people's hearts and souls, sometimes hidden very deep."

"One better than the other," Kal recapped and we all burst out laughing.

"Let's move to the following evidence before our bellies hurt so much that I will be forced to send you home," Semjase joked and continued her lecture, "Another piece of evidence left behind by ancient civilizations is the Nazca Spider which is a mapping of the constellation Orion. The drawings from Nazca viewed from a bird's eye view resemble animals, plants and geometric shapes. They are symbols of the early Nazca culture. It is the largest astronomy textbook in the world you have been left with. Some of the lines stretching for tens of meters coincide with the orbital motion of the stars, and the huge contours of animals seen from above are nothing but a reflection of the constellations. Orion is presented with the figure of a spider."

"Give us some more," Kal got excited.

"Very well. In northern Italy, the city of Montevecchia, forty kilometers from Milan, there is a mountain range. They are three pyramids hidden under a thick layer of soil and plants. If you look at them you will only see hills, but if you look closely you will see regular precise shapes that the earth would not have formed. The highest of the pyramids is one hundred and fifty meters high. These pyramids were built of stone and are very similar to the Egyptian ones as their angle to Orion's Belt and the inclination itself is perfect. Another example is the stone arrangement located in the mysterious zone 51, which is probably known to all, and it also maps Orion's belt. This system has a triangle base which is surprising because most of the pyramids are placed on a quadrilateral. Besides, the difference — the bases in Nevada are like pyramids. At first, the American government firmly denied the existence of any bases in those areas, but then admitted to one and stated that the pyramid was built for research purposes. It was to be used for weather research and for radar experiments, which was just another cover for the truth that could no longer be kept secret."

"One thing makes me wonder, Semjase, " Kal began and I already knew that would be curious, "Why do the majority of such buildings reflect Orion's Belt. Isn't it weird? There are so many constellations in the sky and they got stuck on this one. Can you explain this to us?"

"I'm not surprised that the multitude of precise representations of this constellation makes you wonder, Kal. It is related to the culture of ancient civilizations that were located all over the world and the rich system of their beliefs. However, it is also related to the energy that is very felt in these places. Many of the messages hidden for future generations are found precisely in those places where we deal with the exact reflection of the Orion Belt on the Earth plane. It is in them that you should look for answers."

"Well, let's say that this explains it all. But, anyways, it's hard for me to believe that our ancestors were so unfair towards other constellations."

"And with this sense of unfairness I'll leave you, dear ones. It's enough knowledge for today. Anyway, I've been expected for some time on one of the orbits. So, see you later," she said goodbye quickly as usual and suddenly disappeared.

Pyramids that surrounded us for a few moments were slowly disappearing too and I woke up fresh as always as if the night trip to Egypt hadn't happened at all.

Chapter 13

"Illusion
You come from light
Here, where the darkness seems to be greater,
You try to fight it like your enemy
Finally accepting it and holding it
You realize that you fight with a part of yourself
By crossing new gates of the illusion, you go on to create yourself anew"

Damian Buczniewicz

The dangers
How the darkness wants to defeat the light

When I went downstairs, I could immediately feel a weird atmosphere prevailing in the living room. My parents were sitting on the coach staring at the TV, yet that wasn't odd. They were watching the news with such great interest that I hadn't seen it before. I could feel they were apprehensive.

"What's going on?" I asked in the doorway, not giving them a chance to change the channel.

"The elites are fighting. They want to introduce mandatory vaccinations at all costs," said Daddy.

"Ah... Those with surprises inside?"

"Yes. Exactly the ones. People are not aware how quickly the time is running. How much of it is left to wake up before it's too late for some. And they openly say that the complications after the vaccination are much safer than getting down with the virus,"

Daddy snorted a laugh," This is embarrassing. What kind of world do we live in? "

"Such that it needs to collapse to get up," Mommy summed up, aptly as always.

I would have put it into words better, although I wanted to minimize the effect of the collapsing as much as possible.

"So it will be, Smaisi" Mommy replied to my thoughts,"This doesn't change the fact that the Orion nations, being aware of the imminent awakening of the humanity and huge energies that assist this process, in agreement with the world governments they do whatever they can to block this change for humans or to hinder it as much as possible. They have tricks in stock that humanity hasn't dreamt of. And humans don't even know under whose control and of which technology they are under. Well, but I don't need to tell you that."

"Well, no. I'm already conscious of that. Perhaps even too much, sometimes. The fight for survival is still on. There are no definite winners and losers yet."

"Soon, in a few days, great energy will help humankind, then the scales will finally tilt to the side of light. And all the evil and manipulations that have been brought into this world will disappear from the new spaces of the new dimension that the Earth will enter. They will no longer exist here."

"Can you elaborate on that?" I asked, not entirely comprehending what Mommy meant.

"This means their complete deactivation. Exclusion. The elite agendas will be on hold, erased from the timeline. It's as if someone suddenly turned off the light because on the next level you can already see the sun and artificial light is not needed. This is how it works."

" I guess it's good, then" I stated.

"Indeed, but this doesn't mean change yet. You know, it has to happen in the hearts of people. The sun flare will complete the changes in space."

"The fact that the majority of plans of the dark side will be wrecked doesn't change the fact that people will have to learn how they've been controlled and what kind of foxy tricks have been used towards them."

"I can feel... Oh I can feel the upcoming lecture" I said slightly apprehensive. Dad and humanity control. It could be really heavy.

"Oh yes. As soon as Kal comes, I invite you both for a speech," Daddy joked,"knowledge is the key to awakening. The more you know, the more people will get to know and the more they know the quicker the change is going to be. At the beginning, they will react with anger but that will soon change. They will want to continue without the chains and cuffs. They will see the light in the dark and they will go in that direction. And there, over the horizon, there will see New Earth. And that will be the moment in which everyone will realize that it always belonged to them."

"I think everyone here should write a book", I laughed out, reminding myself of Semjase interjection about my brave poetic sentence.

"That's your opinion, we have a different one here." said seriously Daddy.

"Which is?" I asked curiously.

"Isn't bringing you up a small challenge already?" he laughed, "Everyone has their own," he repeated more clearly, letting me know that at the moment I wouldn't find out anything more.

Reluctantly, I went to school, longing for the Christmas break. I immediately informed Kal of Dad's intentions. Kal, of course, welcomed everything with great enthusiasm. I did not approach this topic in this way myself. Well, science requires sacrifice. I suspected what the topic for this afternoon would be based on, and for the first time since I started my full awakening, I tried to stretch the time.

The atmosphere at school was not interesting at all. Everyone was already suffocating in masks and were tired of the restrictions as if they had lost the will to live. But I saw a rebellion. Rebellion heralding their imminent awakening. They were in the process — not easy, but they were going in the right direction. Kal saw it too. He smiled to himself every time he saw a scene where someone was opposing the orders. Even the teachers had had enough. Especially the biology teacher, it happened that he had several doctorates in science and it was obvious almost from the beginning that the subject was very, very suspicious for him. He was the only teacher that allowed to cheat and keep masks on the chin, and he didn't put it on at all. In class, there was a total ban on talking about the "alleged" pandemic as he called it.

After returning home, I ate my dinner quickly without even picking my nose out of the kitchen; I wanted to slip upstairs unnoticed to rest before Kal showed up.

"Not so fast, young lady," Daddy shouted from the living room.

"What's happening?" I asked, walking towards him. "I thought I'll be able to get some rest before..." I stood in the doorway and suddenly broke off. I froze for a moment.

A creature that looked like Draco was sitting on the couch. I looked at my parents, but they invited me to join them, and Mommy mentally suggested that I should not feel fear. I took a deep breath and rolled into the living room.

"We thought that it would be best for you to learn about numerous manipulations first hand" Daddy began.

"That's why you invited Draco here?" I felt stupid.

"Yes. As you know many beings in recent times have come to the side of light. That's one of them."

Reptilian-looking being bowed respectfully, I looked at him with a third eye to make sure that I had not fallen into some deep illusions but the aura of this being was not dark. It still had an admixture of gray, but there were pastel shades of transformation. The light has dimmed the dark now.

"This will not transform on its own, Smaisi. I need to work out what I did. For myself — in my heart I need to do it. This conversation is one of the steps that will help me. I will help you too."

"I am so curious about Kal's reaction that I will sit facing the entrance" I only uttered because I was still shocked.

I settled myself in the armchair opposite the reptilian creature. From the corner of my eye I watched him closely. It looked exactly like Semjase had described to us. I also saw a few of them in my dream memories from previous incarnations. I was probably extremely unlucky with them.

"Or lucky," he said.

Seriously? Even he could read my mind? That was outrageous.

"What's your name?" I asked him.

"Call me just Draco," he responded.

"Okay," I agreed. I was sitting impatiently, waiting for Kal to come. I was mindful of my thoughts. I wanted our guest to be a surprise for him too.

As was usually the case with Kal, we didn't know how it was to wait for him long. The desire to expand his knowledge always summoned him with incredible efficiency. Entering the house, he expected nothing at all. Daddy stood in the doorway and motioned him into the living room. Kal started toward us and stopped abruptly. He couldn't see the figure that was with us yet, but he was staring at the point behind me. Only then did I realize that our guest is reflected in the glass window.

"Come on in, Kal, don't be afraid" Daddy urged him.

Kal stood right next to me.

"What a surprise! Haven't seen that one... Welcome," he spoke to Draco when he recovered from the shock that was served to him.

"I was shocked too," I said so that he didn't feel lonely with his feelings,"Daddy decided that the best information comes from the source of the problem" I explained to him.

"I guess only this can explain the presence of our guest."

Draco didn't say a word, only smiled a little, although I wasn't sure if that could be called a smile. I did not know the facial expressions of these creatures, but this was the impression I had, and it confused me less and less often.

We sat down comfortably. Mommy and Daddy also stayed. They wanted to listen, or maybe just accompany us to make sure that we are safe. I had to admit that I felt better when they were by our side.

"Would you let me begin?" uttered Draco.

"Certainly," replied Daddy, "They're always ready. Regardless of how shocking the topic or the speaker are," he added wittily.

"Very well, so I will begin. I want to tell you today about the most common systems of control that have been used against humankind on this planet. Everything that surrounds us has its own frequency, it is an electromagnetic wave. We too consist of matter that is based on waves with a certain frequency, only by matching this frequency to the density of our existence in certain matter. Exactly it was this relationship that was used to manipulate humanity. I mean the direct control of people's minds. Once the manipulators of this world understood how to control the processes taking place in the ionosphere and thus influence the operation of all electronic surveillance systems and communications, they would have had little to make a project aimed at controlling the weather into a project aimed at manipulating the human mind. In a nutshell—mind control is all about scanning people's brainwaves and connecting to them. Changing the waves and frequencies sent towards a person allows you to control the way they think and act. Humankind is tortured by governments with this technology, it has a direct impact on their thought forms but also on their biological body. People have forgotten that they have free will and the right to vote—so they can decide if they want such technology to be used in their space. The problem, however, is that this technology is imperceptible, and it is known that what people do not see is considered non-existent or unlikely at best. Therefore, control over people is carried out without their knowledge—even in countries considered to respect the freedom of the citizen. There is no freedom on Earth, in other words, it has not existed until now. Until recently, people were deprived of consciousness without their knowledge or will, and programs were imposed on them. It's like programming a toy or loading a line of code into a computer program. For the elite, the will of the people was irrelevant, but the programs that were to run flawlessly, at their dictation, without any objection. So you see that the greatest and deepest manipulation is well hidden. Invisible to human eyes. Sometimes, however, it happens that someone notices it in others—less often at home. Human consciousness can be controlled by manipulating the waves and frequencies flowing into the human brain. People mistakenly believe that they would notice if they were manipulated. Nothing could be more wrong. The subconscious and consciousness are two different spaces of the self. The manipulation of consciousness is carried out with the greatest care. An individual subjected to it reads new signals as something of its own. They are not external promptings and are treated like your own thoughts. That is why it is so difficult to detect any traces of mind manipulation. It's as if someone put two people in a person's head, but he or she still identified them as one. He or she would not notice that the latter person is not the same individual. The change in consciousness takes place through the combination of signals and waves of appropriate frequencies flowing through the human brain. The brain is frequency responsive because itself is a very complex bilocation energy cell that operates at many frequencies. It is both a receiver and a frequency transmitter. The brain's abilities allow this organ to process very quickly enormous amounts of information contained in coded signals of a certain frequency. In fact, to understand how it works, you would need to understand the structure of the human brain. However, this knowledge is not widely known. How the brain works is very difficult to describe in such a way that everyone understands it. So people have to take their word for it that such mind manipulation is possible and widely used. The brain is a unique system of interdependencies between brain impulses and signals, which together with the development of a given being create its intellect, personality and way of thinking. In addition to electromagnetic waves, it is also possible to implant a nanotechnology implant. It works like mind in mind — by exchanging frequency signals between the human brain and the implant that introduces programs that are not easy to identify as thoughts that are not yours.

It is not known why, when we were talking to someone else, we asked a lot of questions, and then Kal and I sat quietly listening to what Draco had to say. And he kept talking, and he was speaking very quickly and sometimes chaotically.

Manipulation through consciousness is the most popular method of managing the human mind by the external mind which is applied to the brain using the appropriate wave frequency. The use of this technology is nothing but psychological terror and the submission to the doctrines of millions of people. Over the years, newer and newer technologies have been introduced, giving more complete control over this process. Even on the Internet you can successfully find information about a technology called v2k that allows you to manipulate the human mind with an implant placed in it. And that's just the tip of the iceberg. People do not realize how high the level of technology is hidden by the elite, not to mention the extraterrestrial."

"Have humans any chance of feeling these manipulations?" Kal suddenly inquired.

"In order to do this, they would have to watch their emotions very carefully. Manipulation is done by imposing a wave that is either euphoria or fear. The body reacts immediately showing emotions that have been implanted in the brain that works on them. Fortunately, more and more people will start to notice these manipulations and stop allowing them. People must understand that the energies of space and those in the human body are something completely natural. The body is somehow an electronic device through which pulses of electromagnetic energy of various frequencies pass. Artificial interference in this energy causes everything to spin out of control. Humanity must remember, however, that every stick has two ends and the knowledge of this type of technology can also be used for its benefit. However, the intention to use it must be luminous and transparent to each of the parties. In the coming time, it is humankind who will decide what to do with this knowledge and whether to transform it into something that can support technological evolution."

"And how does it work? Is it a wave of energy that is directed in one way? Can it be dispersed?" Kal was in his element.

"At these times, the most commonly used mind control technology is a beam directed energy weapon that is based on the action of an electromagnetic wave. The operation of this weapon can be used against both an individual and a crowd of people. In the case of an individual, the frequency of the wave hits the given fragments of the body and is thus activated. This weapon can be used in various ways. Not only to control the mind itself, but also to destroy the human organism. It can affect the human nervous system and the resistance of the body. A wave beam directed at the heart can even lead to a heart attack. It all depends on its frequency."

"Are various waves used for this purpose? Or does each of them have their own use?" Kal kept asking.

I didn't know what he was heading on but I sensed that he knew.

"You're right. For example, microwave waves operate in a very wide range. They heat up the tissues of living organisms. They can also be used to send voices directly to the skull based on radio frequencies. It has been widely used recently. What do you think is the cause of the rapidly growing psychological problems in society? It is more and more difficult to find the causes of skin allergies and numerous diseases of internal organs, because they do not reside in humans, but come to them from the outside. These waves can cause almost any disease. From mental illness to cancer. Respiratory problems and heart failure are other ailments. The high intensity electromagnetic field causes numerous changes in the bioelectrical functions of organs, which causes rapid destruction in the nervous system, damage to organs and tissues, and disruptions to the human endocrine system. Ultimately, pathological changes in the human biological shell occur. Waves of this type are usually emitted from radars and their strength is up to a million times greater than that used in cellular telephony. Humanity is dealing with completely natural electromagnetic radiation, but since the introduction of artificial programming of waves and their frequencies, there has been great confusion in human minds and pharmaceutical companies are earning a fortune on an increasingly diseased population. The entire cellular telephone system is also not without its side effects. Humanity has literally become addicted to it. Unknowingly, they cook their own body, constantly heating it on this type of wave. It is especially dangerous for children who should not even fall asleep near a phone that is switched on, because it emits waves all the time, regardless of whether it is in use or when it is resting. Adult people often have more than one phone in their possession. And children...? Well, that's a completely different story. The influence of technology is also important for their development."

"Why?"I asked.

"Apart from harmful radiation... Do you think that a child from an early age, taught to use the telephone and to type text with his fingers on a touch keyboard, will learn to write with a pen with the same precision as children had a decade ago? This is just one example. But let's go back to the damage caused by phones. Radiation is harmful to humans after thirty minutes of conversation. If you regularly conduct conversations lasting several hours, which concerns a large part of society, the waves can affect a person in such a way that he or she suddenly notices difficulties with communication and with proper understanding of the content he hears. In addition, there may be physical symptoms such as headaches, migraine disorders, visual and hearing disorders, and difficulty concentrating. They are also accompanied by persistent fatigue and insomnia. It is a result of the excessive absorption of these waves by the human body. And when you hold the phone directly to your head ... Well, I don't need to say that after a few minutes the ear is sweating. This is how the process of tissue overheating begins. And the body saves itself as best it can—cools itself in the only way it knows, producing sweat.

"People can't just suddenly eliminate mobile phones from their lives. Is there a chance to minimize the risks of using them?" I again stepped out. Daddy looked at me proudly. I was drilling in search of solutions to minimise the results.

268

"There's always such a possibility. It's enough to switch off the phone for the night or at least move it away from your head and place it at least three meters away. It's not an accident that there's been headsets invented thanks to which the distance between head and phone is increased and the phone doesn't bombard the brain or the tissues around the head with direct radiation. The better the connectivity, the greater the radiation. That's another possibility of reduction. Ideally, to use it only when it's necessary. This will soon change but before this happens people will have to know about the harmful effects of the waves."

"Can you tell us when this all started? When mind control was introduced on a mass scale?" Kal asked a question this time. He loved historical references of this subject and I felt that Draco would not let him down.

"With pleasure," said out guest and took as on a journey to the past, "Slavery on Earth has long been rampant, but mind control technologies began to be used for this purpose with the end of World War II. It was then that, as part of a government project, Project Paperclip was launched, as a result of which over two thousand high-ranking Nazis were resettled to the United States. As you can imagine—not without reason and they were not random people but scientists who, under the Nazi rule, began the first serious research on human mind control based on traumatic experiences that people experienced. You've probably heard of Josef Mengele. He is responsible for conducting experimental studies on thousands of twins and many other helpless victims. Everything under the flag of the Kaiser Wilhelm Medical Institute in Berlin. He was called the Angel of Death, rightly so. He earned this nickname. He was one of nearly nine hundred scientists and medical researchers who were smuggled into the US after the war. There, having support and financial resources, he continued his research, entering increasingly darker techniques allowing him to control the human mind. Governments, however, are in the habit of taking over the work of scientists. It was like that then. All documents relating to this issue were seized by the CIA and codenamed "Bluebird" and "Artichoke". In 1953, these two projects were combined into one with the famous name "MKUltra". The programs were successful and they are taking their toll directly or indirectly to this day. However, the original assumption for using these projects was different. It was intended to create programmed killers. The CIA got obsessed with this. Almost one hundred and fifty sub-programs have been created, implemented in many fields of science: biology, pharmacology, psychology, physics, as well as 5G technology. Countries that agreed to implement 5G in the first place are considered experimental because no one knows exactly how huge the effects of this radiation will be. Each frequency has an impact on the human body because it affects the human electromagnetic field. Ailments of people struggling with a personality split or persistent absent-mindedness should not be called that, because in fact they are memory gaps that are a side effect of radiation to which they were subjected. It's used deliberately to limit human abilities and have power to exercise even greater control over them. This is the twenty-first century holocaust. Unfortunately, it cannot be called otherwise. However, this is still not all. 5G technology plays an incredibly powerful role in the blueprint of the elites that are striving to depopulate humankind. So, as you can see, this technology is not human friendly. All undertakings aimed at controlling the minds of people over the years have been made available to successive governments and heads of state. More than once, however, they received truncated documentation, which showed that the side effects of using a given technology are not so tragic, it is indeed so. Many rulers do not even know how much harm they are doing to their citizens. As you can see, the tentacles of manipulation reach even the highest powerhouses. Today, everything that has to do with controlling human minds is based on a new project called "Monarch". It is attended not only by the CIA but also by the army and navy. Many tests are carried out in the oceans with dire consequences for the animals living there. Dolphins and cetaceans in particular are sensitive to high frequencies. Millions of innocent lives die during the experiments."

"I've read that they used to control drugs in experiments of mind control in the past, and trauma, that you've mentioned, was a crucial part of this process."

"It's true. Project participants were given numerous drugs and substances that supported this process. Probably the most popular was LSD. Especially in the initial phase of project development. And you are right, trauma has a great effect on the split of a person's personality. It was created through ritual violence and terrifying torture. Even the children were sexually abused. All this to create a slave that can be controlled. It is not a myth that there are organized groups in the world responsible for kidnapping and violence against them. The Illuminati is a group that boasts of it the most, and the practices that its members commit at numerous meetings chill the blood in veins. You need to be devoid of a soul and have a heart of stone to be able to see what they do. This is a great pedophile sect whose wounding claws are aimed at the youngest of the most innocent."

"That's horrible, " I confessed. Once it struck my ears. It was difficult for me to believe it then. I was not able to swallow the information that such a beast can hide inside a human. Literally.

"It's true, Smaisi. Sometimes, as they say, the less you know the healthier you are. This is a subject that will shake humanity when the truth comes out. I would like you to know that during the experiments there were many states of generating personalities. The programming was usually conducted in alpha state, which was the base of the rest of types of mind programming. Beta state was used to program sexual services, it was called sexual slavery and was mainly with women. Usually such women were programmed slaves for high-ranking politicians. Another state, delta, was responsible for programming killers who killed unscrupulously on commission, bodyguards who didn't hesitate even for a second to sacrifice their life for their client. Another state was theta which was directly connected with the development and use of psychic abilities, it emphasized these skills. The energy of magnetic waves allows for a wide spectrum of usage. It works not only close, but also at long distances. This is why it is so dangerous when in the hands of the wrong people. Do not forget that waves of given frequencies can also heal both mental states of a person and the biological body itself. So nothing is completely black and white. Oh I would forget. Theta programming involves another activity, namely using the energy of thought to kill at a distance."

"How does it work?"

"This technology is to be introduced on a greatest scale and widely used yet, but the mechanism of it is quite simple. By emitting large amounts of the energy of hate, it's directed at the potential victim. Then, the internal organs of this person implode repeatedly, leading to self-ignition. Sometimes it causes heart attacks. This has a wide range of applications depending on the skill of the energy sender themselves. Most often this technology was used to create for governments people to do "dirty work" who operated almost like programmed machines. They are now quite commonly called assassins."

"I was always wondering where this name comes from," Kal interjected.

"I'll tell you," said Daddy, "An assassin was at first a member of a religiously-political Islamic sect that existed in times between eleventh and thirteen centuries under the name Izmailici Nizari. It was known for the fact that their members were killing their enemies believing that it was their duty according to their religion. Before they left for "hunting" they smoked hash that induced in them visions of paradise they were to go. The ecstasy and happiness that they were feeling let them go on a mission without fear. It was important for them because many times they didn't return alive. The term assassin was then brought to Europe by the crusaders and since then it has been used synonymously to the person who fanatically kills important personas. It's like a murderer to hire. Additionally, at the current stage of the development of mind controlling technology, there is a possibility of segregating memories of such a person, erasing what should stay there and replacing them with different experiences. Such people can be easily controlled. It's enough to know the code assigned to that murderer. The code, that was repeated many times during torturing, activates in him his second personality, putting

272

him in a state of a trance — there appears then the personality of a murderer that has been manipulated into him. There are various triggers of such behaviours: from short sounds, individual words, to whole phrases like kids rhymes."

"But aren't they conscious of what they are doing? At all?" I asked, it was difficult to believe in that.

"This is the whole point of mind programming: to create two separate personalities in one body that cannot have the capacity to merge in one consciousness. They don't know each other. It's as if there were two separate people living in one body but interchangeably. One of them is not aware of the existence of the other."

"But how is that possible?" I could comprehend that.

"During the process many times, as Draco mentioned, there are tortures inflicted and horrible things," Daddy continued, "then these people create something that can be called a wall of amnesia. They don't want to remember these horrible experiences. They get into the trance. A word assigned to an individual is enough to trigger an automatic switch to the state of being on the other side of the wall. The person doesn't control themselves or their body. They belong to the person who wants to use them. This wall allows them to stay hidden for those who give orders."

"So the pain and suffering make the human cut off completely," Kal explained in case I still didn't understand.

"Thank you." said Draco and slightly nodded at Daddy giving him a sign that he wanted to continue.

"Of course, continue!" Daddy slightly lost countenance.

I wasn't bothered by Daddy's interjections at all. They were more clear to me.

"It's of utmost importance to understand," Draco continued, "that the use of such a type of wave and frequency brings downfall yet it can also save lives, it can heal. Many beings use such electromagnetic waves, they accumulate the energy in their hands but with the intention to heal and cure. I don't want you to abort some possibilities and so that you know that even though they carry a risk, it's only in the honest and grateful intention that they will work for humanity's merit."

"I understand that this technology can be used literally against anyone?" Kal asked out of curiosity.

"Yes," Draco responded shortly.

"Even against heads of state, as you mentioned?"

"Yes. Even heads of state and people in top positions are often unconsciously manipulated. Sometimes I have the impression that the manipulators don't know who they're manipulating and if they are not under the influence of manipulation themselves. With the use of the brainwave frequency one can pass on a thought to the other, it will be received as their own and publicly spoken. You can't be undone. The words have been uttered. You can reach in this way to individuals as well as masses. Many times, when someone was subjected to the influence of such waves, they started to behave like a madman. He or she was unpredictable. None on the side was aware that he or she was acting like this under the influence of frequency waves of a given intensity bombarding him or her and that they caused him or her to behave in such and no other way. That was the way of activating silent killers too. The trigger is sufficient to activate their alter-ego. It's a very easy way, you can admit, to eliminate a public enemy. When someone digs too deep, the elites know what to do to get rid of such a person in a way that doesn't arouse suspicion. What's more, when someone is publicly announced as a madman or insane, his or her findings become classified in the same way. And they are, most times, very true in fact. Remember that! I know that for many such pieces of information can be like extracted from a science fiction movie. However, it's not true and humanity exists in such times when such technology is still used against it to a certain degree. For army, police and governmental agencies it became a defensive weapon. How easy it is to dispel the angry masses of protesting people with a weapon that they don't even see... "

"Much easier than spraying them with water cannons," Kal summed up mockingly, "One can expect what such degenerates can resort to..." Kal interrupted and glanced at Draco who, let's face it, until recently, he had probably stood on the other side of the barricade.

"Go ahead, boy. I know what I did and what I should do to repay my karma. I was there and I saw that. I took part in that, feeding off the energy of humans enslaved by cults and religions. It's not fantasy. It's not a movie, it's reality in which ritualistic violence, horrible tortures and sexual practices and satanic rites are a daily agenda. Humans in such circles tear off the hearts and livers of their victims, eat them when they're still warm. Children are sacrificed many times. Those people who belong to these circles justify their behavior with the knowledge derived from antiquity. For even then it was known that every living thing is an energy storehouse. The amount of energy in the body depends on the size of the animal and its health. Mental and moral character is also of great importance. Energy is released rapidly upon death. When the sacrifice is made in the act of the highest rank, the individuals with the highest and purest energy are selected for it. I'm sorry to say this, but these are children. Innocent and intelligent. This should come as no surprise to anyone, as this information has been circulating on the web for a long time, but it is being superseded by the human mind because it seems improbable. Nobody can believe that there is a group of people in the world responsible for kidnapping, sexual abuse and sacrificing them. There are many such groups, but the leading one in this respect is known to many people and the aforementioned organization called Illuminati. They are real and cannot be given any positive credit, even though they often seem able to atone for their horrible karmic obligations with money. However, it doesn't work that way. This is a group whose motto is: "Do what you want, that's the law". It can therefore be said that they consider themselves gods, they decide about everything and everyone about the life or death of each individual. Neither human law nor the laws of the universe are important to them. They put themselves above them and break them on the agenda. Illuminati have tentacles stretched everywhere, the power of money has made them masters, and they are untouchable. Even the CIA gets to grips with this murderous practice."

"And what can you tell us about a phrase that is also in fairly common use, namely the New World Order?" Kal inquired. I knew that he was interested in such topics. One time he even told me how many children die every year and he kept asking the question how it is possible that none finds them.

"I'm telling you. Firstly, I would like to refer to Smaisi's question. Many children are kidnapped but you need to know that a great part of them is voluntarily given. They're bought. There are women who give birth for money and they give their children to Illuminati. It's that far. The New Age Order is also the work of the organization, although not only of this one. This is the work of many joining in one agenda groups who want to bring about a single world government ruling the world that has an impact on everything. Thanks to this, they will be able to do whatever they like. The elite believe that the planet is overpopulated, although this is not true. Humanity just doesn't care about the planet as it should. The New World Order in its plans assumes the depopulation of humanity. It has been introduced for decades with drugs and vaccines that contain heavy metals and destroy human DNA. They also cause infertility, which will ultimately lead to a reduction in the world's population. For years, a technological or biological warfare has been planned that would make it easier for the elites to reach their destination. What is it that is happening now? What do you think? Just another point in their plan and the entire population trembles with fear. Their trick up their sleeve is the ability to use mind control technology. Nobody will see it or teach it, and the plan will be carried out. The governments of the world, as they call themselves, have not foreseen one thing. Pretty significant. Many people in high positions knew about the processes that would take place on Earth, but no one took them into account. The elites have shown arrogance to the Creator's plans, and this will cause them to fail miserably."

"You mean the ascension of the planet, right?" I asked, happy that the self-proclaimed gods of our times missed this important fact.

"Exactly, yes, Smaisi. Even a lot of us… believed for a long time that technology would stop the ascension of the planet. However, the light has been fighting for decades so that our interference had no bearing on this process. The light has already won. The space is almost completely cleared and in a few days the energy of awakening will reach the Earth from the Central Galactic Sun. All the wonderful inventions of the dark side, even the before mentioned and described technology of mind programming, will stop functioning at the moment when Earth enters the higher density level. It wasn't even suspected that the methods of elites will work as they planned during the change of the vibration and density, which will take place on a fourth quantum level. Moreover, in the new space, people who have been subjected to mind control will have the opportunity to recall externally controlled events. It will also open the eyes of many people. These recollections will prove how numerous and massively the law of human freedom was violated and how strongly it was controlled. People are poisoned in many ways. Artificial clouds left by airplanes are poison sprayed in the air. Many governments, including the United States, have bombarded the sky with streaks of chemtrails and energy rays from extensive antenna installations for many years. The same is true of Europe and other parts of the world. What they allow is more than just spraying substances that are hazardous to human health. You don't realize how one interacts with the other. All technologies are interconnected and create one great combo against humanity."

"Can you describe to us in a nutshell how it works more or less? What exactly is happening and how does it directly affect the human body? " Kal asked because the subject was interesting to him.

"The towers emit energy rays which are reflected by the ionosphere due to particles sprayed in the upper atmosphere. Electric waves have extremely low frequencies. It's called EFL. These low vibrations are able to penetrate people's minds. Directly directed, they immobilize the victim or drive them mad. The same goes for animals. These waves are able to penetrate even steel, nothing is an obstacle for them. They improve radio contact even in bunkers deep underground. They can also be used to detect underground bunkers. They can be used to track and target aircraft rockets and other flying objects even on the other side of the globe. At this exceptional time, it is hardly surprising why the elites want this frequency to work efficiently. Many spaceships enter the Earth's space and these waves allow us to detect at least some of them. Apart from the danger that these waves pose to the human body and mind, the effect on the planet itself seems to be forgotten. These frequencies are not natural for the Earth's atmosphere. Nobody even tried to understand how the Earth's ionosphere would react to the repeated hitting it with radiation of this type. The ionosphere of the core is a very sensitive layer, in addition, it is assigned to human organisms and the frequency that the Earth has at the moment. Together with the ozone layer, the ionosphere protects your planet and all life forms on it. Since the impact of these waves has not been studied — and even if it has been completely ignored for the higher good of the elites — it is likely that projects such as chemtrails and HAARP will destroy the protective layer of the Earth. I don't need to say what this means for any form of life on Earth. Many military groups that have done any kind of testing refuse to confirm the security associated with it. They assume that nothing will happen. To tell you the truth — they assume a miracle. The extraterrestrials warned heads of state about the dangerous effects of these guns, but it did not reach people who are focused only on their own goals and striving to achieve them no matter what. The special antennas of HAARP technology are spread around the world and form a web of death, but humanity doesn't even know this. The test stand that was built in the Alaska mountains was one of the first. I will now introduce you to how it works so that you understand well."

"We'd appreciate that," Kal interjected shortly.

"As I already told you, the ionosphere is under the ozone layer. It's a layer of gases enriched with ions which are electric particles. Scientists intend to heat the ionosphere using HAARP technology by directing powerful beams of radio waves into space. And a wave is a wave, it reaches not only where it is directed. It penetrates and travels further, when the ionosphere is bombarded with these strings, it will create artificial curved clouds of ions that can act as optical lenses. These lenses will be used sequentially to reflect the low frequency EFL waves. Humanity does not know what it is doing. Even our race looks with fear at what they are doing, experimenting with their planet in fields and spaces that they have no idea about. A long time ago, a similar fate befell Mars which lost its atmosphere. It was a tragedy for the creatures inhabiting this planet. Many people who at the moment watch what is happening from the sidelines and sense what the effects of this technology may be, they are trying to intervene but are silenced by governments. They present chemtrails and HAARP as a purely scientific experiment, while this is nothing more than implementing a radiation weapon project on Earth. And while the use of these waves for tracking airplanes may seem like a great benefit to the military, for the entire planet and all creatures that inhabit it, it is a huge threat. I'm telling you that so that you can warn others that these projects may affect the spatial layer of the planet, and it will not end well for humanity. Humanity has been warned yet it still takes the risk of creating a huge catastrophe. This shows how much humans don't care about the planet, themselves, or future generations either. What can happen with the ionosphere of the planet is not the only risk. HAARP is also a weapon with a huge power that no opponent can handle. There's a war over which country has the greatest weaponry and is unbeatable. HAARP can lead to an explosion that is similar to the explosion of a nuclear bomb detonated at different heights. However, this is still not all, although as you can see its operation is already shocking. HAARP and wave beams can penetrate deep beneath the Earth's surface — into the layers containing oil reserves or the secret bunkers I have already mentioned. It is accepted unscrupulously that this type of radiation is lethal to humans and animals as well as to vegetation. Even if you take into account that it will destroy flying ships and protect people from attacks by extraterrestrials, radiation still poses a greater risk to the population. If this project is not withdrawn, it will become very possible for extraterrestrials to intervene in this matter. This is because humanity cannot be allowed while playing gods to stab the atmosphere of its planet with huge gigawatt devices. There can be no irreversible disturbances in this field, nor the destruction of the Harmony of the Earth's atmosphere, which has been created and improved for millions of years. There will never be permission to acts that could destroy the planet. The project poses a huge risk. By heating the ionosphere, the weather conditions on Earth are changing. The reversal of the planet does its job, but people add their brick to it, which only makes everything worse."

"How much power does this device achieve?" Daddy asked this time.

"Imagine that only one gigawatt of power per unit could burn a hole in the ionosphere. However, when using its full power, it turns into a beam weapon with a power of one hundred gigawatts. This means that at full power, the waves will damage the entire consciousness of humans and animals and adversely affect the genetics of the biological human body, which will lead to numerous previously unknown mutations. With such high doses of radiation, the sensitive energy field may be so manipulated that the poles may shift. However, it will not be a natural process related to the Earth's cycles, but an interference from outside, the effects of which cannot be predicted. So as you can see, the danger is enormous and yet underestimated."

"It's not the first time when humans would be given a warning and they didn't listen, " Daddy interjected again. He was sure Draco knew what he meant by that.

"That's true. In 1945 humans for the first time detonated an atomic bomb. Before it happened, the extraterrestrials had come to Earth and warned the president and managers of the United States of the enormous risks they take. Despite the warnings, they did not listen, and there were nuclear attacks. The truth is that after the fact they admitted that they did not take into account what could have happened during the explosion, they had no idea that there was a risk of a nuclear chain reaction which could result in the incineration of the whole Earth. They were so overwhelmed by the desire to show their strength that they ignored the consequences of their actions. At these times, they will develop a similar attitude. Once again, they only focus on what they want to achieve and, once again, forget about the potential uncalculated consequences. The chances of a nuclear disaster or HAARP and chemtrails are fifty to fifty. So it's quite a risk being taken on behalf of the entire human population. Despite the fact that the darkest of scenarios didn't take place, the game with nuclear bombs brought many other terrible events at that time which humanity tends to forget about. After the first atomic test they built new bombs. They were used in turn and dropped on densely populated areas. I mean here Hiroshima and Nagasaki. Hundreds of thousands of people were killed then, many were burnt and hurt. Until now their descendants bear the stigma of genetic mutations caused by radiation. It cannot be undone. There are huge contaminated territories all over the world where tests have been performed that you don't even know about. The land there will remain radioactive for the next thousands of years and will become uninhabitable. Note that atomic materials used for peaceful purposes also contributed to the deaths of many lives through radiation pollution, either as a result of an accident or deliberate action. One of the most famous examples is the explosion of the Chernobyl nuclear power plant. How long was the information about what had really happened concealed? Too long. And people absorbed dangerous radiation like a sponge. To this day, only few live in the vicinity of the nuclear power plant. Various experiments using radiation for the alleged treatment of humans can be added to this list. The only result is death, often much faster than the disease itself. And how many experiments were conducted in small villages away from human eyes before these treatments were introduced, and how many people suffered torments being the guinea pigs of the medical mafia. You don't even want to know. Nuclear power plants must disappear because they still pose a huge threat to humanity. And now very, very hypothetically, imagine a situation in which a shift manager who manages all parameters in such a power plant receives an electromagnetic wave beam and, manipulating his mind, leads to a tragedy. How little is needed with such technology ..."

here Draco broke off and I felt that it was even difficult for him to talk about it," and added to the atomic risk there are next ones: HAARP and chemtrails. Despite the objections of many scientists, the project is being implemented with more and more force. The opponents of these ventures are well aware of the great danger to the planet from the use of this technology. Let us also not forget about all living organisms. The list of potential ailments and effects is very long. From skin cancer to climate change including violent storms, droughts, floods, earthquakes and volcanic eruptions. Already the top mass of the Earth's atmosphere is damaged. Without any consultation and without the knowledge of people — substances containing not only numerous elements dangerous to human health, but also technology are sprayed in the sky. They are called Morgellons. Unfortunately, the people in power who make all these decisions care about themselves and their interests only. They are madmen and megalomaniacs."

"Has the ionosphere been really damaged already? Can this be repaired?" I asked.

"It has already happened," Draco confirmed, "Partly it has been damaged indeed which increases the amount of cosmic radiation that reaches the planet. Unfortunately, it's dangerous for humans. Yet the rebuilding of the ionosphere will take place as soon as the planet enters a new frequency of the fourth density. Then, all the damaging projects of elites will become deactivated and won't be able to threaten humanity. It will happen in a few days. It will be completely stopped after the solar flare when the frequency of the planet will change permanently."

"Are there any examples of events that were triggered by the use of this technology without human consent?" I kept asking.

"Of course, there are some big events that left a big mark. One of them was the detonation of an atomic bomb in the atmosphere in 1958. This eruption was supposed to affect the weather. Within two years of this event, a whole series of climate disasters have occurred. The next event took place in 1916 when three hundred and fifty thousand copper needles were shot into space, each of them was one to two centimeters long. The result of this interference was a powerful earthquake in Alaska with a magnitude of eight and a half on the Richter scale, at the same time in Chile a large part of the coast slid into the ocean. There are many such events. Everything is harmonious energy, any interference with this harmony causes the effects felt for the Earth and for all humanity. One of the main threats to the HAARP and chemtrails projects is their location. Three hundred and twenty kilometers northwest of Anchorage, in an isolated corner of Alaska, a forest of antennas has been erected. It's ultimately three hundred and sixty towers with a height of as much as twenty-five meters. They were created so that they could be used to shoot beams of high-frequency rays towards the ionosphere. It is a serious threat to all life on this planet. Fortunately, the Earth will soon enter higher frequencies and all the evil caused by this technology will be neutralized. I would like you to know about one more thing that has influenced the quality of life of the human species for decades. It is genetic manipulation introduced under the disguise of the safety of the youngest."

"I know what you're about to tell us," I confessed and saddened because it concerned the most innocent beings on this planet, that is children.

"You feel well, Smaisi." Draco read my thoughts, "On Earth, consciously and with full premeditation, genocide is carried out with the use of vaccines. Some people will die and young generations will be mutilated for life and become slaves of Big Pharma. This has been happening globally for many decades, but in the last one it has been exacerbated to such an extent that it has led to the awakening of the awareness of people who have witnessed the side effects of vaccinations, that is, numerous diseases of their children and even their death. Many doctors are aware of the dangers of such a number of vaccinations that introduce toxins into a young, not fully developed organism. However, any attempts to speak out about it result in the doctors losing their jobs, so they keep quiet. All vaccines are contaminated. They cause autism and cancer even in the youngest. Nagalase, a dangerous enzyme that stops vitamin D from attaching to the Gc protein, is added to vaccines. You do not realize how the child suffers when he or she receives the next doses of vaccines and the vaccine calendar is bursting at the seams. In such a young body, the brain swells, which is the result of a cytokine storm in it, which is the result of a lack of vitamin D. Children cry for hours, unable to calm down and doctors tell their parents that it is normal because the body has started to fight the virus in the vaccine. They will prescribe painkillers when the baby needs to be given vitamin D immediately, in the right form — from the GcMAF protein, the production of which is blocked by nagalase. As a result, not only do many children become autistic, it also destroys the body's natural ability to kill anti-cancer cells. The human genome is anti-cancer, but it effectively protects the biological body by blocking its proper functioning. Most autistic children have large amounts of the enzyme nagalase in their bodies. It can be said that nagalaza completely turns off the body's immune system, which is why vaccinated children become ill much more often. Nagalaza also causes type 2 diabetes. It's not the genetic changes, but the vaccine gifts that are causing the epidemics of autism, cancer and diabetes all around."

"Why does it affect children so much?" I asked. "Adults who take vaccines don't suffer from so many side effects," I stated. I was in the subject. My schoolmate's brother was a victim of such unnatural interferences in the human body. From her story, I inferred that he was a wonderful bright boy until he got vaccinated and everything changed then. Since that day, the life of their family has not been the same.

"The young body does not yet have a fully developed immune system and does not have a fully functioning myelin sheath of the nervous system, which means that the substances contained in vaccines can freely get anywhere in the body without causing its defense reaction. Often compounds such as mercury or aluminum, which are some of the ingredients of this "goodness" served to humankind, are deposited in the brain. It causes a number of diseases. In addition to heavy metals, vaccines contain formaldehyde viruses and animal DNA. So how are such toxic substances supposed to have a positive effect on the body of such a little human? The consequences are terrible: Parkinson's disease, Alzheimer's, Asperger's syndrome, epilepsy of various types, asthma, and allergies to everything, eczema, cancer, autism... I could go on and on. Young mothers trusting health service doctors, give their children poison with the intention of protecting them from childhood diseases. Meanwhile, vaccinated diseases last a week or two, and the vaccine diseases last a lifetime. Of course, they can be cured by administering the protein that binds to vitamin D, that is, the aforementioned GcMAF. However, this possibility was taken away from people, and the laboratories involved in the production of this protein were closed very quickly."

" Another block, " Kal summed up.

" I need to go now. I said everything that you needed to know. This knowledge is available on the Internet as well, you need to know that it's not only a theory," said Draco and quickly disappeared.

"I knew quite a lot of that already," Kal boasted. He was proud of himself and of the knowledge he had and I needed to admit that there were not many things that could surprise Kal.

"OK, OK, no boasting," Daddy said, "I knew that too," he added and everyone burst out laughing.

After such type of information I guess we needed to relax.

Chapter 14

"With the increase in the level of our consciousness, the way we look at the world, the way we think and are changes. Something we have not noticed before becomes quite obvious. This happens with every area of life. However, to see things as they really are, we must cleanse everything we knew so far, we thought we knew. Open up. The deeper we can reach ourselves, the deeper we perceive the world, we begin to understand that we create every second, at the same time being aware that we are an observer of what we create. We begin to see ourselves in everything that surrounds us... We see God who works, creates through us..."

Damian Buczniewicz

Multidimensionality of the soul

Christmas was coming in huge steps. Since the Draco's visit there had passed only a few days but the harm done to humanity and the multitude of them all the time sat deep in our thoughts — especially Kal's, who searched the Internet for information and tried to break everything down into prime factors to, then, put it all together — more compact than what our unexpected guest had served us. Draco was right — if you did a really good search, you could find a lot of evidence of the crime. Most times, though, we were looking under the tags of conspiracy theories. I regretted that it wasn't a conspiracy theory that people are so blind and manipulated. I had a hope and it was still alive in me that soon everything would change. It was only a few months until the entire planet reached a higher dimension. The energies were shifting rapidly which triggered weird sensations in the body. Sometimes I felt dizzy and I was disoriented. I knew though that it was temporary and as soon as the body got used to, everything would come back to normal.

That day I was very glad when I returned home from school. It was caused by the fact that one of my schoolmates started to ask me questions about awakening. I hadn't known before that she was into this subject. I felt it straight away that this process started for her. I was happy about that and I was very excited. All my hopes for saving humanity got winged at that very moment. I didn't forget to tell it to my parents as soon as I returned home.

"The high energies that are coming down from space start to influence more and more people, look closely at what will be happening around you," said Mommy with a smile on her face. She was happy with every breakthrough on the plane of awakening of humanity. Every next person was gold and could do a lot for the collective."

"Do you really think that there will be more and more of them?" I continued asking.

"Of course, Smaisi! That was the reason why these energies have come down—to start a new age. Many souls, really many, have come here as a symbiote to experience this beautiful transformation of the planet and humanity. This is one of a kind event. Precedence."

"You're right, Mommy. They're gonna make it," I said confidently, using one of Mommy's advice that I should look at my desires in a way that they had already come to fruition and were part of my presence.

"Keep it going!" Mommy winked at me, "Are you seeing Kal today?" she asked.

"No. He promised his mum he would help her with the Christmas shopping. I'm seeing him tomorrow," I replied and felt a prick of longing.

"Don't exaggerate my daughter or you'll get addicted. Spend some time with yourself. Meditate, take a cleansing bath in salt water. Believe me, with the current changes it will do you well."

I decided it was a great idea and as soon as I ate my dinner I ran upstairs. I added quite a lot of sea salt to the bath tube and turned the water on. Before the bath was full I went inside and immersed myself in the noise of the pouring water. I liked the sound, and although it couldn't compare to the hiss of a waterfall, shivers ran down my body. The energy of the water filled every cell in my body. The hot liquid dissolved the salt very quickly. I dived as deeply as possible, I regretted that the bathtub was not long enough for me to fit in all of it. My knees remained slightly bent and protruded above the water. I lay there for such a good thirty minutes and my thoughts drifted back to my past lives. I relaxed, remembering only the most beautiful memories. Mommy's voice pulled me out of my reverie, apparently checking if I had not melted.

"Are you going to sit there long? It's not good for too long either."

I guess Mommy was right because all my skin was wrinkled so badly I had never seen it like this before. My palms were almost white. And the water? The water was as dirty as if I hadn't had a wash in a couple of weeks. I soaped myself up and all the old skin peeled off, leaving perfectly smooth skin. I felt the depths of this cleansing bath. I hadn't felt so fresh and clean for a long time. I dried myself with a towel and embalmed my body well. When I left the bathroom it was steaming. Dense steam burst into the hallway causing the mirror hanging opposite the bathroom to fog up almost immediately.

"Holly Molly!" Mommy summed up the event, "Did you have a bath or intend to boil yourself alive?" she joked.

"I definitely rocked it," I admitted and I painted a bug beautiful heart in the mirror, "That's for you, Mommy!"

"I love you too, Smaisi," she replied and if it hadn't been for the fact that I was standing in the corridor in a towel, we would have surely sealed our love declaration with a hug."

I went to my room and put on a loose and comfy pajamas. I sat down in front of the computer and opened the file with my book. I was in the chapter on the symbiote. I wanted to write and even started, but I realized that I didn't know everything about it. It seemed to me that the knowledge that was passed on to us is truncated and very general, and I wanted to sneak in deeper. I felt it was very important to understand who we are and where we come from as the symbiote incarnates into a body on Earth. And I somewhat already knew something, but I felt unsatisfied. It bothered me to such an extent that I was unable to concentrate on writing.

Semjase — I said in my mind, hoping that she would read my silent request.

It's OK, Smaisi. — she replied — *Tonight* — she added and I felt how her energy left my space.

I went downstairs happily and for the rest of the evening I spent on watching a hilarious comedy with my parents. It had been a long time since we last spent free time together in such a way. I was either with Kal, writing, or simply meditating and spending time on my own. That day though after spending a few hours with them I felt that each of us needed that in a way — remembering that the mission is a mission and it needs attention and devotion but not to such an extent to forget that you are a human. Each of us understood the importance of our tasks and waited patiently for such moments together. Hot and cleansing bath and a huge dose of laughter tired me to such an extent that I didn't need to calm myself down to fall asleep quickly.

When I opened my eyes I was in cosmic space. Surrounded by the stars and planets, I was floating in space, enjoying the views. I knew them so well, I missed them so much. Kal flew up from my right and prodded my arm. The force of the nudge, although small, knocked me far into space. At first, Kal was a little panicked when he saw my facial expression, but then he noticed the wings adjacent to my back and pointed at them with his finger. I unfolded them and after a few solid swings I made it back to where I was just a moment ago. Semjase was still gone. We took advantage of this and began to move freely in space, spinning like little donuts devoid of the force of gravity. I was getting slowly dizzy and that was the moment Semjase showed up.

"Welcome, my beloved. Are you ready for another trip in search of the truest truth?"

"Of course," said Kal, "What subject are we going to talk about?" he asked.

"Smaisi asked to broaden the knowledge on the soul, the symbiote and its multidimensionality. And this is what we're going to focus on today."

"It's a bomb for me. I also felt a slight hunger in this matter. I don't know why."

"Perhaps that was my hunger and you've picked on it?" I laughed.

"Highly probable. Although if you believe that you need it, let's dive deeper."

"Let's begin this beautiful lecture, then. I must admit that I love talking about it. The soul, its origin and multidimensionality is such a beautiful knowledge that you have never enough of it. Maybe that's the reason for your hunger, Smaisi."

"Who knows. Everyone is interested in their own origin. And so it's even logical that you dig and dig all the way to the spring."

"I love your metaphors. I have an impression that with every day they're getting better and better. I can see that writing goes excellent; if this goes on, you'll end up writing earlier than planned."

"Than I planned?" I was slightly surprised.

"Well, yes. Your soul. She's planned everything."

"Ah, yes!" I tapped my hand on my forehead as a sign of how I could forget such fundamental knowledge.

"Let's begin. I would like you to understand from the very beginning that the symbiote and therefore your soul is not you. It is an ether that has existed for billions of years and experienced multidimensionality. The symbiote is not something local, it is assigned to a specific space in which it wants to experience and exists completely independently of the physical body. It is nothing but pure existence. In space, this existence is defined by quantum decoherence, which can be determined by giving it the final force that determines the direction in which a given quantum system is going. You could say that the symbiote is an awareness of existence. When the soul locates itself in a physical body, it is only temporarily assigned to a given time and space. Thanks to resonance, it can assign itself to local or non-local spaces in multidimensions. In a way, it blends into the space in which it has decided to take the next stage of the soul's evolutionary path. The quantum reality of the soul is therefore variable and, depending on space, it determines its existence in a given dimension or density. The symbiote is the existence of many types of light energy, thanks to which the soul can choose and use just the one that is useful for it, depending on what being and from what dimension it has decided to incarnate in order to experience. The symbiote can be energy from the most subtle, immaterial to the one where it has the ability to vibrate itself to dimensions and physical densities. Every creature in the universe has souls, no matter what level of evolution it is on. The symbiote has as many as forty levels of penetration of vibrations and frequencies in one dimension of space and there are billions of dimensions. So as you can see, the symbiote has a lot to show off when it comes to its evolution. There are as many as four billion visible star systems in our universe. There is life in half of them. The rest is beyond the perceptual spectrum on which consciousness resonates."

"Two billion planets is enough to choose from. I think so," Kal scratched his head as if he was trying to remember on how many planets he had already existed.

"The symbiote is linked to a multidimensional alert of vibration and frequency. In the space of the third dimension alone, it can have up to twenty connections. The more aware a person is, the more connections between the symbiote and the mind become active. Each level allows you to resonate in different spaces, for example — only one of many frequencies is assigned to a human being. The symbiote very quickly reaches the level of vibration and frequencies that are characteristic of a human being. It can resonate with the space and field of the planet on which it resides and tune in to them. Thanks to this, a continuous development process is possible. The soul is permanently connected to the heart chakra. It does not reside in the physical body, but in one of the subtle bodies gathered around it. At the beginning of human life, it is located in the nearest layers of the subtle body, but as a human being grows up, it moves away and passes to the next layers. In each of them, he shows a different way of influencing and influencing people. This leads to a change in the way of thinking and the expansion of perception skills. This is why it is said that a person changes, grows up and becomes smarter, and the space around them is more and more familiar to them and they can move better in it. Souls do not draw energy from the human body. They always use an external source. This source is one of the many energies that surround a human. The soul is connected to everything around. We talk about four connections with the source in case of existence that is strictly human. They are constant and are able to fulfill all the needs of the symbiote. The symbiote exists billions of years and its evolution and experience are planned for that time."

"Is every symbiote the same?" I asked, "Since so many beings have existed in all the universes, have they got the same source of existence which is the Creator-Of-All-That-Is? We were part of it. Little sparks of a flame of eternal creation."

"Initially yes. However, there are special souls which, thanks to their experience gathered during numerous journeys across the universes, have gained many skills. They've gathered a lot of information and connected with many entities on many planets. This allowed them to grow fast. These souls enrich the wisdom of the whole universe. They're called luminous souls and they comprise approximately ten percent of all the souls. The universe needed a lot of time to create the first symbiote — the original pattern of the soul. Symbiotes are pure energy that they come from. From the moment the first symbiote was created it was much faster and souls started to birth in masses."

"But we incarnate not only in human bodies? " asked Kal.

"No, not only, but because in this incarnation you're human beings I would like to tell you specifically what a human symbiote is. Every human is a shelter for a soul. A vessel in which the soul feels safe in, dwelling in its subtle bodies. However, it's not always that beautiful. When there are many changes in the life of a person, especially emotionally, the frequency of the heart field and of the whole body including the subtle bodies changes. When the human enters low frequencies of fear, it simply gets very difficult for the soul. It's not able to stand the low-vibrational impurities, especially when the human dwells in them for a longer time. The build-up of these emotions makes the soul feel more and more overwhelmed. She is then forced to go beyond the subtle layers of a human and detaches from the body. The protection then that the human body gave her is disappearing. The soul suddenly becomes easy prey. And believe me, many beings are waiting for this situation. Being outside the subtle bodies of a human being, the soul can be snatched up, decimated and transferred to the lower astral layers. For many beings, the soul is of great value and they will take advantage of every possible situation to be able to possess it. When this type of situation occurs, the soul slowly loses its connection to its source. The lower it goes and the farther it is from the human body, the more connections are lost until there are so few of them that there is disintegration at the energy level, which weakens not only the energy of the soul itself, but also the person to whom it is assigned. The symbiote then falls into a lethargic state and separation is created. The soul is energetically detached from the body. There is no longer the connection it should have. Of course, the soul, as I mentioned to you, does not die, it is immortal and limited only by the duration of your universe. However, the quality of its existence changes and its own vibrations, which depend on the relations in which it resonates with the human body. It is dependent on coexistence. Each soul has its own personality, consciousness and its own story to tell you. Many times, these stories are a component of the billions of years of existence they have lived. Some people's souls are unique because they have accumulated many experiences from the universes in which they previously existed. When the soul has a good connection and vibrational interdependence with the body of a human being that it has chosen for its experience, then exceptional people are born who can significantly change reality and have a positive impact on the fate of humanity, because they transmit the wisdom collected during previous incarnations. Thanks to a good connection with the soul, they do not start everything from the beginning and intuitively feel what they should do, what they already know and use this knowledge in a given incarnation. It is just connecting with that awareness of your soul. Tesla had such a connection. You know how much he's done and how much will be done thanks to him, even though he is no longer in the timeline at this point, or at least not in the body he had before", Semjase ended in a little puzzling way.

"With the current descending energies and ongoing changes, does every person have the opportunity to raise their vibrations?" I knew that the soul had a choice and many times it made it before it even connected with the human body, I was curious though of not only the possibility to make a choice, but also the possibility of the process of ascension itself that was reliant on the soul plan.

"A very good question, Smaisi. Many people use a very known term vibration not knowing entirely what it is. Vibration is, in other words, the frequency of the magnetic field of a given being. The vibration of the frequency is fully dependent on the being."

"So it directs it and can change it on its own?" Kal interjected.

"Exactly, yes. It depends on them what vibration they want to have. Every human being is multidimensional, luminous. The possibility to ascend is not dependent on the level he or she is in the given incarnation. Always, whenever they choose to, they can raise their vibration to their natural level, to their original vibrations of the zero point. It can happen even if they are on a completely different level and it's not even dependent on whether their being is based on the DNA matrix of Shiru code. Currently, the world which is ascending to the fourth level, is surrounded by natural processes which assist it in this change. Orgones, crystals and other natural minerals that have a high level of personal empathy, they

294

too help in this process. The soul itself, if it chose to ascend, has its own ways to invoke the awakening of consciousness of a given being, that's a human body in which it incarnated."

" In what way? " Kal asked and I immediately felt warmth in my heart.

"You feel well, Smaisi. The symbiote produces the energy of the heart. It's a magnetic field of the heart which is up to five thousand times stronger than the magnetic field of the brain as well as the rest of the human vessel shielded with biofield. There's more. The energy of the heart has its own intelligence. It's exactly where energetically the subconscious is located. The heart not without reason is co notated and embodied with higher feelings, such as love. What is called the subconscious is closely connected with the right hemisphere of the brain, the more intuitive one. That's why, I often repeat that in some cases you need to switch off the logic, at least partly because it's not possible to do it entirely, and try to feel everything with the heart space because it's not contaminated by the external manipulations. Logic and mind are like plus and minus when plus is a problem and minus is the lack of the problem. From the level of the energetic matrix you can connect these two states."

" In what way? "Kal asked.

"By concentrating on those two states with the power of your superconsciousness you can reach a point of energetically quantum merging of both of them. The key here is to use your awareness. Many times it's enough just to express your wish for it to happen, you need to call the superconsciousness. Then, the subconscious will call the power of your superconsciousness and in result what you ask for will be transferred to your consciousness. Then, your logic will be suppressed and feeling with the heart will be possible. It's therefore the interference based on your free will. It's a quantum leap. Change of the level of consciousness," Semjase laughed, "The change in the logic and mind can be also directed via the ultrasound resonance with the right frequency. It's commonly known to heal with the frequencies and vibrations of sound. It's music therapy. In music therapy, thanks to the right intensity of sounds, the quantum fields and light photons are excited. Many times this contributes to spectacular effects and leads to healing. Depending on the scale of the changes in the tissues of the human body, the healing process will be either faster or longer. The resonance takes place gradually and adapts to the extent of the damage. It happens very often that after the first energetic resonance one can see beneficial changes. However, the dosage here needs to be carefully planned so that the process can take place in a harmonious and complete way. Soon, such ways of healing will be becoming more and more popular. Medicine will develop in ways that have been blocked until now even though their efficiency was proven to be greater than of the current methods of treatment. There will also be created replicators that will be capable of restoring tissues and even the whole body. The changes in the health state will be done immediately in the near future. It depends on the identity of the quantum field space in which a given person resides."

"Any useful advice in this matter perhaps?" I asked. I wanted to describe as much as possible in my book but also, focusing on practice, help people with the introduction of some behaviours in their life so that they can reach a desired level of consciousness in a short time."

"Of course. Firstly, it's important to find a quiet place in the house. It has to be a place where no other flatmate will disturb you for at least half an hour. Before I move to the description of the process itself, I would like to make you aware of the fact that it shouldn't be done all the time and there should be a few days of break in between the energetic resonances. It's connected to the fact that the human body needs to have a time to rest to achieve a level of homeostasis so that it can undergo the process again. And so, I recommend doing this no more than two times a week and not day after day, but rather with breaks applied. You should experience the readiness of the body after some time. During the process, it's important to switch off all the media and transmitters that would cause disharmony. Lie down or sit down comfortably. It's important that neither your hands or legs are crossed and the spine should be straight. At first, focus on the breath for a while, rhythmically breathing the air in through your nose and out through your mouth. The breathwork should last a few minutes. You can do that with your eyes either open or closed. After that time, stretch your right hand forward and imagine that your thumb marks you the point A. You need to assign the ailment or the place you feel pain or discomfort. Next, with the power of your superconsciousness, place the point A in the field of your awareness, focusing on it."

"That is, on the thumb, right?"

"Yes, Kal. On the thumb of your right hand. When you do that, stretch your left hand forward and the thumb of this hand will symbolize point B. And here, you assign to point B the matrix of a reality which is the level of your symbiote soul and its energy. This matrix determines the state in which your sick organs are completely healthy and working absolutely properly. In the energetic matrix there are all possible states so you need to choose the one which will be most proper for you. In case of ailments there will be a state of lack of them. With the sick liver — a healthy liver and with the heart problems — no problems and its ideal functioning. The next stage is visualization in which you place point B on the level of the energetic matrix. The next step is quantum merging of those two points, that is point A and point B. With your act of will you express your desire that these two points connect. You move both fingers closer to your heart and making another act of your will you express the desire that these two quantum connected points come into your heart space. This is the moment when you should feel the energetic connection between your thumbs and your heartfield. You can feel the sort of a bond and pick up the waves of energy flowing from your heart towards those thumbs. You can also feel the energy flow from point B to point A. However, even if you don't feel these energies, you don't give up and continue the whole process. Stay in the thumb-to-heart position for several minutes, or longer if you observe an energetic connection between these two points. Keep going until you feel like yawning. This is a signal that the connection should be terminated. The resonation finally ends with the expression of your will that the quantum leap takes place from point B to point A and from point A to point B and that point A takes over all the health properties of point B. Finally, you should clap your hands several times vigorously to complete the process of energy resonance. Then, forget about what has happened as soon as possible, do not think or analyze if it has happened or not. You leave it to energy. It will make it on its own. Your will has been expressed and the energy has been set in motion."

" Thank you, Semjase, I think this knowledge will be helpful to many people. I think I know this method as two-point. I've read about it."

"You're right. They call it this way. Let me quickly tell you about the soul's non location factor. Soon I will have to leave you, I need to attend another space, I would like to finish this topic with you today though."

"Of course, continue." I uttered although I was slightly saddened that our meeting was about to end.

"Remember when I told you there is no death, that it is only a change? So it is a change in vibration, a kind of change in the quantum state while preserving the information it contains. The body dies, it was only the carrier of the symbiote, but the symbiote's memory does not change, it remains, only the form in which the symbiote is stored changes. Consciousness then becomes part of the universe until the next incantation in a new body. You must remember that the symbiote is not permanently assigned to any space, therefore it is multidimensional and non-local. The symbiote is the pure essence of existence and at the same time the creator of energy for a given existence or the life it causes for its experience. People have always associated the soul with something luminous, and this is a very good association. The soul is composed of quantum biophotons. The luminous being must go through the often difficult path to unlock the human brain cell memory and lead to the connection with the awareness of the soul. It's not easy to break through the layers of programs inculcated in people from an early age. They are the cause of energetic irregularities in quantum

298

alignment, they are pathogenic, but also energetic programming, which is difficult to reprogram afterwards. However, the most important thing for people is that they always remember that they have souls. Beautiful and individual. Located above human heads, a silver particle that is the main source of power supply to the pineal gland and forms the entire heart's energy grid. Always remember that everything you experience in your numerous incarnation cycles is part of what then makes up this special and one-of-a-kind gem which is your soul, which rises in its beauty and contemplates every moment that has lived. There are no more important and less important moments. Each of them is just as important and unique for the soul as it is one of a kind, " with these words Semjase said goodbye to us.

First she disappeared from space, and then Kal. He didn't even have time to say anything. I was hovering for a moment, delaying the time of return, but the reality caught up with me.

There are only two polarities: love and fear | light and darkness | information and no information — everything else is a symptom of this polarity. One gives away life and the other takes...

We decide which one to follow. When you delve into your essence, you recognize yourself. A person who has fully recognized Oneself will be guided by love... Because in the final analysis he or she understood that fear doesn't exist, it's an illusion... Paradoxically, fear is something that pushes a person towards love... Towards Oneself. It pushes us through suffering to self-understanding... Like the smallest candle flame visible in the darkest darkness... The only condition is honesty and acceptance of the rejected part of ourselves.

Integrating the dark side... The dark night of the soul. While it may not seem to us at first, it ultimately all tends to balance and reconnect. Both polarities complete each other (Yin Yang). And all this just to give yourself the opportunity to experience, create... For is the journey about achieving goals if, during its duration, we admire the most beautiful views?
Is it the goal or the journey itself that builds us the most? You create yourself anew. From a complete Place and Space, a perfect Paradise, full of love, and wanting to experience it fully, you created the opposite pole. For do you have any idea what light is if you don't know darkness?

Although at first you may think that you are a crumb in a cruel world, remember that this crumb is made of the same atoms that make up the stars in the night sky.

Damian Buczniewicz

Chapter 15

The heart awareness—intuition and ascension vibrations

Harsh rays of sunlight streamed into my room through an open window. I felt their heat on my face as if they were much warmer than the ones I'm used to. Energy, I thought, and only then did I open my eyes. The light almost blinded me and — most interestingly — the rays of the sun were breaking through in one place only in the hole that was formed between the thick clouds which obscured the sky that day. I thought it was luck and that I had to enjoy it for a while. So I lay there and soaked up the warmth until the sun went down and the well-known twilight of the cloudy morning returned.

Charged with positive energy, I came down to eat breakfast. Mommy was sitting in the kitchen, preparing nutritious fresh fruit juice as she did every morning. Mommy made so many juices that each juicer was with us only a year and they did not accept returns under the warranty. Mommy was just crushing them with the amount of work. We also had a brand new juicer at home almost every year. The gallons of juices that came out of each of them contributed to maintaining a high level of health for our family. The juicer had been making strange noises for several days and we knew that this was its last twist. Parents were even looking for new models available on the Internet. They always hoped that the next one would last longer, but it never happened.

"What an antique," I said to Mom, when I heard the juicer hissing and gasping as it was squeezing the beetroot juice out.

"Yes... Unfortunately, it's time to buy a new one. Daddy has to do it on the weekend. I hope that until then this antique, as you called it, will do the job."

"May it... Lack of fresh juice in the morning it's like the end of the world," I laughed out.

Even Kal got so used to it that the first thing he did was go into the kitchen and pour himself a portion of juice. Only then did he look for me at home. He always greeted me with a glass of juice in his hand and more than once with a colorful mustache formed after already drunk sips.

"Today is the 16 of December. Get ready for beautiful energies from space. They'll get more powerful. Receive them with gratitude and give them intentions," said Mommy.

I only nodded my head and grabbed a glass of juice. I took it to the living room where Daddy was already sitting on the sofa. He was watching some sort of a documentary

"What are you watching?" I asked.

"They try to prove with every possible means they know that Megalodons have become extinct," he laughed.

"What's so funny about it?"

"What do you mean? The fact that they haven't gone extinct but they're searching in the wrong places."

"Aaa... I see. However, I have a strange impression that some scientists know well that they still exist. And since they cannot reveal the whole truth, they wrap it up in numerous speculations. Maybe they are counting on the fact that people will come to their own conclusions. Or maybe to prepare us for numerous surprises when there is a great disclosure? When humankind gains access to the underwater depths of many species and their existence will be a real surprise for them."

"It's true. They do the same in all these extraterrestrial programs. You're right. Perhaps it is good that they are sowing a seed of truth. Even if they themselves question it in the programs or treat it as a hope for future contact."

"And past," I added.

"They have lots of evidence on that and they don't need to

speculate. They just look but they can't see."

Daddy was right. We recently learned a lot about the existence of previous civilizations, much more technologically advanced than our own. I didn't even want to guess how much more evidence was hidden underground, buried under the mud and rocks that had been brought ashore by the great flood."

"Plenty, Smaisi, " Daddy answered to my silent question, "and you'd better hurry up before you are late for school."

It was only then that I looked at the clock. Perhaps these bright radiant sun rays took me off guard because I felt as if it was the weekend.

"You could give yourself a break if it wasn't for the geography test."

"Yeah…Right before Christmas. No mercy," I was agitated. I went upstairs to get ready to leave.

At school, as is at school, only boredom. The test went great for me and I didn't expect any problems with the evaluation of my work. After school, I made an appointment with Kal in front of the school building. We went home together.

"What's the plan for today?" Kal asked.

"I have no idea. It's so grey that I don't feel like doing anything," I answered.

"Same here, that's why I was hoping you'd come up with something," he laughed.

"No way. Although we'd need some entertainment.

I can assist with that — I hear in my head a well known voice — *I know what kind of entertainment you prefer* — it added.

"Yriah," Kal uttered, "I can hear Yriah"

"Me too. No boasting, please," I turned to Kal, "When and where?" this question though I turned to Yriah.

"Every time and every place is good" she answered and in front of us appeared a small luminous sphere.

I looked around, checking if anyone else could see it.

"Follow the light, " she added and the luminous point started to move very quickly forward. It was flying with such a speed that we needed to run to chase it.

We knew very well the place where Yriah was guiding us to. Recently we spent lots of free time in the nearby forest. We felt the connection with Mother Earth there and it was always so quiet there — as if people forgot how wonderful it is to stroll in the trees. This forest though was unique, the majority of it was filled with old huge trees and one could ideally feel their energy. You could literally feel the wisdom and ability to heal and cleanse. We went hundreds meters inside the forest and a small luminous ball stopped and after that it completely disappeared. We looked around. Behind our back Yriah was standing, smiling radiantly.

"Hello, my lovelies. I've missed you. I'm glad that Semjase has got so many responsibilities these days. It gives me a chance to take over in passing you some information."

"We love to listen to you, too," I confessed. I liked Yriah's company very much. I felt very safe with her.

Yriah sat on the canopy of a big fallen tree and she patted the seats next to her.

"Before we begin, I would like to tell you something, Smaisi. Totally from me. From my heart. Because you've chosen this form of transmitting the truth I would like to assure you that word is one of the most beautiful things that you can offer."

"I'm all ears," I said. I couldn't wait to hear what I was going to hear.

"Every word is like a spark. Spoken, written, read — It sinks deep within us, illuminating the paths previously unavailable many times. It explains and allows for deeper understanding. It builds a new way of looking at many things, thus awakening people. The word is like a microscope that allows you to get a better look at the tissues of your own being. It is like a voice that tells you how to change reality, if it is not the same as the one you would like to be in. It guides you towards happiness. The energy with which you speak and write will go around the entire universe, be reflected in the glow of your eyes, in your gestures, in your voice. Ultimately it will affect your actions and those who will read it and take your energy. This energy will strengthen them, there will be a spark of awakening. The spark of soul consciousness. A fuse that will allow them to kindle a fire and burn everything that is distorted in it. When this energy touches the light yourself and you embrace it fully with what you gave to others thanks to it, it will come back to you strengthened by everything that it has been able to accomplish. The way you write passes your energy on. It is extremely important. People will be able to pick up this energy, and its high vibration will allow them to open up to the truth."

"Thank you for these beautiful words, Yriah..."

"Truth is always beautiful. Even if it initially is shocking, the recognition of it will always be connected with a positive effect, both for the side that presents it as well as receives it."

"When will you take us today?" I asked.

"At first, I'll take you into your heart space. Then... Who knows where the truth takes us."

"I can't wait," I clapped.

"So let's start so as not to test your patience any longer," she laughed soundly, "As you know very well, everything is energy. It shows up in various forms, it emits light. Consciousness is the emanation that is expressed through many different ways. Of course, when talking about consciousness, I mean the level of it that is eternal and infinite. The primal state that is all knowing, all possible, and infinite awareness. In its original state, everything is an expression of this one awareness, it must be so, and that's because it is all that exists. However, not everything and not everyone are on the same level. Consciousness in its original state has no form, it is simply conscious. The terms of the conscious and subconscious mind are often used on Earth. There is also talk of regaining consciousness. It is also well known that to be aware of your existence is to be aware at all. However, this is not true, and it is not the same as Primary Consciousness and Soul Consciousness. The human mind has a self-awareness, it creates a closed circuit, then we talk about a closed mind. Unfortunately, most people's minds are still locked to the truth at this point. Consequently, we cannot speak of eternal, infinite consciousness, because the mind will operate with very limited access to it, which will block its possibility in many fields. If the information that you are getting from the beings of light were to be conveyed to people, the intellectuals would undoubtedly react the worst because they would consider it to be unconventional. The mind is the template. The closure in it is that people are as if trapped by their own mind and are unable to process information and concepts that only their consciousness can understand. For many, it is therefore a foreign world, a fiction that is completely unacceptable. Notice, furthermore, that these intellectuals, locked by the barriers of their mind, usually stand in power and deal cards in a game called life. Thus, a mind-made system becomes simultaneously dependent on the management of that system. And it goes on and on — for decades and centuries. You have to understand that the mind communicates with thoughts, while consciousness speaks to you as wisdom. The knowledge that is your inner wisdom can also be called intuition. Notice that when you talk of intuition you are not using words such as think or believe. You just know, even if you are not aware of the origin of this knowledge, it is just within you, and nothing or no one can question it. Sometimes your intuition tells you to meet someone or do something. You don't know why, but you feel the need to make it happen. You just know it has to happen this way. Then in your mind you are not able to find the basis for explaining this feeling and the knowledge that you actually felt in yourself with great strength. It is the impulse of consciousness that directs you to do something, but it is not a product of the mind, but the promptings coming from within you, from your consciousness. These are messages from your soul that cannot be ignored. However, not all listen to these promptings. It's a pity. The dominance of the mind that guides and defines your sense of reality, of course, in the mind, closes the door to your intuition, into the space of the heart. The mind knows that if you follow this inner feeling, it will lose control and no longer rule, and that's not what it wants because it was created for the purpose of control. This is where the fight begins. The mind will not give up so easily and will stubbornly stick to its version, trying at all costs to keep an advantage over the opponent who is intuition. The mind is also referred to as the ego."

" Is it always like that the mind fights? " asked Kal.

"Of course, it is. And would you surrender without a fight? Remember how many situations in your life there have been when something intuitively came to you but your mind successfully blocked it, sent you to other thoughts, or made you think that intuitive feeling is nonsense. Your ego will always find plenty of ways to take you away from doing something that has been received intuitively by you, especially when your intuition works in a very out of the box way. And now your mind will attack you with questions that you will try to find answers to. For example — What will your parents or family say? Is it appropriate? It will say: You have responsibilities, you can't do that, you'll neglect other duties and let yourself and people down, you can't just follow your whim. There'll always be a "but" whose purpose is to block the message from the soul. Many times these clues are crucial to our lives. For example, it turns out that our intuition tells us to go visit someone but we don't listen to it, so we take away the opportunity to meet this person possibly for the last time. Or we don't listen to our intuition telling us not to go somewhere and an accident happens. Often, even very often people spit regret because they didn't listen to their gut feelings, but when further prompts come, the diagram is duplicated. Few can beat the mind. The mind is cunning and can influence our emotions. It plays with them and often doesn't work in our favor. It places on the pedestal the ability to think logically, but none will think that real logic is actually being blocked by the mind. What should be logical in many cases is not. Human reality has been dominated by the mind, which means that everything is defined from its perspective. There is no room for foreboding coming from within the heart. But now look at it differently. What if your mind — especially the third dimensional human mind — only knows a fraction of what it should know? Unfortunately, that's the way it is. It is intuition that is real knowledge. Would you like to follow someone who has such meager knowledge and is labeled "idiot"?

"Well, I guess not," Kal said and I knew what Yriah was getting at.

"Exactly. It would be madness. And now have a look at

what billions of people are doing in the whole world. Exactly this.

There is a huge gulf between the levels of perception of consciousness and perception of the mind. As people open their minds to their consciousness and allow it to impart information in full force, they will realize how limited the system is. In the mind's illusory perspective, everyone and everything is judged and must pass through the ego filter. It has nothing to do with seeing from the heart. We are at a point in the timeline where any person that is perceived as crazy by others can be absolutely sure of his or her complete mental sanity. It has passed through the barriers of the mind."

"From this it follows that we are also fully sane," I laughed.

"Unfortunately, the mind is not the only block that the consciousness needs to face. There are swirls in space. It's another level that connects with the web of neurons. These webs and energetic fields are like various expressions of the same beliefs of low vibrations. They close the connections with the infinite consciousness, keeping humans in the reality of five senses. They're like electric and vibrational levels of processes of filtering pieces of information through the brain in order to adjust them to beliefs. And these, as you know, have been manipulated. When there's a situation in which you're capable of breaking through the template thinking, the neuron web breaks and a new one is formed that fits into the new reality. This influences the changes in the filtering processes and the decoding of previously unavailable possibilities takes place. What used to be impossible suddenly becomes possible. It's a point which many people describe as a turning point in their life. Only after some time, as the connection with consciousness awakens, people realize that the energy of these possibilities has always been in them, but they did not use it in an appropriate way. It is the power of creation from the heart space."

"It's true, creating from the heart space is a beautiful energy and its manifestation is very fast."

"Because it's the energy of high vibration. Only beings that started their process of awakening open this possibility for themselves through unblocking the higher chakras in their bodies.

You need to remember though that a close control of the mind and blocks have been maintained for centuries by the elite families that belong to a global conspiracy against humanity. It's not in their favor for humans to be guided by their intuition, their soul, their source of truth. They use written by themselves the only real knowledge to close people up in the prison of their own minds. They destroy the silence because in silence the soul screams loudest. They're afraid that it will be heard. This quiet voice of the soul has the power of a loud scream that calls for awakening. It's not a coincidence. The consciousness speaks through the heart that's why in its place the intuition is most often felt. Of course, I mean the spiritual heart that can be felt in the middle of the chest, in the chakra of the heart. This circle of life connects the physical level with the higher levels that go being the scope of five senses."

"It's obvious then why the heart had been used as a symbol for love and higher feelings for such a long time; the feelings that grow beyond what is seen and what we can touch. Love goes beyond our basic senses, therefore, we often can't even define it with words, you can just feel it, " I confessed.

" Yes, that's true. It's the source of the heart symbol. It's been derived from the long forgotten understanding of what heart and feeling with it really means. When you feel enormous love inside you or compassion, focus for a little and turn your attention to the feelings near your chest and heart chakra. The soul can in a physical way send you messages. Very often people before they make an important decision ask themselves questions: What does your heart tell you? Do I feel it's right? They don't refer to the mind then but to their consciousness, to their soul, they look for advice from the inside. They trust it. The heart chakra is a main connection to the consciousness which is beyond the world of illusionary forms, whereas your head is caught in a trap of thinking and boundaries of the five senses. Many people, majority of them in fact, are enslaved by their minds and these minds are, in turn, enslaved by those who want to control. So, there are superimposed patterns of thinking: what is wrong and what is bad; what should and what shouldn't be done;what is normal and what is normal and what is not a norm. So they think not in a way they should. Everyone has their own individual feelings. When you feel inside what is good and what is bad — you're yourself, you free yourself from the puppet show. Most often, people hear what they can't. And who forbids them? Instead of looking for the guilty, they look for a reason they shouldn't do anything. They're based on paralized and fearful mentality which keeps them in a mental and emotional cell which is the mind. You already know on what scale humans have been manipulated and controlled. You know what ways and technologies have been implemented to do that. Although it's easy to manipulate the mind, the space of the heart is a completely different thing. It's not that easy to instruct it. Heart is an Intuitive connection with the infinite consciousness which has its own electromagnetic field and its own sense of reality. You can't impose anything on the heart. It simply knows. It doesn't need a second hand confirmation. It possesses the source of wisdom and it is wisdom. When someone often listens to the guiding whispers of their soul and trusts them, they're very often perceived by others as someone who has an innate intelligence. These people — their behavior, ability to quickly identify dangers, sensing situations and many more abilities — they're not unnoticed. On the contrary. They become unique when they cross the barrier behind which they were called insane because they were trespassing norms. Whereas the majority of people fight a constant war between what they think and what they feel — and the head wins—these unique just flow with life. They are like a current of a river that none can stop. Of course, being like the rest of the society will always be simpler, but none said it's better. I don't judge people, far from that, I know from the experience of my incarnations on Earth how many programs have been uploaded in human minds from the youngest age. The educational system itself directs humans fate, media and crowd battue is another huge counterpart to the willingness to individualistic feeling and break through. I know what it's like to be a rebel and a free-thinker ridiculed by the crowds, condemned by the followers of the lie. But this is not the way. Not anymore. The time of manipulation has come to an end

310

and I am trying to make every part of me incarnating on Earth awake to the connection with the awareness of my soul. Sometimes it's a hard and painful awakening, but I know it's necessary. The moment of mass awakening of humanity has come. It is the time of the vibrational frequency for ascension."

"Exactly. Can you describe it to us? We know more or less what will happen and that the frequency of Earth will change. But we don't have greater knowledge about the way these processes will take place. We know the influence of these changing frequencies on the human body but it has been presented to us in short, " Kal said. He didn't feel like saying goodbye to Yriah and she, as always, received our willingness to gain more knowledge with a huge enthusiasm.

"Aw, how I love your questions and inquisitiveness!", on Yriah's face there appeared a beautiful radiant smile and, smiling, she started to introduce us to the secrets of the energetic processes of ascension taking place on Earth — "So as the planet enters a higher dimension, it needs to raise its vibrations. It's important for you to understand what it means. The ascension of planet Earth is, in reality, the gaining of an energetic equilibrium. Humanity on the whole planet is receiving beams of light that create holes inside the energetic webs of the planet. These energies, mixing together, create whirls on Earth, and these in turn create sources of which purpose is to cleanse the Earth from all the old and faulty patterns. They cleanse humans as well. They release negative energies which welled up in humans. However, these changes cause some blocks in the energetic systems of the Earth, in human bodies, and in all the beings living on the planet. It means that the old patterns won't be purged one at a time and the process of purging can create a temporary chaos. When the process of clearing ends, human existence will be full of peace and harmony. The inner truth and the desire for freedom will be revealed. Long asleep powers will be awakened in humans. Higher energies will activate the consciousness of the soul, giving access to higher wisdom flowing from their intuition, that is the wisdom of the symbiote. Humanity will receive the necessary energy to again integrate their systems of chakras.

311

During this process humans will receive the resonance of merging and the changes in the heart and mind will occur. Energy of the Earth will help in this process since it shifts to a higher vibrational state as well and changes its frequency which will influence the level of awakening in humans. The Earth started to vibrate more intensely which means that every living creature in the planet needs to lift their vibrations as well to adjust to their Mother. Unfortunately, not all the living creatures will be able to sustain such highly rising vibrations. Initially, humans will feel confused, almost lost. Then, chaos will creep into their lives. Many of them will start to get ill because, despite the possibilities that the raising of vibration will offer them, they won't be able to make the connection with their symbiote. It's a very difficult period for humans. It leads to the Golden Era but it's not an easy path. There will be re-sorting of human DNA and a new, more developed nervous system will be formed. In the final stage of transformation, it will give people access to inner information and will give people a higher awareness. This will happen thanks to the awakening of the previously inactive DNA segment and brain cells. Human bodies will take in more light, so they will begin to evolve into a fully conscious multidimensional being. As you already know, the degradation of the DNA strands of the human being led to the fact that people began to be driven by selfishness and this contributed to the closure of their heart centers. Due to the lack of these strands, the human has become, in a way, a hybrid being and most of their abilities have been lost. Until now, humans have used a very small amount of the DNA segment, which has prevented them from developing their full potential. You already know that the human body is the carrier of the soul and how important it is for the human being to take care of it properly. People don't realize how important information their own body stores for them. It is information thanks to which it is possible to unlock the full potential of a human being. All connections of human intelligence are stored within this segment, in the human body.

It is the gateway to connect with the universe. If humanity allows it, the gate will be opened. Human genes containing light codes will be activated, giving access to all latent and lost abilities. They will allow the body to regenerate itself, transfer the healing ability and give access to all the latent and lost abilities. They will allow the body to regenerate itself, give the ability to heal and access all the energies and powers that your symbiotic soul has, depending on where it comes from. This transformation, however, will not take place if the intention of ascension does not come out of the will of one's own being. Do not forget about the fact that the human has received from the creator a free will which is respected in every case. Many people will experience short visions and flashes of memories that they will not be able to identify because the transformation process will not be completed and the body will not adjust to the new vibrations of the planet yet. Many people, due to the space and density in which they have lived so far, lack harmony, the desire to sow good not only for themselves, but also for others. Such beings will have a hard time opening up to these new pure energies.

It will require from them a great internal change — a change in perception and way of thinking. They will also need to awaken their consciousness leaving numerous programs and manipulations behind. First, however, they have to come out of the matrix space that they have been stuck in for so long. Without it, there will be no transformation. In addition, man must put in an effort to self-purify the body so that the transformation process can be completed as quickly as possible. It also requires self-discipline and persistence in the pursuit of goals. In one word, a person must really want it. He or she must consciously desire to ascend and this desire must come from the space of the heart because only then will the new Earth open up to them. Confidence in change is also needed here. People sometimes think too much instead of feeling within themselves where they should go and what to do. Thinking too much, which is the ordinary of the day for humans, is a huge waste of energy. The same is true of fear, which literally drains your energy. People have millions of brain cells that can improve in any way and make them grow and develop. However, it is impossible to do it right without knowing what energy affects human life and how to use it for your own growth. People have become slaves for energy and were once experts in it."

"What do you mean by that?" I asked, "It's actually nicely put, " I added after a while, I was wondering if I could borrow it and use it in my book.

"Of course you can do that, Smaisi. They're just words. They don't belong to anyone. Nothing belongs to anyone. Everything is common because we're all one. And coming back to the topic... The difference between the expert of energy and its slave is huge. The expert of energy can make use of it, manage it, even play with it. When it comes to the slave, the energies manage them and play with them. Humans can't control energy and so energy controls them. How? It's easy. Thoughts are energies. If you're an expert, you know precisely how it works, you think and create for your benefit and for the benefit of others. If you have no idea though, how the energy works, negative thoughts and grumpiness in which the majority of people reside, become energy, which creates the reality of a given person. How is the universe supposed to give something beautiful to the person who all the time sees everything in black color, looks for traps and tricks everywhere, is filled with fear, lacks a sense of self-worth and if he or she could, they would hide in a deep black hole? How? Energy does what humans tell them to. When they tell it to be fearful and grumpy, this is what they receive. They do it to themselves. None else is responsible for that. Their lack of knowledge about energy makes them slaves instead of experts and powerful creators of their reality. Humans need to understand that there are no accidents. Everything that happens is the creation of energy, in majority the one that they send out themselves. The process of creation takes place in space where the human consciousness dwells. This can be called the flow of movement between the energy of light which is a thought and the material world and all the universes in the torso-vibrational field. Energy is like a stream of water that flows freely through different areas. Likewise, energy flows lightly from one world to another. Sometimes there is turbulence in the energy stream that changes the flow, but it continues to flow. Energy is ubiquitous, and energy is ubiquitous only when it is faster than the speed of light. This is how fast energy works. In the end, people must understand that whether they like it or not, there will be a sudden energy alignment in their lives. It will only depend on them how they adapt to this change. In times of great change, humanity will join the Earth's torsion field on the rise. This is already happening and human beings together with the planet enter the energy space of a different vibration and frequency. "

"I have an impression that the vibrational frequency has a different meaning. Perhaps as a level? I don't know..." Kal suspended his voice. "as a channel of a mutual agreement? I have a strange feeling, but I can't name it. I don't know if I'm right."

"You're right, in a way it can be said so. Hmm..." Yriah pondered, "Perhaps I'll explain that to you with the example of water. Water is a source of a given vibrational frequency. People can hear only its splash, that is a sound that it makes. Neither the source of water vibration is analyzed or the intelligence and memory is read and that's because it's a frequency of vibration that is because it's a frequency of vibration that is adjusted to the level of the existence of water. It's like communicating with different languages. You hear the words, sounds that the other person makes but you don't understand them because it's not your vibrational frequency. If the human would tune into the frequency of water they would be able to understand it and know how intelligent it is and how great memory it has. Energy is the source.

The rustle of leaves or the noise of the wind are the source of a certain frequency of vibrations. When a dog yells, people hear barking, but if they tune in to the frequency of the sound made by dogs or other animals, they would understand that it is a communication system. The frequency of vibration is like the radio waves common to a species. Just because we don't understand the water or the noise of trees doesn't mean that these sounds don't store information. People just don't perceive them because they are not in tune with them. Each vibration has its own frequency, often multiple frequencies — they define how we perceive information.

"So everything around us speaks to us?" I asked to be certain.

"Yes, Smaisi. If you at least once tuned to the vibration frequency of a tree and heard its cry when it is cut, you would never buy a real Christmas tree again."

"So the people who can communicate with the trees... So how do they do it?"

"It is commonly referred to as clairvoyance, or clairhearing. However, this is a resonance. A person is able to tune into the vibrational frequency of another being in each density and dimension. The space is filled with information about both the past and the future. All you have to do is learn to tune to these frequencies in order to be able to connect with them and the power to download the knowledge contained within them."

" Unbelievable! Kal I think I know what we're going to do this evening, "I said.

" Enjoy your practice time, " wished Yriah and I sensed that it was a goodbye,"See you later, my lovelies. We shall meet again," while saying that she disappeared and I started to feel cold. As if her presence was making the surrounding space filled with warm air.

Only now it dawned on me that it was winter and we spent almost two hours in the cold, in addition sitting almost motionless on the trunk of a fallen tree.

"Are you too...?" I muttered and didn't get to finish.

"Yes, I've just felt the cold too. Let's go home. Hot girl, this Yriah" he laughed and I joined in knowing perfectly what he meant.

Chapter 16

The seeds are sprouting in the white glow
Already growing leaves with green healing
Plants go straight towards the Sun
Striving to connect with God
Silence is wrapped in the day
As if time has stopped
Time will not move forward anymore
But will change direction to the stars
From this stopping, a new world rises
Above the chaos that has reached its peak
Let the confusion remain in it
And the harmony will reign in the new space

Elizabeth Krajewska

Age of Aquarius

Christmas passed very quickly. Fortunately, I was able to get Kal a gift that he liked very much. I gave him an electronic sketchbook that could be used both for taking notes and for practicing his drawing skills. He gave me a set of skin care cosmetics, perfume and warm pajamas.

During the holidays, we were allowed to rest and nobody took us anywhere. Beautiful strong energies were descending from space. I absorbed them with my whole being, opening up to the processes of change. Despite the new era just around the corner, governments, while still manipulating the toll, introduced further restrictions and tried to appropriate our freedom. All of this was

317

done to force people to accept a vaccine of questionable content. Few were willing, so the government had to push the public by exerting more pressure. I knew that in the end their plan would fail, but I felt sorry for those who took the vaccine because of fear or lack of awareness of what it really is.

It was very much in my favor that I didn't have to go to school from January 18th. It allowed me to spend more time writing and I had to admit that I was very close to finishing the book. It turned out to be quite an extensive work. However, considering the amount of information to be communicated, it still seemed quite thin to me. How do you fit humankind's stories into four hundred pages? It was not easy, but I tried. I didn't want the book to scare away potential readers with its thickness. People subconsciously stayed away from such works. There are only a few more topics left for me to write about.

Recently, I have noticed the actions of other star children more and more clearly. Many set up YouTube channels or posted important information on their private profiles. Nobody was hiding anymore.

The Age of Aquarius began with the great conjunction of the two great planets Saturn and Jupiter on December 21, 2020. I was counting on the fact that the year 2021 will start with a great pump and many changes will take place very quickly. The energies helped make this happen. The old matrix was disappearing at an alarming rate and the elites were clinging to what was left. And there wasn't much left, and it was conscious.

People were slowly waking up, starting to see outside the programs, reading between the lines and noticing the manipulations. Increasingly aware of their free will and independence, they rioted. The time was coming when humans were to stand up for their rights, and nothing inconsistent with the highest principles of the universe could be imposed on him. All over the world there were organizations whose aim was to restore order with full respect for the human and the whole of nature. They are to take care of people who, during many changes taking place in a short time, will be able to feel lost at the right moment. These organizations will not support governments because there are no higher or lower in the universe. Everyone is equal and has the same rights to life, therefore, in the first place, they will call for the purification of the environment in which we live. The purification of soils, water and air, is essential because their pollution has so far had a destructive effect on human health. I couldn't wait for the space to be cleared so that when I go outside it feels exactly like on Earth without humans where Semjase once took me. The humans themselves are not a problem for Mother Earth. It is their destructive actions and their pursuit of power and money at all costs that contributed to all the harm to the environment, and ultimately also to themselves. Everything is connected with each other.

I went downstairs. I expected Kal to appear soon. That day we had an ambitious plan to prepare for the Age of Aquarius in which we had been already treading. Kal wanted to make a concise note of the changes so that he could post it to several Facebook groups. People needed preparation and information about this great event. We wanted as many people as possible to find out what to expect in the near future. The new year 2021 was to be a year of many changes. I felt it with all my heart and had no doubts about it. It was a new start and although humanity still had a quite bumpy road to the finish line, I knew that when they got there, they would feel great love and gratitude for everything that had happened.

"How's your mood?" Mommy asked me as soon as she saw me bustling in the kitchen.

"Okay. I can feel the upcoming shifts. Their energy is amazing."

"It's true, you can feel that the spaces are almost entirely cleansed from dark, low-vibrational beings," she replied, "Is Kal coming today?"

"And what do you think?" I asked playfully.

"I think yes. I can't remember the day when he wasn't here" she laughed.

"And what are your plans for today?"

"Actually, no plans. Everything is closed so we'll pop out only for a small grocery shopping and we'll stay at home."

SIRIAN

That was the moment when Kal strode into the house with a big smile on his face. I felt that something had happened, something positive because of his facial expression.

"What are you showing your teeth at?" I joked, amused.

"You won't believe who visited me last night" he announced in a puzzling way.

"Surely I won't believe it. Will you share? Or will you stand like that and smirk like cheese?"

"Of course I'll share. I was visited by the being from Sirius. I received a message from it," he confessed and I felt a tinge of jealousy," I'm supposed to tell you everything that I've received. And don't be sad. The being tried to pull you down but it looked like unconsciously you had a different task and you didn't show up."

I was slightly surprised by that but I knew that the soul as a multidimensional being penetrated through various dimensions. Perhaps I was really doing something very important even if I was unconscious.

"I have it all recorded so let's sit and listen to it together," Kal consoled.

The "Let's listen together" part didn't miss Daddy's attention who almost instantly appeared next to us.

"We'll gladly listen," he announced; Mommy only smiled, and I knew we would spend this time in foursome.

"The living room will be most comfortable for that," Daddy suggested and since none objected, he led the way there, waiting for us to join.

"It's quite a long monologue. I warn you" Kal said.

"We're not bothered by such long monologues.

Humans learn all their life. It is possible that today we will learn something completely new. It is important to supplement your knowledge. We will never be at a point where we can fully consciously say that we know everything. Our perception also changes sometimes things that we already have suddenly take on a completely different meaning under the influence of new information. Everything we've seen so far shatters and begins to put itself back together. Many times on the way of awakening consciousness we come across traps in which at a given moment we are sure of our knowledge, but this knowledge evolves and is good only at that moment. That is why everyone has their own path that must be respected. It is also worth being able to admit that you were wrong sometimes because you did not yet have the knowledge that you have now because your perception has changed. It will always change. This process will not stop."

"Let's listen then," Kal suggested and switched on the recording.

The space of the universe is multidimensional and all energy has the ability to penetrate these dimensions just as light penetrates through water and coexists with it or as radio waves of different frequencies flow through data spaces. The record of the information data exists everywhere, every living thing carries it along. Currently, only four dimensions are observed by humans. The first three are width, length, and height or depth. The fourth dimension is time. For this dimension, there are as many as ten dimensions or even eleven dimensions if you take into account the zero dimension, which is the quantum dot. The fifth dimension is the branching of the timeline, here people have the choice of which path they want to follow. The sixth dimension creates worlds in parallel or, to put it another way, those in which the choice of the fifth dimension was different from yours. In this dimension there are all possible paths for the development of the universe, starting from the formation of the first particles in it. The seventh dimension is the beginning and the infiniteness, it is the point at which our universe began to emerge. The eighth dimension is even more intricate and extraordinary because it has different infinities, which means that there is a whole multitude of universes there, and each one is different from yours, and they have their own laws. The ninth dimension is a space-time gate that allows you to move between all universes. The tenth dimension is where all possible infinities and universes are. Humanity is currently ascending to the fifth dimension and this journey is a personal energy shift. It happens at the level of the chakras which are responsible for human connection with the Earth, rooting in its energy and understanding who is Mother Earth for humans. It also connects to the higher dimension in which the human symbiote resides, and this gives an insight into the entire knowledge of the universe. The age of the human population is currently struggling with increasing energy-

related problems. It is connected with too much attachment to the past and worrying about the future. This means that their focus has no point in the present and that the present eludes them. They are unable to be in here and now, they keep reminiscing over what has been or analyze what is to come. This leads to an energy disturbance that ultimately causes people to feel fear and over-worry, aggravating the problem more and more. It's a closed circle from which it's hard to get out later. Fear and bad energy manifest later in the everyday life of a person, and he or she perceives it as bad cards from fate, even though they're responsible for their creations. Humans should understand that they will find all the energy at the level of their crown chakra. It is the connection with Mother Earth and the cosmos which is the great order of the universe. People got the opportunity to ascend with the planet now, but for that to happen, changes in themselves are necessary. Their bodies must be cleansed of any lingering toxins that have accumulated over decades. Toxins are blockades made of negative energies. It is impossible to enter higher dimensions without being cleaned. In order for a human being to ascend through the body, light must flow, animating the whole organism. If the energy field of a given being is strong enough, it begins to build a shield-like matrix around the entrance hall. It is then that a powerful stream of pure scrap of paper flows into the crown chakra and a tremendous connection is made. In the crown chakra there is a luminous diamond which appears as a blue pearl emitting a bright blue beam of light. It is pure energy. Many people, however, are trapped, stuck to the timelines and clinging to old paradigms. They forgot that everyone with him has a guide, a guardian angel and a healer who is with them all the time and helps to connect with the higher self of man. It is thanks to their help that the heart chakra opens and joins the field of universal love, and the human being enters the higher dimension of experiences and possibilities. Consciousness is awakened and the soul symbiote is no longer closely related to time. This is the moment when a person cuts himself or herself off from paradigms, begins to live in the here and now, stops worrying about tomorrow and does not dwell on the past. He or she knows that all that has happened are the things they should be grateful for because they got them to where they are. Usually then people stop fearing death as well. For the knowledge that it does not exist, and not in the sense that they know it. Such a person's life suddenly becomes better and more comfortable, even though there has been no major change in the material world. People stop being interested in what they have and focus on their feelings. They depart from matter, assimilating only with what they consider necessary in their further journey of experience. They then close themselves in the blue energy that protects them. They feel safe thanks to it, and in fact it is just like that. Due to the individualism, the healing processes of the mind and body will be different for each person. It cannot be reduced to a single version of events. Children of the stars also go through these processes differently, it is easier for them to regain connection with the soul, but it is they who usually take on the worst incarnations and the most pain. The ascension process offers everyone the same, but everyone will ascend as much as they have earned. While some will open their full potential, others will only partially succeed. There will be those who will stay in the third dimension that doesn't really exist anymore. Not everyone will always get insight into the higher dimensions. However, a new era is coming for everyone, filled with love, wisdom and conscious awakening. Human energy will be anchored in the heart and will open a window to your consciousness, activating additionally the human crystal body. This will allow human beings to evolve very rapidly. Their chakras will reach a completely different level, which will translate into consciousness, wisdom, feeling and perception, humanity will finally start to be active on completely different planes, will start to properly care for the body, will feel the full strength of the spirit, intuition, and develop the mind and its capabilities At this level people will feel abundance already understood by them in a completely different way, they will take responsibility for others with love, respect and gratitude that fills them. This is a completely new journey for humankind. Until now, all energy vortices on Earth were blocked, which effectively withstood the potential of a human being, therefore the world lacked the vibrations of pure and unconditional love for everything that exists. However, this will change and a person will be able to feel it again in himself and in others. A new nation of human beings will be born on Earth, which will give rise to completely new possibilities."

Kal switched off the recording for a moment. We looked at him surprised.

"What? I'm thirsty."

"How is it possible that you didn't ask any questions?" I wondered.

"I have no idea. This entity was speaking in such a way that I felt hypnotized. I think though that it has something to channel and it was not necessarily open to our inquisitive questions."

"Highly possible. Is this the end of the monologue?"

"Of course not! There's a lot."

"Let me have a glass of juice as well."

When Kal returned with a glass of juice for each of us, he again switched the recording on and we focused on listening. He was right there was something hypnotizing about the speech of this being. You just felt compelled to listen.

Every person is a wonderful creature, curious about life and its secrets. Many people want to ask questions at some point. Who are they and where do they come from? Are there other worlds and other civilizations inhabiting planets, of which there are billions all over the universe? Do they have souls? What Happens After Death? They come to a point where it becomes unbelievable to them that there is nothing else but them. As many questions, as many answers. Humanity greedily searching for information about its origin, unaware of how little they know, have made many mistakes. One was the recognition of human evolution according to Darwin. Many people have already noticed the complete omission of the soul aspect in his theory, which only focused on the evolution of the human body towards more and more advanced forms of physical life. So I want to remind you that a human being has never been able to influence its physical development by itself, and in truth — none else. You've always had outside help. It is the universe that has interfered with your evolution, the universe is everything and you are the universe. Humanity must break out of its mantle of vanity and open up to the truth. The universe has always given humanity everything it needs. Now, after a thousand years of enslavement, this also raises the question of how humankind will take advantage of it. Humanity has to believe that it was never alone. There are billions of different lives on the many planets in the universe. And although they are different from each other, in a way they are the same and always stand on the side of humanity from the very beginning. Our entire common history is recorded in the energetic diagrams of the planet Earth's field. Humanity has this information at hand. When they open their hearts and minds, this information will come to them on its own. So understanding the existence and origin of the human species will cease to be a secret or merely a speculation. The universe is reopening to the human generation inhabiting Earth. Let it look for the truth for it has always been waiting to be discovered. When humankind removes its blockages and bow its heads to the truth, then it will get it. It will be a time when old theories will be forgotten and new theories will only be built on the truth. Earth is also not alone in this process. There are as many as 383 ascending planets currently in the five local universes. Earth is one of them. Everything is based on a dependency of coexistence. This means that between the universes and the planets there is a connective tissue that coordinates their evolution and makes them one universe. In 1994 the process of planetary evolution was accelerated and already then there were many significant changes on Earth. With the beginning of July of that year, humankind felt an increase in fears and negative images of reality. Old traumas returned and diseases began to attack human bodies.

It was the effect of accelerating time and events on the planet, as humankind made bolder steps towards self-destruction. The light body activation processes have started and are still going on. The successive phases of activation may take years or seconds, all depending on the will of the soul's symbiote. It is completely independent of the human level of individual development. It is the soul that decides which horizontal celestial body best suits your being at any given time and matches the height of the planet itself. If the human looked at the planet from the perspective of his symbiote and oversoul, he or she would understand the dependence of all existence where the beginning is the end and the end is the beginning, and everything is connected together. He or she would then see billions of parallel realities and the entire holographic web of their incarnations. From the symbiote position, all these incarnations now continue. In all dimensions and spaces at the same time. So by getting connected, they will get access to the knowledge of their soul that exists and experiences in the past, present and future. The entire structure of space is contained in a membrane that we can call a holographic bank of three dimensional realities. Today, this membrane is more than two-thirds behind it through the fourth dimension and is rising rapidly, old structures are decaying. These changes can cause a variety of reactions in humans. Let me explain this a bit more vividly. Imagine a spherical aquarium located in the center of a much larger aquarium. Fish in a large aquarium can freely look inside a small aquarium, but fish in a small aquarium cannot see what is outside of it. Their perceptions are limited to their own, let's call it the backyard. Only goldfish swim in the small aquarium and the water is sweet. In the big one, the water is salty and there are many species of fish. Unexpectedly, the wall of a small aquarium becomes unexpectedly thinner and slightly cracks, which causes salty water to pour into the freshwater. Goldfish must quickly adapt to changing living conditions and the degree of salinity of the water. Due to the fact that the walls of a small aquarium are getting thinner, something else is happening, goldfish are able to see the fish in a large aquarium better and better. Some goldfish treat other fish as a threat, others as controllers, and some gods suddenly find themselves victims of a conspiracy, and still others feel a kind of excitement. Due to the fact that the wall is becoming thinner and thinner, goldfish start to feel increasing fear, mood swings and experience a whole range of different emotions, depending on how they perceive the fish from the big aquarium. More and more often there are goldfish that look with delight at the multitude of types of life in a large aquarium, are not afraid and feel that behind this increasingly thinner wall there are their distant brothers with whom they will finally be able to connect in their common existence. So they are waiting in joyful anticipation for this moment to come. They look forward to being able to swim in the larger waters without the limitations they've had so far. This holographic sphere disintegrates even more, causing the two spaces to merge. Linear time is decaying and slowly moving towards the eternal now, where the notions of time constraints simply do not exist and are not part of reality. The time of infinite presence is coming. And although the end of the connection process is beautiful, just going through it is associated with irritation and many difficulties. Many times, when the process appears to be too fast and abrupt and could lead to too much shock for the human body or its psyche, interference occurs. Big fish from a larger aquarium, that is creatures from higher spaces, send out complex subatomic wave structures that influence the human body in such a way that it is able to absorb the energy of other dimensions. There were many such interventions, which allowed for the inevitable breakthrough and disintegration of old structures with a complete breakage of the aquarium walls to be more delicate for human beings. The synchronization of the waves of human reality is still in the process of ascending — first to the astral level and then to the next higher levels. Due to the fact that the ascension process has been adjusted and adapted to the possibility of human transformation, the transition between dimensions will not be such a shocking experience for people. I feel it for many. As a dream, but everyone experiences this transformation within themselves. People allowing themselves to release the old forms create conditions for the emergence of new ones, better for them both in the short and long term. Space, as if it adjusts to your new image of reality. So what does humankind want most? The human *symbiote put humans in a new evolutionary position, believing that they would accept the changes and let the sweetness emanate from them fill their souls. When people follow their own soul and its whispers, they will begin to live life to the full with each new step and breath. This is what the human soul wants to do, which has decided to glow on Earth at this special time. It is important for humans to understand that they are in the midst of a complex process of planetary transformation and ascension. Thanks to their understanding of this, they will manage to reduce the fear and confusion they may feel during this process. Each time the planet moves towards the light, this process is unique and exceptional. It is different for each planet. The model I was trying to present was about the Earth and the human species. As I said, besides the Earth, 382 other planets are now moving towards great changes for them. The land, however, is special. This is due to the fact that she was the only one to experience the greatest possible separation from the source. Earth and humanity will triumph. There will be no apocalypse. There will be a great disclosure of the truth about humanity. It has already happened and time is only filling up. Humanity and the planet are catching up with themselves in the events that have already happened in the future, currently there are about eight million people on Earth, whose task is to support the ascent of the planet and humanity. They are referred to by some as the planetary transition syndrome. Each of them came down to Earth with their own task to fulfill. Many of these people have helped with these processes in the past in their previous incarnations. They have done this many times. So knowing exactly what to do, although each time it is a unique phenomenon. However, they can intuitively adapt to it and lead it. The game played on this planet was intended to achieve the greatest possible distance from light. The goal has been achieved, so the planet can return to light again and continue its journey in full connection with the source and humanity will follow along with it. The process of returning began in 1988 with the first activation of the luminous human body. As humanity, you are moving towards the point of Oneness. Mother Earth, turning towards the light again, ascends to higher planes. However, this process is gradual, one second cannot matter and the next one light. Most people, however, already have half of the process behind them.*

"Are things more clear in your head now?" Daddy asked and Kal automatically switched off the recording, "Because it should."

"I think so. A lot of this we've already known, but here the perspective is slightly different" I responded thoughtfully.

"That's why, sometimes it's worth looking at things from different perspectives as not only the whole image becomes more sharp, but also the spectrum of perception is greater,"Daddy explained," Is there anything else?" he wanted to know.

Mommy was sitting and focused on listening. I could feel that this knowledge was totally in resonance with her. She liked to listen about the new era and about the transformation of the planet.

"Of course, I do. Now it's time for the most interesting part for me" Kal said mysteriously so all three of us started to nag that he should switch the recording on again.

The Earth is entering a new era, the Golden Age of Aquarius. All religious interpretations of this era are erroneous and misinformation, heightening the fear of an apocalypse that will not happen. Religion deals with the last days in its legends, but these are only the last days of old age. It starts new and it will not be related to looking at humanity. It is a time of great changes and this is how you need to look at all the processes that will take place on the planet and in human beings themselves. This new epoch into which humanity entered just a few days ago unfolds new perspectives for it, including the existence in existence. However, it will take many centuries for humans to reach a level as advanced as other extraterrestrial nations. The most important thing, however, is that this time has begun and humanity will now only go up. The transition period will be quite difficult, especially for very religious people, because many biblical and church lies will come to light and this will make people feel lost. They will forcefully look for something to confirm the faith that has guided their lives so far. Scientists will begin to use the newly introduced facilities very quickly. The elite, along with the false prophets and the rulers of the countries, will begin to publicly offer liberation, fanatically seeking their followers and victims. And there will be less and less of these. In the early days of the golden age, many people will unfortunately fall into these traps, and the transition period will culminate in 2028. The power of the new era began to grow long ago, in 1844 to be precise, and since then, vast changes have taken place on the Earth. The first half of this period lasted 92 years until 1946, when the Earth emerged from the end of the Age of Pisces. Then there was an acceleration. Numerous inventions and technological discoveries began to appear; humankind was moving forward even though it was held back. Big disclosures will also mark the present end of this transition period. Information and truth that will come out will shake off everything that was known and blindly believed so far. The entire SOL system is now under the control of a new era. All the movements of the planets and all the companies of life in the universe are already subjected to new energies. The Earth follows this path in line with the evolution of the creation of existence. The source of this great epochal change and somehow the culprit of beautiful transformations is the radiation effect of the Central Sun which orbits the solar system once every 25,860 years. The Earth has already entered the outer limits of this high radiation. Time for changes in a human, so now a moment about it. A human hearing the word "creation" or "existence" reacts to it intuitively and in his or her senses they see it in a spectrum of beauty and changes. However, this will not happen until he or she deepens the true knowledge of creation and understands existence as it really is. However, the very words themselves influence the idea, directing them towards the truth. Humans at first perceive the essence of creation as omnipresence, being omnipotent and omniscient. They strive to learn more about the specificity of the creation of existence. People with low vibration levels show no interest in this topic. For them, these words do not exist, because they do not know what existence is. The worst part is that they don't want to find out. Millions of people are enslaved and blinded by the self-proclaimed god religions in which the words "existence" and "creation" are distorted. By pronouncing the word "god" they believe that he is the creation. They are not aware of how wrong they are. It is very important for people to know as much as possible about the essence of the existence of creation. They should bring their knowledge to life and translate it into experiencing this existence by themselves creating reality. Existence and creation are infinite supreme beauty, boundless happiness, and absolute love and truth. Wisdom beyond all knowledge. When a man understands what the existence of creation is, he or she will recognize it in themselves, they will bring each of their joys to the source. Wherever he or she looks then, seeing something beautiful, they will relate it to the infinite beauty of the creation of existence and express their gratitude for it. Then the way a human being perceives everything that exists will change. When he or she sees any life, the slightest movement, the softest vibrations, will fully perceive the infinite eternal and creative creations of existence. They will also understand their own existence differently and will expand their understanding and feeling about the surrounding spaces. They will realize that they are a fragment of the creation of existence and its integral part. When a person knows the creations of existence and the awareness of what it is, it will penetrate their thoughts and the heart will never feel fear anymore, and all doubts will disappear before it appears. They will know that existence or creation is omniscient and they will trust it. They will exist in a state of harmony with all that is and with inner peace in their heart they will walk through life. This peace and trust will allow them to develop even more. The way they feel and think will change. The more light they consciously accept, the more their potential will increase and the space around them will materialize in the way they only want. In people who are aware of the creation of existence, there are even paradoxes (in human understanding) that what is creative is much more real than the sensations of the body. A human lives in accordance with the ether and his or her space is pulsating with the dynamic power of the existence of creation. Nothing is impossible for them, their actions are dynamic and full of creative thinking. I want and desire to do everything right now, because for them what they planned has already happened in the present and they make every effort to make the energy materialize as soon as possible. A human who knows about the existence of creation simply becomes it themselves. He or she is an existence that nothing can limit.

Kal switched off the recording. For a longer period of time, none said nothing. Each and every one of us wondered at their own awareness of existence. And each of us came to different conclusions. This meant only that we were on a patch of awakening the consciousness of the soul, but each of us on our unique one. Exactly in a place we should be now.

Chapter 17

The octaves of vibration and density

The day before New Year's Eve, I was awakened by strange noises coming from downstairs. I got up and quickly slipped on my robe. As I descended, I heard voices that were unfamiliar. Or maybe familiar... Yes, I knew them. Fear pierced my whole body. I ran downstairs as fast as I could. Kal's mother was standing at the doorstep. She glanced at me quite meaningfully.

"I don't know what's going on, Smaisi. Kal behaves as if..." she could finish her sentence.

With the corner of my eye I saw Daddy making a phone call. Mommy was supporting Kal's lost mom. I did what I could best and I connected with him telepathically. When I entered his feelings, I froze. Kal, the one I knew and I loved and that was with me the evening before wouldn't have had feelings like that. He could have had various feelings but not like that.

"Where is he?" I asked.

"At home. I chained him to a radiator" she broke, "I'm sorry, I didn't have a choice," she stuttered through tears.

"I know" I let her know quickly and I already knew who Daddy was calling.

"He'll be here in an hour", he said, "I'll go get Kal."

"I'm going with you" I said quickly and threw a jacket on my robe.

There was no time to change clothes. I knew Kal didn't intend what had happened. He had so much hope for this incarnation. I felt that something heavy and dark was sitting on it. But despite trying, I couldn't see it. It was hiding. One thing was for sure. It somehow clung to Kal and took over his mind enough to order him to take his own life. And then I only thought of one thing: Was it the final attempt to eliminate the luminous beings living on the surface of the Earth? If that was the case, how many other people besides Kal are in that state today?

"Many" Daddy answered to my thoughts, "Mariusz has had plenty of such calls in the last few days. He was even caught in one. They try everything. Everything will be alright, Smaisi. I can see that. You don't need to worry. We only need to unhook it and Mariusz will do that most effectively."

"That's good" I replied.

Kal's mother, upon hearing Daddy's utterance, calmed down as well.

"Perhaps my presence will help him," I added.

"Create a protection. Now, ideally. We don't want to rescue both of you."

Dad was right. I focused and closed myself up in a cocoon of love and light.

"Done." I let them know. A few moments later, we were parking at Kal's house.

When we got inside I immediately headed to the bathroom. Something told me that was where his mother had left him. I was not wrong. When I opened the door he looked at me hostile at first, but then his soul recognized me. The only thing he managed to whisper was:

"Help me, Smaisi." his voice was soft and it sounded like someone was squeezing his throat so he wouldn't be able to say it.

I could feel his fear. He was fighting with himself. Or perhaps with what the entity being all this was ordering him to do. It must have been strong. Kal wasn't that easy to be trapped. I knew that he meticulously lit himself up and made protection. He did that more often than I.

"Help has just arrived. Everything will be okay" I calmed him down and despite the hostility that again appeared on his face, tears started to flow down his cheeks.

Daddy took Kal and escorted him to the car. Then, he again tied his arms to the seat and asked me to make sure he didn't hurt himself. I could feel Kal was fighting. I could hear one of the orders that the entity was asking him to do. I even didn't want to know what would have happened if his mom would have reacted in this way and come to for help. We arrived right on time. Mariusz just parked in the driveway. I didn't know one could get so happy in the sight of a stranger.

Mariusz sensed straightaway what was going on.

"Come on in" he ordered and everyone obediently went inside. Even Kal which surprised me a bit.

Mariusz asked us to put Kal on the couch. So it happened and right next to him Daddy sat down because he was still belaying him. We couldn't be sure what the entity would order him to do again. He could be a threat not only to himself but also to others.

"I need your consent, Kal. Do I have your consent?"

I could see how he must have fought relentlessly to squeeze out a silent:

"Yes, I give consent."

Mariusz closed his eyes and focused on his task. He didn't say anything. He was in complete silence. So was Kal.

I lasted a good thirty minutes. Only after that time did Mariusz come back to our space. I looked at Kal and knew he was free. I lunged towards him, hugging me tightly. He put his arms around me. Daddy reacted to my move, but I think Mariusz called him behind my back because Daddy suddenly stepped back, allowing me to be tender.

"What was it?" I asked Mariusz.

"You don't want to know. Either you or Kal. This information stays with me. Sometimes it's just better not to know.

I created a special protection for him, they won't come close again."

"Thank you" Kal expressed his gratitude and stood up to shake hands with Mariusz.

"No problem, boy. You'll be thanked for it in future too. I'm just doing my job. I'd love to stay but not only you have such problems."

"We understand. You're surely invited to a more favorable date."

"I hope that soon there'll be more of such in my calendar," he laughed softly.

"There will be." I stated confidently.

"And that's why you'll change the world, young lady. That's the reason…" Mariusz said goodbye to everyone quickly and left.

"That was awful. I know that you want to know and, to some extent, you already are aware because I feel it but can we not talk about it for now?" Kal spoke to me.

I remembered my energetic attack very well too. Then we always did everything not to dwell on that.

"Sure. You know very well. We never have to talk about it. This is already a past that is of little importance, " I responded and hugged him again.

Mariusz was right, I could clearly feel an energetic shield that protected Kal's body. It was thick and dense but the sensation was very pleasan t— as love and light as usual.

Only then did Kal's mom come over to him. For her, everything that happened was quite surprising, despite her awareness. She hugged Kal and suggested that he stay with us for a day or two so that she could calm down mentally and her son would be safe. Kal agreed. Anyway, he was to spend tomorrow's New Year's Eve with us. The parents also had no objections.

Even though it was morning, I could see that Kal was tired. I was sleeping while he was fighting with the being that possessed him. I think that was a good word for what we were dealing with.

"Do you want to have a nap?" I suggested, seeing that he could barely sit.

"I won't hide, I'm exhausted. Do you mind?"

"Of course not. Perhaps I'll even lie down with you. I'll ask someone to take us on a short journey for relaxation. Perhaps this will allow us to forget about this whole situation," I suggested and Kal nodded. I did what I promised and asked Semjase to show up.

Kal fell asleep almost immediately. He was really exhausted. I embraced him and for some time I could relax enough for the sleep to take over. There were many various thoughts appearing in my head. I wasn't sure when but I finally fell asleep. When I opened my eyes, I was at my favorite beach. Semjase chose a perfect spot. Especially for Kal. I looked around. Kal was strolling on the sand, wading in water which was washing away all the negative emotions. He even looked a little bored.

"It took you a while," he said, noticing me.

"I couldn't fall asleep. Have you been long?" I asked.

"I don't know but it looks like for a few hours," he responded, "I feel that I needed that, though. All the negative emotions subsided. Water has taken them," he added after a while.

"Semjase knew what to do," I smiled and that's when she appeared.

"Hello, my beloved" her radiant smile always triggered the same emotions in me, "As per request, I'll take you today to a few places. At this stage, your education is almost accomplished. Not much has been left to absorb."

"We will always be ready for another dose of knowledge in case you're bored," Kal said and all three of us laughed out loud.

"Yes, that's something we all know. Let's start then, my dear. I would like to begin by presenting to you the circle of existence. You know it as alpha and omega which are the infinite intelligence. Everything is in the circle, and the circle never ends. In this circle there are cycles, which are densities as well. The first density is your cycle of awareness, the second one is the expansion, in the third one there comes self-awareness, the fourth one is filled with love and understanding. In the fifth one there's light and wisdom, the sixth one is the light and love that creates oneness. The seventh is the cycle of transition into the perception of nature of all that is in

336

which when existing with all that is you become one with it. The eighth is dwelling in the existence of creation. And the existence of creation is everything that is. Humans can't comprehend it yet that stones are alive. Stones exist in the first density that can be also called the density of consciousness. The first three densities of the conscious forms of existence are at the moment perceived by humans. Now, I would like you to imagine this movement inside everything that is created. In matter, we deal with energy that is limited, despite the limitations of density, this energy is quite high. It is intelligent, and one might even say hierarchical. Just as there is a hierarchy of bodies as vessels for the soul, every atom that makes up a stone has such a hierarchy. Once you enter the stone's vibration frequency, you can communicate with it. The exchange of Information between densities is possible. Not only that, it can have great power. For example, let me tell you that just one human, purged of all low vibration blemishes, would be able to move a mountain. So, what would the minds of the masses be able to accomplish with simultaneous determination and the same pure intention? I leave it for your consideration. I am telling you this for a reason. This is an introduction to a piece of your history. About seventy-five thousand years ago, your planet was in the second density. There were only second density beings on Earth. This density is the life density of higher plants and animals that exist without ever rushing towards infinity. In the very distant past, there was a third density population on the planet that existed in the SOL planetary system. Their civilization was similar to that of Atlantis. Due to the war, their biosphere was damaged, which disintegrated the biological network of life of this planet. The creatures inhabiting the planet have experienced such a traumatic experience that they have entered the knot of fear.

No one has been able to help them despite attempts to intervene with other beings. None of them were able to reach them and persuade them to change. After all, six hundred thousand years ago, a certain spherical-etheric race originating from the ER'Ra system made an attempt and succeeded. She managed to untie the knot of fear in which that civilization got stuck. This led to the

337

return of the consciousness of the beings. After their planet was destroyed, they came to Earth. It was then the only planet in the SOL system that could sustain life. This was the beginning of the human form known as the Neanderthal. At first they incarnated on Earth in second density, going into forms that were not human. This was to lead to an evolutionary change, that is, a transition to the next level, which they could only do by wanting to serve others. At that time, they only had a body that humans consider as ape-like. However, this is not entirely the case. This is the only similarity that holds true for the Neanderthal man of the past. It was not a third density evolution in a third density body. These beings have gone through a process that can be called the harvest. They were reborn in the higher realm of this density. Many of them have been reborn on the planet without the second density consciousness complexes they had when the world they once lived had problems. There are three races that still use the type of a second density form. One of them comes from the planet Maldek. It lives inside caves in underground passages and tunnels. They are known by people as Bigfoot. They continue to work through their karmic redemptions. The second race took up residence in a body that could cope with nuclear radiation. However, a human would not be able to do so if there had been a nuclear war. These creatures live in deep forests in many places on Earth. However, they are extremely rare and very skillfully avoid meeting people. They have glowing eyes and are most closely related to humans. It is important to realize that all three races are collectively referred to as Bigfoot, although they are somewhat different from each other.

The third is the thinking company. In the near future, it will be found in caves in the western coastal mountain region. Scientists will think that they have managed to find a new evolutionary human strain. However, it will not be true. About half of the Earth's third density beings are of Mars. One fourth is from your planet's second density and the rest is basically a mixture of beings of different origins. The fact is, the more balanced a being becomes, the less he needs parallel incarnation experiences. Many think that the soul experiences on many densities simultaneously, that is, at the same time, it is stone and man. Of course, this may not be the case, but it often does not happen because souls do not feel the need. The will to move from one universe to another and then these beings can occur on a parallel plane, that is, at the same time but in different universes. These parallel incarnations are then programmed by the higher self to which they use all the information and knowledge that the symbiote has. The nature of oneness is that everything happens simultaneously, but it is impossible to comprehend this by the human mind. The higher self, which in all parts supports each being over the soul: it assists it in programming further life experiences and leads to physical, emotional and spiritual healing. The higher self is free to communicate with the being between the oasis incarnation cycles during incarnations if the proper pathways have already been opened and the soul consciousness has been awakened. The Self is the set of everything that can happen. It is like quicksand and each time it is some part of the parallel development of the same being in multidimensionality and infinity. Because of this, she is able to correctly program her incarnations based on experiences that she already had and those that still need to be experienced. It is like the synchronous programming of many elements simultaneously allowing the self to evolve in many parallel universes. Is it understandable to you?", she asked us which was very rare.

"Yes," I replied confidently. That was my feeling. I already knew that the same wisdom can be perceived differently in our further stages of our life and evolvement.

"Good. Let's continue then. I want to tell you about intelligent energy as well. It's oneness, and this oneness is everything that exists. It has kinetics and expresses a great potential when it is focused. The intelligence infinity is the potential. The intelligent energy is a being, it has oneness that is free from any distortion. However, it must be perceived by whoever enters it. Since I am concerned with the subject of intelligence, I will go to intelligent matter which is in space. It's called Black Goo. In fact, it is an entity assigned to the planet Earth. This intelligent matter travels using electromagnetic fields. It usually moves within the line system, with the exception of when the aurora appears. It then travels through the apple-like structure of outer space. This matter also resonates in the ether like a radio wave. Waves are mechanical-electric vibrations transmitting their frequency, they contain the vital essence of humanity placed in its information field. Black Goo creates a grid of lines all over the planet. This grid charges the entire Earth and has a direct impact on the people it is connected to. Any interference with this intelligent matter causes it to process data in its own way. It can contact all creatures that are within the range of its waves by creating a frequency appropriate for this contact. A famous example of an attempt to use this intelligent matter was its discovery by the Falklanders and the British who claimed to have had Black Goo derived from blue-gray aliens — the Grays. These creatures can properly use and program Black Goo for their purposes. The Grays once collaborated with the Argentines on an island called Thule. The Brutis acquired this intelligent matter and brought it to England. This became their main trophy in the Falklands War that took place in the early 1980s. However, people made many mistakes again because they did not understand certain relationships. The British did not take into account that this intelligent matter is adapted to the frequency of a given region. Therefore, taking Black Goo to another place could stimulate its activity and lead to negative effects on the new environment. Black Goo adapts by converting hydrogen into carbon. It is intelligent planetary consciousness. Other planets also possess such intelligent matter as Black Goo. Each planet has its own. Many such transmutations take place on planet Earth in the natural environment. Magma, when it is no longer in a liquid state, is subjected to the flow of subcutaneous waters. They are sucked in and transmutation chains are formed within them. The water in these places is transformed into substances similar to vegetable oil. Pt, by loosening the transmutation process, silica is obtained and then precious metals. Even gold can be obtained from water, but it is not liquid gold, but its colloidal or monoatomic type, depending on the method used. Many frequencies with specific values are used with Black Goo and are the source of many beings inhabiting the interior of the planet. Scientists on Earth have no idea what the Black Goo structure really is and how it can be used. This intelligent matter is eternal, it does not pass the dying cycle, it can encode everything that stores any information contained in the biosphere. It is empathetic towards the biosphere and is able to remember all the records that are in it. Scientists are working hard to understand this knowledge and access the records preserved in Black Goo. Governments spend billions of dollars researching it. Black Goo also has a different name, more popular. These are the Akashic Records. Black Goo is a collection of information written by itself. All information contained in Black Goo can be retrieved. And there is literally everything there. Every second of every human being's existence is preserved like a movie in intelligent matter. A person who had access to all the information stored in Black Goo would be able to see again all the crimes that happened on Earth and pinpoint their perpetrators with perfect precision. That is why there is such a great struggle between the governments. Every government wants to find a way to access the information contained in this intelligent matter. This is because it accumulates in its memory everything that has ever happened in the world. It is a race for truth and disclosure. There are many beings on Earth who have the gift of connecting to the Akashic Records. However, they never use the readings from the Chronicle that evil motives and the matter itself will not allow them to do so as they are fully aware."

"I've read a lot about Akashic Records," I said at the end of the lecture, "It's a very interesting subject."

"Now you know what the true name for chronicles is and how to search for it."

"Semjase, I have a request" said Kal,

"What is it?"

"Could you tell us about the Sun?"

"Hmmm… I think I still have a moment for that. The Sun… What to begin with…", Semjase was wondering while Kal was rubbing his hands, "The Sun is the star of the solar system and is electric in nature. Scientists who bring forward a hypothesis of an electric plasma model for the entire universe are right. The torsional field in the universe includes not only stars but also planets and entire galaxies. In fact, one could say that the entire universe is a gigantic gravitational torsion field. There is a very small nucleus in the Sun. It consists of magnesium, sodium and all other elements that are mostly metals. The inner shell of the Sun is made of similar materials but functions like an anode and a cathode. The sun is electric in nature, so it can be compared to a common light bulb. It has sunspots running towards its center. They are like individual vortex threads that travel inward, or into the denser parts of the star, to a point located at its core. It can be compared to an energetic tornado. These tiny tornadoes intersect each other as they spin and finally meet each other at the star's core. When you observe sunspots, they are ring-shaped explosions that come out of the sun. This is nothing but toroidal bursts of energy. This phenomenon is called protuberance, and the bursts of energy do not just affect the surface of the sun but go down to its core. There are stellar gates in the sun and their use may cause such phenomena, especially since these gates are used by many extraterrestrial civilizations to reach and leave the SOL system. There is also a wide open and quite empty space within the sun. Its outer region manifests itself as a fiery warm shell. And although this may surprise you, the temperature outside the sun is much more severe and it is the hottest. Until now, it has been perceived as a scientific puzzle. The sun is an electric generator powered by various kinds of waves that hit it. These impacts cause increased activity and a higher temperature on its outer layer. The sun is also powered by the cosmic network and is connected by electromagnetic filaments to other stars. This is why chain reactions often occur in the universe, as a result of which an event in one solar system causes feedback throughout the entire lattice system and may affect other stars in the solar system or a given galaxy. This is why when the Sun, Orion's Belt and the Earth intersect, extraordinary things are happening, as if some gates were opening. This event is some kind of energy transition that affects the nature of matter when the Earth cuts this beam of energy passing between the Sun and Orion.

The plasma beams then influence the matter of the Sun and this is how the opening of the gate manifests itself. I think this is enough for you to know about the sun at the very beginning."

"What a pity. I was counting on more" Kal became gloomy.

"Get some rest. There's another nightly adventure ahead of you. See you soon" as she was saying it, she disappeared. She already knew perfectly well that dragging on goodbyes with us was not a good idea because we would always come up with a question that can be asked to extend the conversation. So it has already become normal that our star lecturers immediately after passing us the necessary information disappear almost as quickly as they appeared.

Chapter 18

"The need
Life will not unfold the way you want it to.
Life will unfold the way you need it most.
If you want to know what you need most you need to get
to know yourself better."

Damian Buczniewicz

Tiny pieces of history

Our nap, as it turned out, lasted a bit because we woke up for dinner. Kal looked much better now. You could also see an improvement in his mood right away. He ate such a large portion of Mommy's dinner as if he hadn't eaten in a week. I had no idea how it fit into his stomach. When I told Mom about it in the form of a joke, she told me that the energetic struggle with the entity that attached himself to him exhausted his body. He needed to get stronger from such a large meal. The organism demanded that. Full of understanding for his gluttony, I suggested a midday walk. We were strolling along the paths of the nearby park, we were in no hurry. In fact, we didn't even talk much. We had such a nostalgic moment of the time when the mind calms down as much as possible and the soul enjoys the pleasure of existence itself. It had already been announced by Semjase that she would visit us, so we were excited about another opportunity to meet her. After such a long break, we enjoyed it even more, but I felt that, just like me, for several days, Semjase sensed that time had sped up a bit. This could have caused a sudden increase in the intensity of the messages that she had yet to present to us.

"I feel it a bit, too" said Kal, reading my thoughts, "It's not a clear acceleration but still it is".

"The time is clearly not in our favor. I need to speed up with the project of the book. I didn't even consider how I'm going to publish it. I have no idea how to do it. Writing it is one thing and publishing it and doing everything possible so that it reaches people is another thing and I suspect it's the most difficult one."

"Focus on writing for now. I'll search in free time what the options of publishing are and we will analyze them together," Kal's words made me emotional

I was happy that I could count on his help.

"I feel that your diary of extraterrestrials would become a book one day as well."

"Rather, a guide about the races of the universe."

"A guide is also a book" I said and laughed out loud, "So, once we publish my book it's going to be easier with yours. We will have clear paths. Practice makes perfect."

We walked for a while longer, but due to the drop in temperature, it got so cold that our noses were already the color of a vivid red. Upon my return, aware of the speeding-up of time, I sat down to write while Kal was surfing on the Internet. In fact, I didn't even know what I was looking for. I focused fully on my task. According to the agreement we had, Kal was supposed to have a sleepover at mine, so we could sit together until late at night. Usually, when we wanted to fall asleep, we played a boring movie. That day we did the same because the morning nap meant that despite the late hour we were not tired. Even the boring film that Kal chose could not handle it. Resigned, we turned off the TV, turned off the lights and hoped for a miracle. And it happened, although the fact that Semjase acted on this matter appeals to me more.

Again, we found ourselves at our favorite beach. I loved the peacefulness and harmony of this place. It was like a temple of beautiful luminous energy.

"Welcome back. We saw each other not too long ago." she

smiled radiantly as always.

"We're very pleased with such frequent meetings. I can feel shifts in the space. Everything has accelerated."

"You're right, Smaisi. Slightly but still. Therefore, I would like to pass onto you everything that is needed. There's not much left."

"But I don't know so many things…" I was saddened.

"In the near future there'll be a time when you stop needing my help. You'll connect to the universal wisdom, Smaisi, and that's where you'll find all the answers to the questions concerning the past as well as the future of humanity."

Semjase surprised me then for real. I didn't know what to answer.

"You don't need to say anything, my dear," she responded to my thoughts, "It's time to tell you that. You're unique due to many reasons. Who you really are though will tell you your parents at the right time."

That was the time even Kal opened his mouth wide open.

"And now, let me. The time is running," Semjase continued.

"Of course" I stuttered out, although after what I had heard from Semjase, emotions were running wild inside me.

"Today we will go back to some significant events in history that were falsified to humankind yet they influenced their entire lives. You already know very well that what is made public in the mainstream media is in fact — at best — a narrow version of the truth, and most often it is just lies that are served to the people so that the elite can achieve their own goals. The history goes the same. Humanity knows only the part for which they are allowed. And believe me, this is a tiny fraction of the truth. You also know that humanity is in the clutches of elites who keep numerous technological discoveries in secret and deny people access to them, even though they would solve almost all problems of humanity. We will move to the end of World War II, the image of which has been very seriously distorted. First of all — World War II is not over. It only took a different, carefully planned unofficial direction. On the one hand, there were Germany in this conflict, but not those in

346

Europe, but only some of their inhabitants who evacuated to Antarctica to positions specially prepared for them. Their goal was to develop secret projects and programs that were never presented to the public. The Second World War did not end with the fall of Adolf Hitler in Berlin. The Third Reich was very well prepared for a possible defeat. The Germans were supported by a certain civilization which they considered extraterrestrial. Before the Second World War, there were two lodges. One of them was the origin of the SS order, which already then participated in secret space programs and projects. You must know that Yuri Gagarin was not the first person to leave Earth and go into space. Such trips took place much earlier in antiquity. Civilizations back then were much more technologically advanced. Space projects and programs have always been secret operations, even the military and aviation industry have no idea about the technologies that are owned by Earthlings, but are carefully hidden."

"What happened to the ancient civilizations? How is it possible that they disappeared so suddenly? Did they experience the process of ascension?" I asked.

"The ancient civilization which remained and which should not be confused with the Aryans was forced to evacuate, they hid underground. It happened while the Sun's crown was expanding, which caused the temperature of the Earth to rise. The temperature rose to unbearable limits. However, thanks to technological development, civilization had a chance to survive. Its members built underground systems and settled there. In fact, they are still there today. Deep beneath the surface of planet Earth, there are entire network structures inhabited by many planetary communities and life forms that humans have no idea about. These creatures have completely separated themselves from life on the surface and from the civilization that lives on it. However, sometimes these civilizations pretend to be extraterrestrials and manipulate society on the surface. Already in times when people still had no idea what electricity is, underground references had highly advanced technologies that allowed me to freely fly into space and move through outer space."

347

"What are these beings?" Kal asked because he was curious if he had included them in his atlas.

"These beings look like humans. They live inspired by the beings of the astral plane who pass the wisdom into them and give them free will if they won't to evolve and ascend or stay on a certain level. They teach and assist. They never order, they respect the fee will of every being."

"Unlike what religion does to humans" I stated.

"It's true. There are no bans or orders. Every creature is free as long as it does not break the laws of the universe and harm other beings. Even the Ten Commandments should not be read as a commandment but as a proposal to act. Notice the words — command, prohibition and proposition. You can live as you like. Nobody can forbid or order anything from anyone. It is the religions that have manipulated the people they are to submit to. This, however, is not true. People always have a choice. I will come back to the topic of spaceflight if you please."

"Of course," said Kal quickly.

"So, space flights from Earth into space have always been going on. This also happened after the Second World War. Two types of space flight can be distinguished. One of them is what has been shown and declassified to the public. That's Gagarin flights and Apollo flights. The flight to the moon, although somewhat falsified, was also declassified so that it was known that things are happening and that humanity is developing and conquering space," she laughed, "I'm sorry, but at times it just makes me laugh. The second type of flight is everything that has been concealed. That's thousands of flights to other planets already taken. To the Moon or Mars, where for decades there have been bases in which people currently reside. The elite treat these bases as bunkers, it is their ability to escape if something goes wrong on Earth. So whoever should know, knows and the rest is cheated into unawareness. The Nazis received help from the Draco beings, as well as from other groups of extraterrestrials who are called Aryans. Aryans are an ancient race that developed civilization and technology that allowed them to travel into space. They have a space program called Silver Flora. They have set up huge bases near the Himalayas. The most interesting of them is in Tibet. The underground systems, on the other hand, are called Agartha and its dwellers are called Agarthians. These are the ancients I have already mentioned — those who hid in the depths of the Earth due to the rising temperature on its surface. They are not Arians then, which is often confused. There are factions and secret societies on Earth that work closely with the Draco civilization. Thanks to the technology of this civilization, they are able to control and manipulate the human population more efficiently. Of course, like any contract, it must be profitable for both parties. This is how a system was created in which an ordinary person loses. Secret bases were established not only on Mars and the Moon, there are also many of them on the surface of the Earth. I once mentioned briefly to you about bases located in Antarctica. These bases were created a long time ago and they function and are used efficiently to this day. The lodges that I mentioned a moment ago had people in their ranks, who were commonly referred to as mediums. They were people with a talent for telepathically receiving and transmitting numerous information. The medium therefore received the information and then precisely conveyed it to scientists and engineers, who constructed spaceships, airplanes and constructions of unknown origin for ordinary people. In their notes one can find even descriptions of spaceships that moved in the atmosphere already at the beginning of Hinduism. They were called Vimana and they were powered by mercury. The lodges, which of course had their bases in Antarctica, kept in touch with Berlin and sent a mission to support Hitler who was obsessed with the ideology of superhumans and was looking for a perfect model completely opposite to what he represented. He was looking for tall blondes with blue eyes. This is the source of the eugenics video. The secret licks from Berlin also remained in contact with the Cong Pa lodge which controlled Egypt. There was an exchange of information between them in order to build spacecraft, which was done."

"Unbelievable that they have it all. And they keep it secret." said Kal.

"Seriously? You're still shocked by that?" I asked because I was shocked by him being surprised, "the whole world is a one huge lie."

"I'm not shocked. It's indignation" Kal corrected.

"Yes they do. For a long time. The first vehicle was built by the Nazis with the support of the secret lodges I mentioned. This show was equipped with brake lines and anti-gravity engines. But don't think that only ordinary people are constantly deceived. This is going to be funny to you, but to the realities — and so many other people around the world who are in contact with secret lodges — they still think they are extraterrestrial beings. Aryans, beings from the inside of the Earth can create illusions and even the elites of this world successfully fall into these illusions. What is so funny that they are not aware of it, but in fact they are the victims of the manipulation of the old civilization of people who simply separate themselves from the new surface civilizations and pretend to be extraterrestrials whose goal is to help humanity in its evolution. But let's get back to secret projects and space flights. The SS were an order that also had its own secret space flight programs. Also the Pentagon has them, they are often billionaire sponsored programs that very few people know about and everything is kept secret. These billionaires have been to Mars or the Moon more than once and are aware of the existence of bases on these objects and of the fact that they are inhabited by various forms of extraterrestrials. Children who had no one after the war were often taken to the bases as a bull. So no one looked for them and reported them missing. From that moment on, the children worked for those who, in their opinion, were heroes because they gave them a home. Even if the house was on a different planet or in different areas of Antarctica. These children grew up to be minions of the lodge and today they exercise power and sit at its highest levels. I have probably already mentioned to you, although I am not sure, about the Paperclip operation carried out just after the end of the war, in which many German scientists were transferred to America to continue their work there — often questionable and dangerous for the entire human population. All this, however, was

350

a carefully programmed infiltration action that allowed the Nazis to penetrate the structures of the CIA and FBI. It was then that the plan to create NASA was created. This was the moment when they began to successfully infiltrate the American national security system. They achieved their independence and finally the integrity of the US military space programs was completed. Without Nazi scholars, there would be no CIA, FBI, or NASA now. So the question is: Who do they actually belong to?"

"It's best that everyone answers that themselves," Kal suggested.

"I'm telling you that all so that you are aware that as multidimensional beings you don't need to be compliant to any doctrines. The process of ascension of the planet is in an advanced stadium. It happens on the universal level. This process corners everyone and everyone should focus on themselves and on the expansion of your knowledge and awakening of consciousness. Only through the raising of your own vibrational frequencies can humans adjust to it. No government will help you in that. And the one that pulls the strings, tries to disturb only, being delusional that they can stop the process. In order to make you aware of that, I'm taking you to the events in history and I'm abolishing lies that have been considered as true for a long time."

"Let's abolish some more," I requested.

"It wasn't my intention to stop here," Semjase laughed out, "Now I'll take you to places where even more secrets are hidden. To the Vatican. Elites would rather burn the whole city than let the information hidden in the Vatican see the light. This treasury of forbidden knowledge is there for literally everything from extraterrestrial contacts with them, to high-tech projects, to conspiracies and elite plans to enslave humanity to the limit. Simply the whole of what, if exposed, would demolish what the elites and the centuries were building in a few days. The elite are aware of this and will never allow this information to be disseminated. It doesn't matter what it is, however, and you don't have to rummage through the Vatican's secret dungeons filled with files. You just need to sync with the Black Goo frequency or the saves in space and everything becomes bright and clear."

"But you'll tell us anyway, right?" I asked because I couldn't download the information for the space yet.

"Yes of course. Anyway, I do it all the time. So the famous seal of the Vatican, or SS—Sedes Sacrorum, was the seal of the order. The Vatican is home to a cold-blooded old serpent, symbolizing none other than the Reptilian race you already know. Secrets are hidden there because power needs secrets. The elite can do a lot to gain secret knowledge. This is another trap for themselves, but they are too blind to see it. They are so obsessed with their lust for power and their service to die instead of life that they see nothing beyond it. It is them who need disclosure. Only it will be able to bring them healing and transformations that could eat them and save them, but not without consequences. Let me quote you the words of the *Millennium Bible* spoken by Yoshua who was a Nazarene and mystic who foretold chaos, propagated the truth, and exposed the manipulations of the church. However, it was removed by the elite as it was and still is the custom.

Three crowns:
"The absolute power over religion, politics and economy".
Keys:
"Woe to you, scribes and Pharisees, hypocrites, for you close the kingdom of heaven to men."
"You yourselves do not go in and do not allow those who go to it."

This is what the earthly astral-free etherically spirit in the earthly shell predicted two thousand earthly years ago, that is your earthly Christ who spoke through his earthly instrument — Jesus of Nazareth, the greatest prophet of all time. It is this Roman institution that is the shadow of a much larger group — it is a sect responsible for the blood-suckling of small children and innocent victims; satanic groups that are scattered around the world. They've been known for thousands of years for burning people at the stake and breaking with a wheel. This is the so-called Holy Inquisition that boasts of suffering and enforces its doctrines at all costs. From the first century BC, high priests also took positions under the control of a handful of beings from the ancient races. They recognize their ancient title from the times of the ancient republic and continue their crimes through the centuries. After the fall of Rome as an empire, the priests proclaimed themselves leaders and assumed the role previously held by the emperor. After some time, they quite openly returned to the practices of child sacrifice, cannibalism, and belief in the cult of Satana and its hierarchy. All this has happened and is still happening under the banner of Christianity which has nothing to do with the teachings of Christ and the Decalogue, even though the priests flaunt a distorted *Bible* under their armpits."

"But this is awful, what they're doing. So… So inhumane!" Kal got indignant again.

"It's true. And millions of people at tent churches and pay donations for their faith. They're blind. They don't know what they do. This is a sponsorship of evil." Semjase was straightforward. The truth, brutal sometimes, needed to come to the surface for once. There was no other method than for people to finally wake up. This monastery has a very turbulent history. However, a lot changed when in 1929 brother Heinrich Himmler was appointed a member of the monastery in Germany. Then, the Nazi army was created and called Sedes Sacrorum. The creation of the army was aimed at carrying out the largest inquisition action so far. During the inquisition, over 18 million human beings were sacrificed at the altar — both in Poland and in Russia. The German order was officially dissolved after the end of World War II. However, it was created as the American SS or Secret Service. The American SS was introduced as a military-spiritual unit to protect the head of state. In this way, they got as close to power as they could. The order still exists today and still uses the secret SS code. Their symbolism is frightening. Anticipating your question, Kal: of course I'll tell you."

That was the first time Semjase anticipated our questions. We laughed out together and Semjase moved to the before mentioned symbolism.

"And so these Babylonian priests dress in fish costumes,

play and manipulate human DNA. In the hands of the gums, pine cones symbolize the pineal gland and the buckets symbolize advanced knowledge in the field of genetics. Above their heads there is a creature called by them a god, sitting and watching them on his flying vehicle. It is a simplified symbol of a fish. There is a miter on the emblem of the SS, as well as on that of Pope Francis, it was worn four and a half thousand years ago by the Dragon priests. Dragon means fish in Hebrew. If you looked at the miter from the side, you would see that it looks like a fish with an open mouth. It is about worshiping a fish-like creature, a beast that once came out of the water and endowed people with knowledge. A christian fish represents exactly this being, i.e. Dragon, also known as Oannes, who was amphibious. He once gave people knowledge about building cities, taught mathematics and geometry. It was him who for centuries was credited with all the knowledge that mankind possessed. The amphibious god is the same being that the Sumerians called Ea. It was an Annunaki leader and Annunaki in Hebrew means giants. So the group he led colonized the Earth. Later, Ea was called Enki and was said to have landed in his great ship in the water. After charging, it emerged from the water in a fish costume. The garment was actually a uniform that allowed him to breathe underwater. Enki built the first settlement for the Anunnaki "gods" on earth, or E-Din, which was later named Eden. This name means "house of the righteous". Then another city of Eridu was built, meaning "home far away". These names later migrated from one culture to another. Here we come to the creation of the human population, which I have already told in detail, and to Nimrod and his sons. Nimrod was one of the sons of Enki, so the royal blood of the same self-proclaimed gods flowed in him. To this day, it circulates in the veins of many royal families-descendants of Nimrod. Symbolism, as I said before, will be what will destroy these elites, and when the truth is revealed, it will point to the evidence against them. The way in which these beings have long acted, and how they planned to become an orthodox creator, is beyond human imagination. That is why it is so difficult to understand certain events. Humanity, without any insight into any activity of these spheres, is unable to break through the veil separating truth from lies. The elite will continue to rule people until they wake up and accept for truth who they are and understand what their true freedom and free will is all about."

"Is that the end of the story?" I inquired.

"No, Smaisi. It's the beginning. I've got a few things to tell you. There's a lot. I'll do my best to shorten that as much as I can. Earth nations have had help from within Earth and extraterrestrial beings for some time and have used them without restriction. We will go first to Italy, which was a fascist nation during World War II. They worked hand in hand with the German people, they had common goals and agendas on which their work continued. They created many secret societies that spread to neighboring countries such as Australia, Poland and Italy. But to understand all of this, we must go back. Until the time before the rise of Christianity and other religions until all these groups were pagan tribes."

"So it reaches that far?" Kal was surprised.

"Yes. That far. Like Celts or Druids. These are old times, they are beginnings. Their descendants from the present day know perfectly well where they come from and know the entire history of their ancestors. That is why they believe that they are entitled to everything and can do whatever they want. Over the centuries, the dynasty changed, the governments were different, but these groups continued without interruption and did not lose their strength, on the contrary — they quietly gained more and more power by expanding the network of possibilities and ranges. Now they diligently guard their knowledge gained over the millennia. Much of the information they have collected throughout this time has its place in the Vatican. In its crypts, to be exact. Jesuits and these groups and associations, whatever they may be called, still have access to these documents, both from the Vatican and from the many libraries around the world. Old texts have been translated into more and more common languages many times, so this knowledge has never been lost. The information in the manuscripts tells about ancient technologies and extraterrestrial technologies and describes the numerous encounters with them at the turn of the century."

"I would love to get to these writings," Kal confessed.

"You think you're the only one? This knowledge would change the face of the world. First, it would raze to the ground and then rebuild human reality. I have already told you that certain civilizations living in the interior of the Earth have repeatedly contacted human civilization, proclaiming themselves as coming from the stars. It has never changed and is still happening. In each of these groups there have always been selected individuals who stayed in touch, and only they had access to the knowledge imparted by these beings. All the rest of the people were to remain ignorant. Even the kings and emperors had no access to these scrolls. Almost all projects of secret space programs as well as the construction and expansion of underground technologically advanced facilities are derived from these groups. Groups of beings from the inside of the Earth often abducted people, which resulted in the birth of a new race of a human. Today, people are still kidnapped by them. The creatures from the interior of the Earth were mostly blue-eyed blondes with clearly marked features of the Caucasian race. That's why Hitler was so crazy about it. He found such an appearance superhuman, almost divine. The entities from the underground have used people from the surface many times. As they call it "something for something". It was always a bundled deal. Thanks to it, even in the days of the Celts and Druids, these groups had access to space travel and to technologies enabling travel through interstellar states. So there has always been a group of people who know the truth and have access to all that I have told you about. During the time of the Spanish conquistadors, the Mayan priests were chased towards the rock wall with a door with engraved signs. The priests, carrying scrolls in their hands, touched the door, passed through it and disappeared. The door was a portal. There is almost the same door in Turkey. Turkey is one of the countries which, thanks to its location, have distinguished themselves in their civilization. There is also a group of extraterrestrials in this country. You know them. They are Draco and Reptilian beings. Turkey is an area of very high activity of extraterrestrials. As an ancient area of land, it has been controlled by extraterrestrial factions for a very long time. Such civilization groups and elite castes are found everywhere and are scattered throughout the world. In Africa, for example, there is a group called Marduk."

"One moment… I'm trying to understand it," Kal started, "So the Germans and Hitler contacted the creatures from under the ground thanks to the medium and channeling. This allowed them to build the technology thanks to which the Germans flew to the moon and built their bases there, and then pretending to be a defeat in the war and so they won because they joined the structures of the American government. Is that so?"

"Well, more or less. The Germans actually got information and construction plans through channelings. It was on their basis that they built many of their facilities and ships. However, this technology was not transferred to Germany just like that and, of course, not all of it. The civilization from under the surface of the Earth initially tried to force the Germans not to go the easy way, so it pushed them towards the tedious process of archaeological excavations so that they could come to everything on their own. Ultimately, however, as they saw no hope, they transferred this advanced technology to them under certain agreements. However, there was a catch. They could not pass on all the technology to them and the Germans had to develop some of the things on their own. So they got help, but not all of it. This is part of the principles that civilization follows from inside the Earth. The Germans had to prove their engineering and scientific skills. Because having such a technology is associated with the compulsion to understand it. It was a process of proving that they can exceed a certain level of their development. Once they were successful, both the Draco group and the Agarthans began to impart technology to them on a larger scale and with greater confidence. The Germans favored the Agarthans group. They received a lot of very unique technology from them and began to use it to rise beyond the Earth's atmosphere. Their first plan was to go to the moon and begin exploring the asteroid belt. You know the rest of the story about the numerous bases on the Moon and on Mars. Of course, the Americans were no worse, and they also signed contracts with groups of extraterrestrials."

"Did they receive technology as well that could be used as a weapon? "I asked, knowing how self-destructive human species can be.

"Unfortunately, yes. Already in the 1930s, they started working on numerous technologies that could be used as advanced weapons. During the war in 1942, the tactics of the war suddenly changed, which was quite a drastic move but profitable.Hitler then made contact with reptilian beings. Adolf Hitler was always keenly interested in adding lands to his empire. He became interested in lost cities in Antarctica. Numerous archaeological expeditions were sent there, the ground was prepared and bases were built to best explore the frozen continent. Initially, no one else knew about the existence of extraterrestrials except for the religious groups and elites I spoke about earlier. The agreement between the Germans and the reptilian creatures assumed the creation of a cosmic navy similar to the one owned by the Reptilians. When Americans and British found out what the Germans were doing, they were terrified. The technology that this country possessed was able to end the war literally within a few minutes. The Germans had cloned soldiers that they sent to fight on the Russian front. These clones were created using an advanced biomedical system designed to extend life. Later cloning became common not only in Germany but also in America. Work on cloning has continued and is at its best in underground bases and biological weapons facilities such as NBC. The enormity of technology and the potential that was discovered thanks to the possibility of cloning were unimaginable. The SS discovered that people can live longer. They tested their biomedical technology on people in extermination camps around the world. Also in Poland. Huge production plants were built that were built underground, and in them weapons, tanks and submarines were produced. The biomedical project was divided into twenty-four segments 2 of which the possibilities of life extension in various values were developed. For the record and example: Nordics live from 1,400 to

2,000 and two hundred years and they look exactly like humans. Over time, research into cloning and extending human life has increased in strength. However, these programs were quickly closed for fear that they would become available to humans. Nevertheless, what was achieved was implemented and used for the needs of the elite. Thus, few enjoy these benefits to this day. The projects involved five major medical research groups as well as hundreds of smaller ones. And all were kept secret from the general public. Again, only the richest make profit from it. This true story has many threads. It would take decades to review and analyze it thoroughly. All I have ever told you is just the tip of the iceberg, but the truth will eventually reach people. Awakening is coming, it cannot be stopped in any way," Semjase concluded her lecture.

"Thank you" I said, on behalf of Kal too.

"Your welcome" she replied, waved at us and disappeared.

We stayed for a while at the beach and listened to the hum of the ocean.

"Everything that is temporary... When you realize this, you will know the value of freedom... Memento mori or carpe diem takes on a deeper meaning... You begin to realize what attachment really is and how much it took away from you the possibility and freedom to be...
Then you learn that the symptom of love is consent and acceptance that allows you to flow freely with the bulk of life...
The fear that has so often accompanied you in many situations has a much more limited impact on you. It becomes an impulse to change only a temporary impression...This is the moment when you start to take care of yourself, because deep down you know that the only value that will remain from this world is love in your heart...
Love then becomes the only currency that has the greatest value for you...
When you allow yourself to be aware of this, you will see that life is a fun game that has its end only beyond the boundaries of this universe...
Or maybe even further?
The moment you realize what is temporary, you begin to see the value of what is eternal...
You begin to see who you really are..."

Damian Buczniewicz

Chapter 19

Etheric energy — Polish Nation

The New Year's Eve morning was very lazy. Kal was the first to wake up and go downstairs to prepare breakfast. For the first time in my life, I was served a meal straight to bed. I must admit that I could get used to it. Due to epidemiological restrictions, we did not have any specific plans for the evening. We were supposed to sit at home and have a glass of champagne together welcoming the New Year. A year which was supposed to be a breakthrough in my feelings. Intuitively, I sensed that the following months would be like a speeding train to which awakened people would jump. I have seen many of them in several of my visions regarding the year 2021, which begins in just a dozen hours. I also felt that the Polish Nation, to which I belonged, would play a key role in this awakening. There was something special about this nation. It was probably about the origin, although I didn't know what it was yet. But I couldn't shake that feeling.

"I feel it the same way," Kal interjected, "but perhaps it's because we're Polish too and our ego can intrude here a bit."

"Quite probably, but..."I stopped, I preferred not to speculate, "We have to do some research and we will surely find out if it is only our ego or if there is something to it," I suggested.

Someone else, hearing about my plans for New Year's Eve day and night, would probably think I was weird. But not Kal. He took it with a smile on his face and an enthusiasm that lit up his whole face.

We took up the topic right after breakfast. The parents were not at all surprised by our plans. We were entering the key words in the search engine and after a few hours of rummaging it turned out that not only we had this feeling. Many prophets and visionaries long ago foretold that in the future the spark of awakening that would change everything would come out of Poland. We found a lot of information about Poles as a Lechite nation, but due to the fact that history had been manipulated, it was difficult for us to reach reliable sources that we could refer to with a clear conscience. So all we could do was humbly ask for a little help in advance. However, neither of us expected it to come to us in such a form.

It was late afternoon. Kal and I sat on the bed skipping programs on TV. On one of the channels we found the program "Ancient Aliens" and we decided to see what they have to say in this episode. We watched for maybe five minutes when suddenly the light in the room went out. We looked out into the corridor, it was also dark. However, when I glanced out the window, I saw that it was still bright in the neighboring houses.

"It must be electrical plugs. I'll sort it out. Light a candle!" Daddy shouted from downstairs.

Kal lit a few small candles and we waited for the electricity to return. Then a ball of light burst through the wall into our room and illuminated the darkness prevailing in it. I had no idea what I was looking at until I saw geometric shapes inside it.

"It's a sphere," I said to Kal quietly.

Yes. It's a sphere — it responded. I could hear it only in my thoughts.

"Kal, can you..?"

"Yes, I can hear it too," he replied.

"Of course you can hear. You asked for help so here I am and I will gladly answer your questions. Perhaps I will add to it myself," the sphere offered.

"We'll be grateful" I replied. I could feel it had a feminine energy.

"I know, that's why so many beings enjoy visiting you", she confessed, "Your intuition is right, the truth about itself has been hidden from the Polish nation for a very long time. This nation is an ancient great empire from before the eighteenth century BC. The history of their power is much older than the Roman Empire. The truth about this nation is hidden for one reason. It concerns the bloodline of Poles and their stellar genotype. Your intuition also doesn't confuse you with the fact that people wake up. That's true. Poland is waking up and the state of consciousness of this nation is changing. The etheric transformation has started and the Poles will be the first to go through it, even though they have started the transformation at the latest."

"What do you mean?" Kal asked.

"Poles started their wake up call in 2015 and from 2025 they will become an awakened nation. The rest of the world, even though it started to wake up in 2012, will complete this process in around 2028. So, as you can see, Poles will lead on the paths of awakening as an example to follow. The Polish energy signature is unique. We are now in the final stage of clearing space, and all battles in the astral spaces are slowly coming to an end. The light has already won. The effects of this victory will slowly manifest on the physical plane and people will begin to notice these changes more and more clearly. As the Earth's magnetic field increases, everything that lives on this planet will be larger and will last longer. Matter has its own laws and a specific lifetime depending on the space and energy in which it resides. Do you know that there are people on Earth who cannot be killed? And this is not related to the fact that they are immortal. They just have a very strong protective field or nature. This high energy vibration causes that the intrusion of any aggressor into the field of such a person ends badly for the aggressor and may even cause his death."

"Who are those people?" I was curious if they're special or perhaps they work very closely with the energy protection of their body."

"They were born on Earth incarnating like other souls. However, their symbiote comes from higher dimensions. On the astral plane, they keep their high energy all the time, even though they lowered the energy of their spark of life to incarnate in this density. Most of these souls came to Earth with a mission to fulfill. They have a very strong protection from the creator—it is, in a way, a guarantee of inviolability. All this so that they can freely carry out their plan of helping people, when life on Earth is in danger or when it comes to crossing the dimension and during the evolution of humanity on the timeline. The time is right now. On Earth, these souls in human bodies usually lead life and try not to lean out too much from the crowd. Being anonymous is crucial for these people. When the time comes for them, they can reveal themselves and help, they will feel it. These people work hard all the time and raise the vibration of the planet. They are engaged in activating places of power on Earth and removing blockages from the Earth's chakras. It is free to call them employees for the benefit of all humankind. They work in silence, they do not crave recognition for what they do. They do it out of great love for people."

"When you were speaking about the energy signature of the Polish Nation, what did you mean exactly?" I asked.

"I meant the frequency. Raising vibrations of the Earth have an influence on not only the magnetic field. They also affect all information fields, creating certain dissonances in their existing programs, which causes disturbances in the flow of information. Let me explain it more vividly. The graphic designer makes a project in accordance with the client's requirements. He presents the project, but the client makes changes all the time. He changes as he pleases, he does not count with the graphic designer or any canons of beauty. The graphic designer is the creator and the elites are the manipulators. As soon as the Earth's magnetic field increases, all news records return to their original state. There is a revolution, which means that regardless of the client's numerous corrections, the graphic allows the original better version to be printed. So if the Earth's magnetic field reaches at least fifty percent of its original power, all overwritten programs lose their power to operate. They cease to exist. This is why all technology that was directed against humanity will be destroyed. It will leave only sad expressions on the faces of the big losers. Earlier, the Earth and its inhabitants were stuck in a manipulated reality with reduced vibrations. Now it will not be possible and nothing will block the evolution of humankind anymore. This does not mean, however, that there will be no attempts to stop these changes. The elites who so far kept the Earth in low vibrations know exactly what and when is going to happen. Even more. Knowledge of people who will be born so that the change will be correct and that the world will return to the original project of the Creator. For decades, even centuries, the elite had been preparing for this event. They reached with their tentacles to the most important sectors of public life in order to prevent changes and to block the incarnations who were to be seeds of these changes in the most effective way. The elite often uses empathy and a complete lack of knowledge of people. It also affects esoteric environments which, instead of merging, compete with each other. They outdo each other in proving who is right and whose actions are more effective. Instead of joining forces, they treat themselves as opponents, although they are not opponents at all. Many people have no idea what spiritual and astra-etheric development is. They forget that unity is the greatest power and this does not lead to the awakening of humanity. Why? Because then such a man is lost. One person said one thing, another said something else, though the question was the same. So where is the truth? In their hearts. But they don't know it either. How, then, are they to find themselves? How are they to know who to trust? Every knowledge should be analyzed. If you don't understand something, you have to strive for understanding. People have to look for the truth within themselves because it is hidden in them. This is what the elite fears. That people will find their inner powers and awaken them within themselves and that everyone will have access to the truth. Only those who are looking inside themselves have a chance to find it. Outside, he will only find illusions and a multitude of false versions. It is a human who is his or her own source. Their energetic and biological system is like a great library. And the elite has always done everything to prevent humans from learning about their power. It was all about it. This gave them the confidence that I could rule and share with impunity. Human's attention was diverted from his interior and directed to things that were necessary for survival. The human tried to exist, but paradoxically forgot about it. Of course, the real existence—not directed. However, these times are over and soon no one will accuse anyone of anything because the lie will be discovered in one second. Humanity will begin to be guided by the heart and intuition. This will happen because of the interplanetary processes that even the most advanced civilizations will not be able to stop. The increased magnetic field of the Earth raises it to higher regions of outer space, which is why it is called an elevation. The vibration fields increase, the brightness of the biophotons is completely different and the sound changes to different frequencies. This process returns the Earth and its people to their original code of life, their own purest matrix of existence. It only means one thing. Anything that is not a primal projection of existence gets burnt. Any lower vibration other than that of the new space is destroyed. However, the Earth needs the help of its children. For all evil to disappear, and for it to happen quickly, two elements are needed. Increased energy of the magnetic field of the Earth and the people themselves. Only people incarnate on Earth have the power to do this because they are the incarnate spark and creators. They will do this by acting together. And the Poles, due to their stellar genotype, will react to these processes faster and wake up first."

"What should humans do then? What advice should we give them? How to assist in raising the vibration? " I asked because I wanted to lead them in the best possible way.

"They should stop fighting for the pieces of knowledge they possess. They should start to combine it into a logical whole. They should learn to draw conclusions and channel their energy on themselves into their lives and turn the spark of awakening into great flames. People need to understand who they are. They must love themselves as they are. Their creation should be beautiful and should be about wonderful visions of the future. And it's not selfish to do your best for yourself. Because only when they themselves become a whole will there be a strong element creating a whole and unity with others. Here I will give you an analogy again. You are building a log house. The foundations are also made of them. And you have a choice. Either you go the easy way and put the house on logs that have cracks here and there that can weaken the structure over time, or you give your best and work hard, but surely that every element of the foundation is strong and the house will never collapse. It's the same here. Weak individuals will not add positive energy to the entire collective. Instead of strengthening it, they will lower it. The founders of the New World Order were well aware of these dependencies. This is not a new Earth. The very word order should illuminate a warning light. The elites, using their connections, eliminated many precursors of positive and light. As many as they managed. As many as they found out about. They know very well that the spark of global changes will come from the Polish nation from groups linked by spiritual development. It is the elite who consciously set up their pawns to misinform and divide, they are trying to destroy everything from the inside. However, they do not stop there. They interfere with the energy plan — they try to hold back many luminous beings through energetic attacks and hooks. So you are right. Poles are unique. This is guaranteed by their bloodline and stellar genotypes. And nothing will withhold a spark that will come out of this country. When it sparkles in other regions of the world, Poland will already stand in the divine radius of awakening. I am grateful to be able to tell you about it. Good luck star children. Be a spark!", the ball of light suddenly disappeared and the room went dark again.

"One moment and the light will be o," Daddy shouted out from downstairs and then, at the touch of a magic wand, there came light.

The TV switched on and... If It hadn't been for Kal, I would have paid attention to one thing. The program continued from the moment the light went off. As if we had pressed on pause during the time we were speaking to the sphere.

"Look at the clock" said Kal, nudging me, "It's been a minute. Even candles haven't melted their top wax."

"Do you want to tell me that..." I didn't finish, because I

was stunned.

"I guess it's that… We stopped in time. Or rather it was the sphere who stopped us," when he said that aloud it was even more surreal than when I was thinking of it quietly.

"What do you think, should I tell my parents the reason why the plugs went off?"

"Of course. This will be an amazing story to tell our children," Kal said without hesitation and then he got slightly confused; blushed he ran downstairs to tell what had happened.

Chapter 20

"Let the stars shine for you as brightly
as your imagination sparkles.
Let the air you breathe be as pure for you as your heart beats.
Let trees as large as your courage surround you.
Water running down your skin is as clear and pure
as your intentions and thoughts.
Let every moment be a great grace in love like the great universe that
experiences itself through you.
Let the eternal light of consciousness illuminate your path to the
source that dwells in you.
It is done."

Damian Buczniewicz

The message for humanity

The fireworks display was very beautiful, but I felt the sadness of Mother Earth. The air was filled with smoke, and many birds that had been brought out of their hiding place lost their lives. It turned out that people couldn't celebrate without hurting their Mother and poisoning themselves in the process.

We drank a symbolic glass of champagne from Kal and went to bed shortly after midnight. I couldn't fall asleep for a long time and thought about how to finish my book. I wanted this to be a message and a summary of what people already know from the previous pages. Suddenly I felt that I was ready to write them, so I got up from the bed and sat down in front of the computer.

Kal was sleeping quietly, I saw his steadily rising and falling chest. He snored gently from time to time. I was lifted by the feeling of love for him. It gave me energy and my fingers began to flow across the keyboard like a sailboat on the ocean pushed by the perfect wind. The creator himself led me. I felt it. I knew perfectly well what I wanted to convey.

The last chapter of Smaisi's book

In this beautiful world, everything is incredibly simple and unique, only people make everything very complicated.

Planet Earth that I came upon to incarnate to help people with the events in their timeline was the most beautiful planet in the entire universe. Filled with all kinds of life, it was simply teeming with it. There was no other such planet in all the universes. The Earth was special, as were the people on it. She attracted souls who, having met her, wanted to return to her many times.

Earth was exceptional in other respects as well. She had the compositions of all the planets in the universe within her. Good and evil mixed on it, giving souls a choice between them. Having received a planet of emotions to work through, souls experienced the most beautiful here and evolved the fastest. Thanks to gravity, they began to feel truly by entering the full physicality of their form. Although love and harmony have always filled souls, it was here on Earth that they could feel them with full strength. They could feel the energy passing through them on their skin, butterflies in their stomachs as they fell in love with the pain they suffered. The Earth allowed them to touch it all in a completely different way. The Creator designed it to be a paradise of experience. And it is always when souls incarnating on it achieve full harmony, when they consciously experience everything that the Earth has to offer them, that is: joy, knowledge, senses, possibilities of healing, contact with other beings and with nature. They may also experience pain if they so choose. It is therefore a paradise of free will.

Thanks to the Earth and its cycles, people have the opportunity to fully disconnect from the Creator in order to be able to come back to it on the way of their awakening. They go through the stages of understanding and getting more connected with the self. They begin to understand that existence is associated with responsibility — for oneself, for their neighbors, for nature animals, and finally for Mother Earth herself, who in her goodness accepted them and called them her children. This is the path to perfection. The Earth sets them in this direction in their evolution. Just as every mother wants her child to grow up to be a decent human being, the Earth wants it for her children.

Sometimes you have to burn yourself to learn something. We often learn only from our own mistakes. And the universe gives us the opportunity to commit them. Thanks to our small failures, we keep climbing, although we often do not realize it. There are no coincidences, everything happens for a specific reason and is designed to raise us up. Each event is a moment for which we should be grateful. It is these events that create us. Piece by piece until we reach the fullness of our own essence, that strong and filled with love power to connect with all existence of the universe.

We are not alone. You already know about it. There is also no death. The present life and the next and the next are experiences of your immortal soul. And just as the soul has to experience everything, so people have to face their deeds. You always have to pay for evil and receive praise for good. The universe returns energy to us exactly in the form in which it received from us.

Release yourself from all the energy of fear and find the way to your greatness. Your greatness will bring Mother Earth back to the podium and allow her to soar as a mother raised by the pride of her successful child who is strong, loving, compassionate and helpful. Notice when a mother feels the greatest rush of love for her child? Not when it brings a good grade from school — it's joy. As a mother, remember what you felt when you saw your little child helping someone for the first time, giving someone a helping hand and hugs when someone needs it. Yes! This is the purest sense of pride.

People usually define beauty on the basis of what the eye sees, they forget that the soul is the most beautiful to see. As you learn to balance physicality and spirituality, the door to full experience will open for you. You must understand that this planet is the only one that gives you the opportunity to make a full choice, it is your free will here that is the most sacred of laws. Using its full potential you will see the paradise that was created for you.

I know that humankind has fallen — corrupted by governments, manipulated and deceived. History has shown many times the fall of great civilizations. However, after each fall, there is a moment of rising. This is the moment for you, for me, for all living beings on this planet. A time in which, in connection with our soul and all existence of the universe, we make a change together. A change so great and unimaginable that it is beyond comprehension. However, you do not have to understand everything with your mind. You will feel this change in your hearts, the change will happen itself. It's enough.

People have always felt that there is something more, that they come from something greater than themselves. This gave a chance to show off those who wanted to become gods themselves, and they did it. It's time to understand that your only religion is love, respect and gratitude to yourself and to all existence. Each of you is a spark of the creator and together you can change so much. Not by exalting yourself and wanting to become a god — because it has already happened and you know perfectly well with what effect — but by the power to unite so as to awaken a greater power that will contribute to the good of each of you and the entire planet Earth.

There is a symbiotic connection between you and the planet. She helps you and you help her. It's a mutual interaction. When you understand the processes taking place and the great effort of the Earth, you will learn what you should do to help her and yourselves. Nobody said it would be easy, that there would be no complications. It is no secret, however, that in the greatest hardships you overcome the highest mountains and conquer the peaks. We are heading to such a summit. I'm going to. Will you come with me? Will you add your power and creative power to the collective to create a new world? And now I'm not going to ask you what you think. I will ask what your heart tells you? How does it feel what you should do?

Thinking often takes more energy than just acting. Yes. So feel the impulse within you and move forward with the impetus, leaving all the bad behind you. Remember that your actions affect your decision not only on yourselves but also on humanity on Earth, on other nations and planets of the entire Solar System. Because everything that exists is interconnected. So behave responsibly aware that our creation affects the entire universe. Live your desires! But let these desires be sublime, let them have high vibrations, let them flow from the space of your heart.

Humanity, caught up in lies, stopped not only itself but the entire universe from developing. We cannot allow this anymore. The eyes of the universe are focused on us because so much depends on us. Let's show that we want, that we can, that we have the power about which we hear so much now, let's wake it up and use it for a good purpose. Let's do this for all existence in the universe.

The energy that each of you has is like a vortex that radiates the consciousness of the entire planet. Your souls have consciously descended here at this time to experience the transformation process to help others and Mother Earth who welcomed you with love each time. The karmas of your previous lives have been cleansed, it is time to give what you are here for, that is love and gratitude. Let them fill you up. And when this happens, it will fill the space around and spread to the entire universe. Feel the star child within you, let it wake up from a dream and start living truly. It is important that you find a way to balance yourself and connect this beautiful, unique physical world with spirituality, which will ultimately be your full manifestation of existence.

When you understand your relationship with the universe with full acceptance, then miracles will begin to happen. The mind will stop captivating you and a new perspective will open in which you will not only see, but really see. You might think to yourself: So what if I try, if others don't give a damn and are engrossed in their programs? And right now I am asking you not to look and judge others who are still unaware. Take a look at yourself. Who you are. And who would you really like to be? Just be it. You can. There is no force that can stop you.

The disease that was the infection of the elites and self-proclaimed gods has spread too much. But we are not powerless. Time to get it. We have a cure for it! Medicine is our love and the energy of creation in truth. We cannot allow the diseases that digest our Earth to spread throughout the universe. And that's what happens if we don't act.

See the great responsibility that rests on you. That is why you are here now! To change it all. And maybe I'm repeating myself, but I'll keep repeating the same over and over until my last breath. Because maybe not the first time, maybe not the second time, but the time will come when your soul will wake up and answer me. It has no place in itself for medicine. Not a speck. I and the other children of the stars will be here with you every step of the way.

Continued in Star Children Era of light...

Epilogue

*The channeled message hasn't been changed
and is in the exact same form that Semjase has passed it.*

We have come to gift you with existence. So that you would like to learn unity because in unity all paradoxes are resolved, everything that is damaged is healed; all that is forgotten is transferred to the light.

The nature of your tongue is such that what has been distorted cannot, to your knowledge, be fully straightened, but rather slightly brightened up. The path of your learning is engraved in the present moment. It has no history as you understand it.

Image of the circle of existence. You know alpha and omega as infinite intelligence. The beginning is the end and the end is the beginning — everything is connected. The circle never ends. An octave that takes you to the secrets.

By dreaming of large spaces, you want to conquer and explore the Cosmos, yet you forget about your own planet. It is where you live now, it gives you life, you should take care of it. Be prudent and kind to her. Your planet is beautiful, it stands out in the universe. It emanates a thousand colors, glitters and shines in the distance. It attracts many curious space travelers.

We have been sent to you. We have been with you forever. We and others from the Great Space. We are your friends so closely related to you. Now we exist in the crystalline-liquid form.

If you don't understand it, that's fine. Someday your mind will grasp it all. We help you survive.

We charged you with our energy. Crystalline rays penetrated your planet. They have spread in every cell of the molecule in everything that lives on it. Even if you didn't feel it, it happened.

We have given great energy to you and to the entire planet and to all life on it. Earth's energy grid is sealed, you live safely now. The energy we send will still work, constantly. You're shining. Your picture is correct.

Crystalline energy is in constant motion, it changes and radiates glow, it improves your comfort of existence. It constantly changes your inner being. It improves your health and condition. It changes your thinking and feeling for good. You will look at life positively. Crystalline changes are irreversible. Your mind is shining with a great light. It will allow you to change your life on Earth for a better and more harmonious one.

After a few changes on Earth, your planet will regain peace. It is your way of thinking and feeling that will change it. The brightness will be forever. Everything is going in the right direction. Take care of your planet. We have finished transferring energy. Your cells are full. The process of regeneration and creation of new resources of three-fold complex cells is in progress. The processes have stimulated responses in the bodies and all forms of life continue.

Our mission is complete. We have supported your endurance, we have changed your thinking and feeling. On a global scale, the changes will be noticeable soon.

The Elkurians, beings of the highly evolved Errians — Pleiadians of the ERRA system — currently existing as the thirteenth Solar-Crystalline System in the Variod band, in the Taron system, are orbiting the Earth 325 km away in their own etheric object, invisible to your human eyes.

This object emits unimaginable energy that is known as the cosmic percule of time. It is produced in a special crystal-static press. Its task is to penetrate all living structures encountered on its way. The crystalline flux of this energy is now directed towards the Earth. This is to increase the pulsation of your molecules — all living organisms. It is necessary for your continued existence and for the existence of all organisms that want to survive in spaces you do not know yet.

The multi-layered operation of the jet increases its effectiveness. It penetrates into all forms of existence. Its action is determined by the transformation of life forms from one structure to another, while maintaining the purity of existence.

Crystalline streams are designed to bring your existence closer to being divine and pure and energetic. It is a wave action, pulsating and penetrating the deepest areas of the globe. These waves are not reflected, but penetrate deep into particles and structures. The transmission of these waves occurs gradually with different vibration and frequency.

When the reception of these waves is fully saturated, we will stop transmitting them. The nuclear tripartite aims to improve the molecular structures of molecules, not to destroy them. Tripartite is a very important element in the penetration and absorption of crystalline rays. This is to increase the existence of present-day molecules of living organisms to a complex tripartite existence.

The consequence of this is the greater resistance of living organisms to all external factors coming from your cosmos, including espiral and colic radiation. They come from deep space without your knowledge, participation or will. They block the development of your empirical structures, thereby keeping your existentialism on the same level.

Crystalline radiation effectively annihilates and eliminates radiation that is negative to your existence and development. This is our very important project. That is why we approach this task with full respect and determination.

We will support you in your further physical and existential development — optional to other beings we know and are from. We are not just a physical existence. This process was completed many epochs ago (epoch — a relative concept since time does not exist). Our existence is a form of transmission of the universe.

It harmonizes with the most distant species from a distant galaxies. There are many of these lives. In your numbers, there are trillions.

We are an existential, crystal-water form. We are noticeable to ourselves and other forms of the same or similar structure. Your species is currently undergoing changes. They are needed in your existence and in transforming your form from physical to existential. The processes are progressing gradually according to the time plans. The reception of crystalline waves radian radiation is successful.

We will not leave you in this process.

We supervise and regulate the crystalline streams so that everything is in full harmony with the universe.

We are your friends and helpers in achieving this goal.

The world is different

The cuffs of lies locked on our hands for centuries,
Have already rusted.
Eventually the house of cards will collapse, And the broken bubble of
illusion will be consumed by the abyss.

Who we are now, what we are doing here,
What we are looking for, what our purpose is.
What we feel, what we believe in
Its enough to tune into your heart.

This is what they are afraid of,
the power of our love which is greater than a stone,
They will pressurize, they will get angry
They will try to divide us.

For only when we are together can we rise up
from the knees and continue to live.
For only when we are together will we be meant
to thread on a gold trail towards the sky.

Kate Matuschke

Table of contents

Printed in Great Britain
by Amazon

15687026R00222